POSTCARD HISTORY SERIES

Ripley County

In Vintage Postcards

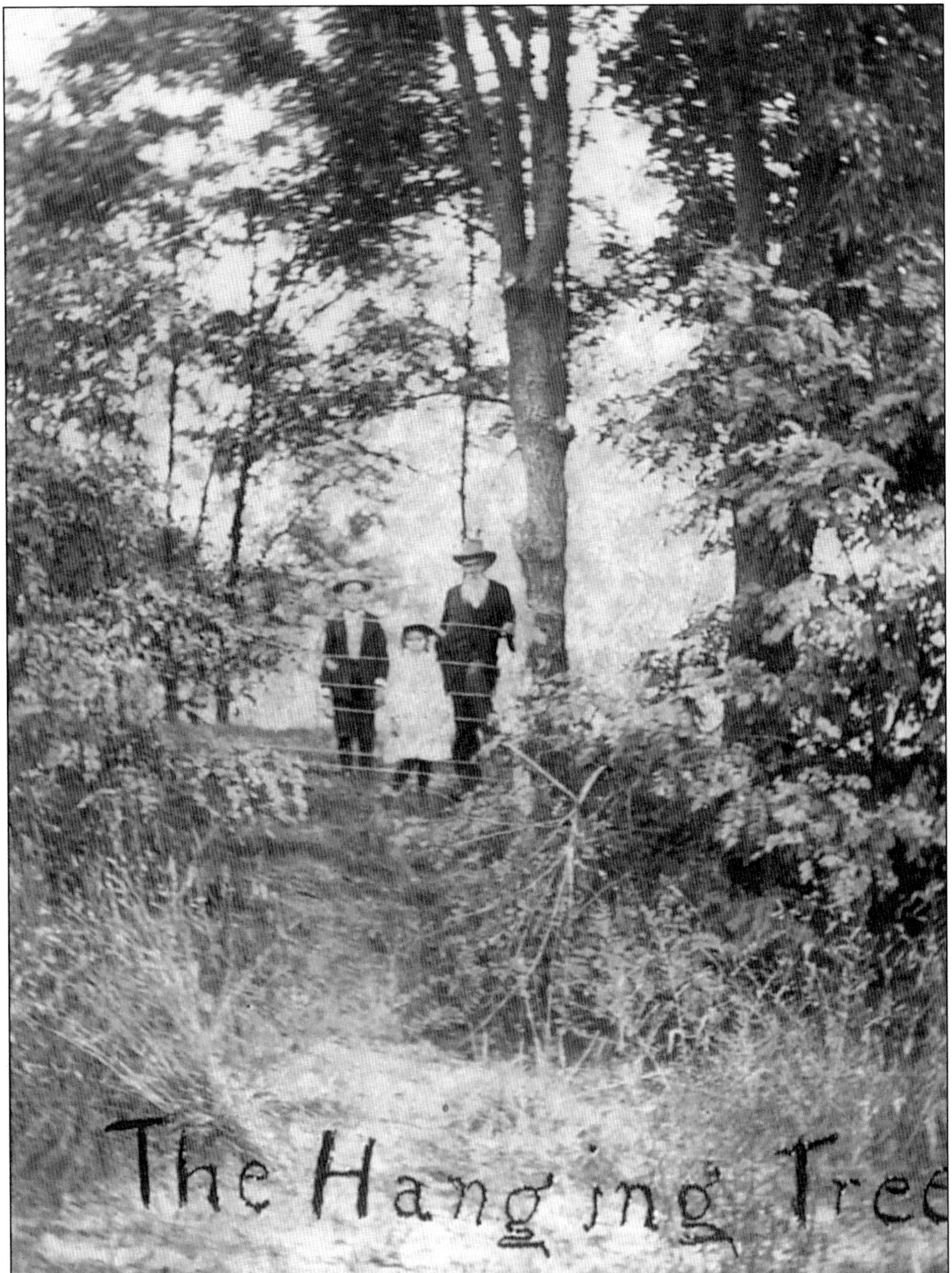

Pictured is the famous elm tree from which five men were hanged by a vigilante mob in September 1897, at Versailles. This lynching made the headlines in city newspapers all over the country. The mob stormed the jail, clubbed and beat their victims, and hanged them near the Cliff Hill Cemetery. The bare stubs of the branches on the tree show where the prisoners hanged. Pictured here are Bess Curran Cole, and Mose Curran.

POSTCARD HISTORY SERIES

Ripley County
In Vintage Postcards

Alan F. Smith

ARCADIA PUBLISHING

ISBN 978-0-7385-0734-7

Published by Arcadia Publishing
Charleston, South Carolina

Printed in the United States of America

Library of Congress Catalog Card Number: 00-107491

For all general information contact Arcadia Publishing at:
Telephone 843-853-2070
Fax 843-853-0044
E-mail sales@arcadiapublishing.com
For customer service and orders:
Toll-Free 1-888-313-2665

Visit us on the Internet at www.arcadiapublishing.com

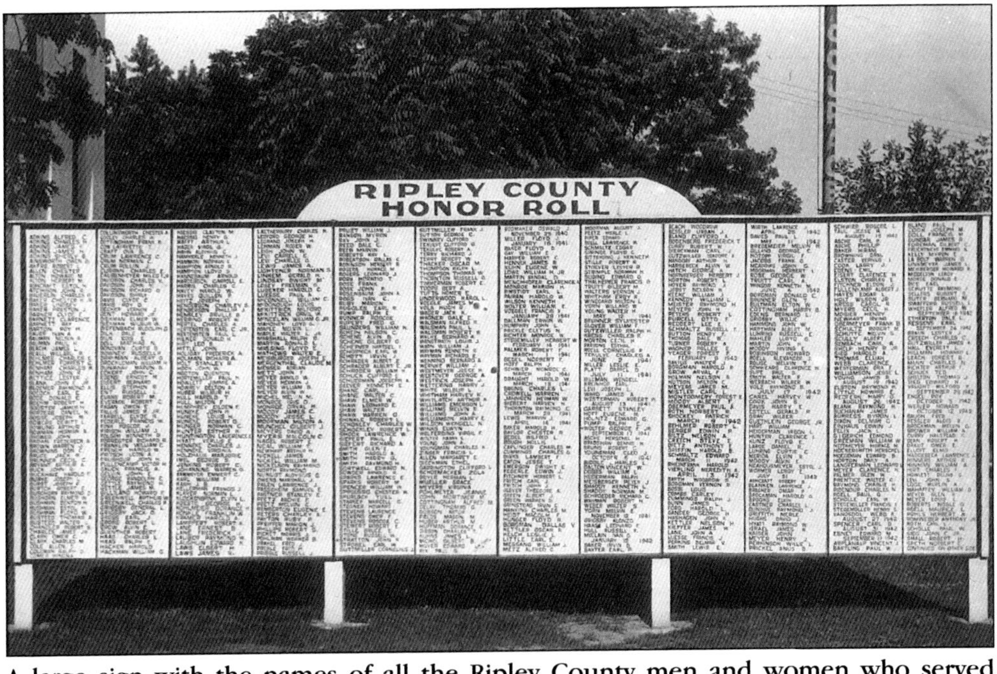

A large sign with the names of all the Ripley County men and women who served in WW II was placed in the southwest corner of the courtyard in Versailles. The sign remained through the war years, then it suddenly disappeared. (Photograph by unknown photographer.)

Contents

ACKNOWLEDGMENTS

I wish to give special thanks and credit to many of my friends who generously shared their knowledge, accurate accounts, and memories of Ripley County. I also wish to thank the Ripley County Historical Society and Lori Huffman and Jack Demaree for their computer expertise.

All pictures and postcards are from my personal collection.

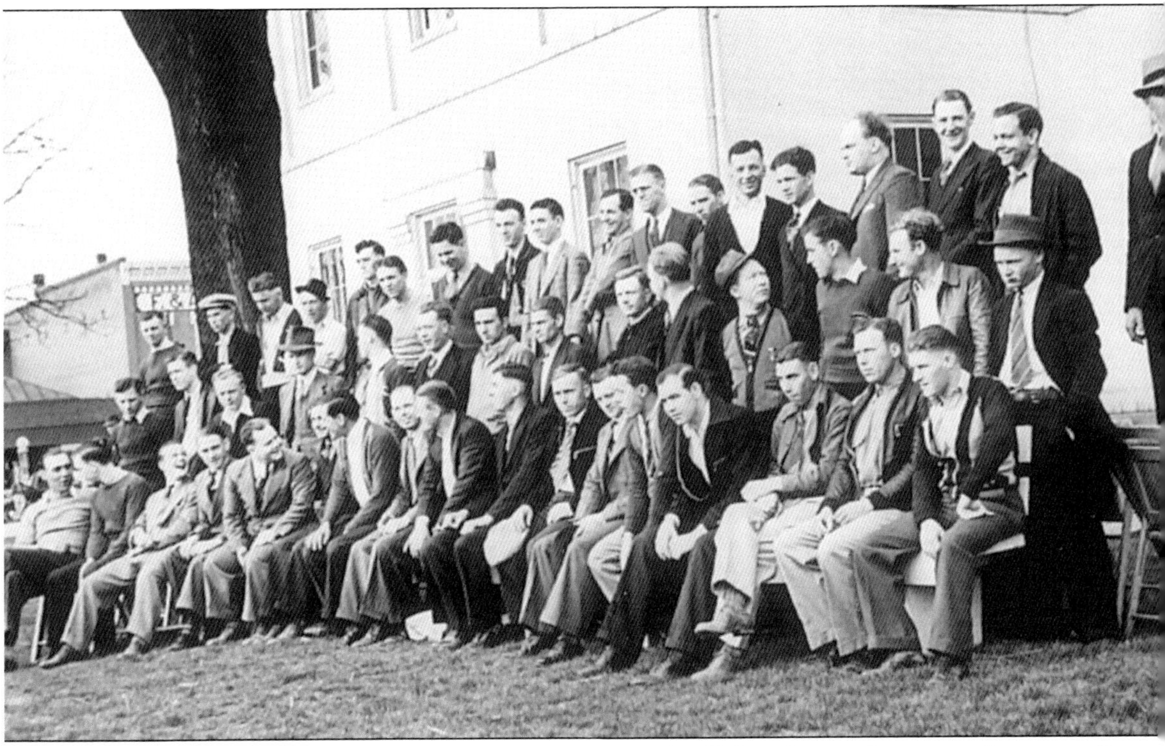

In October 1940, there were 1,932 young men in Ripley County between the ages of 21 and 39, and many were in this early draft. One hundred thirty-six men were drafted in the period between November 1940 and July 1941. Shown in this picture is a large group of these early draftees. Some look glum—as well they should, for many served for five years, and a few never returned. (Photograph by unknown photographer.)

Introduction

The photographs and postcards shown in this pictorial history book will allow the reader to respect the trials, tribulations, and hardships suffered by those who lived in the times pictured here. This book is the culmination of my years of collecting postcards and photographs relative to Ripley County.

How citizens of Ripley County labored, amused themselves, and conducted their everyday lives is revealed in these photos and cards. Ripley County towns and villages, like all rural areas, had their favorite saloons, general stores, hotels, churches, homes, and interesting historic landmarks. Luckily for us, preserved photographs and postcards left us a view of the past.

Many fine colored cards were printed and colored in Germany in the early 1900s, before World War I. Kraemer Art Company in Cincinnati, Ohio, was a leader in this trade. Postcards were a means of both promoting one's home town, and sending a short, to-the-point message to a relative or friend. After the war, local professional photographers jumped into the profitable business.

Each township in Ripley County is depicted in this book, and it is hoped that readers will be enlightened and amused by reading *Ripley County: In Vintage Postcards*.

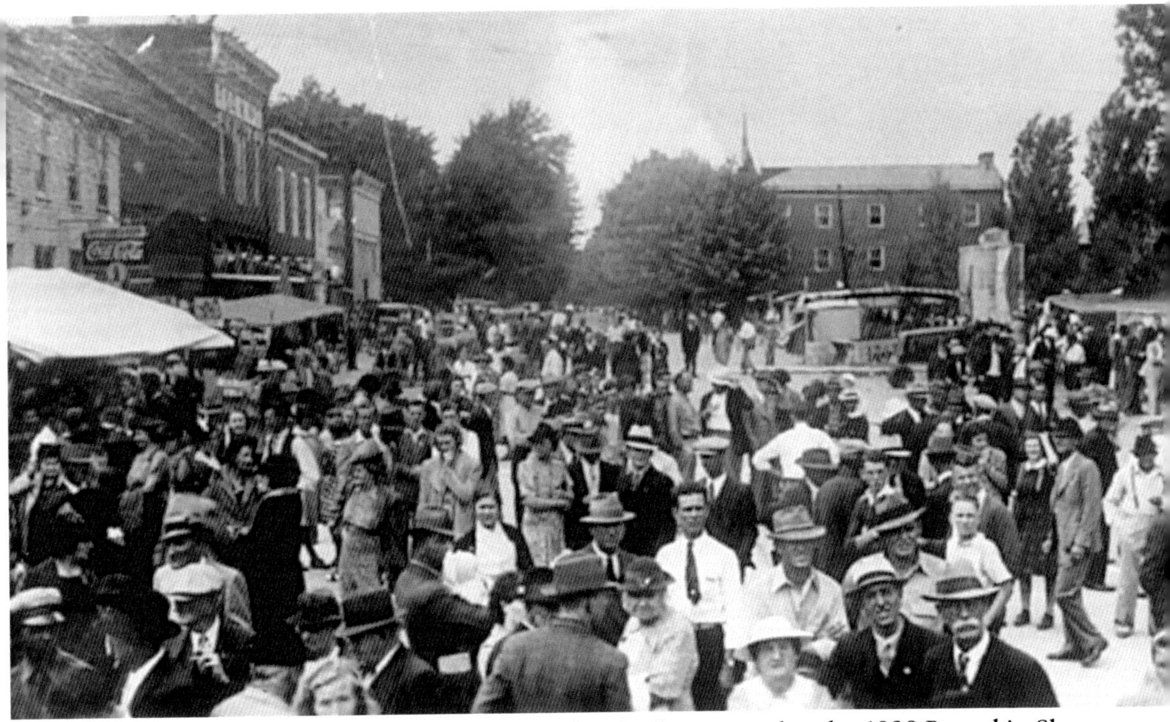

Tyson Street is packed with a rather somber-looking crowd at the 1939 Pumpkin Show. Jane Withers and Monty Wooley are playing at the Austin Theatre, and a ferris wheel is operating at full capacity. This was October—the reason for the hats and coats. A sign within the photo reads, "Hamburgers 10, and Hot Dogs 5¢"...the crowd should be smiling at those prices! (Photograph by unknown photographer.)

One

Laughery Township

On July 23, 1818, the first county officers assumed office, and three townships—Laughery, Perry, and Graham—were formed in the new county. All the area east of Laughery Creek became Laughery Township. From 1825 until 1856, due to boundary changes, Laughery Township failed to exist at all. It was reestablished in 1856. Laughery Township had three towns: Ballstown, Cross Roads, and Batesville. The township was named in honor of Captain Archibald Lochry, who was killed in 1781 by the British and Native Americans at the mouth of Laughery Creek.

BATESVILLE. The largest city in Ripley County was founded in 1852. The Callahan Trust Company purchased land from Teunis Amack, land which now is in the city of Batesville. An engineer named Joshua Bates acquired the first 42 lots from the Callahan Trust, and built a house facing what is now Depot Street. An abundance of fine hardwood in the area gave the new town its principal industries—furniture, coffins, and wood products of all kinds. These were crafted by Romweber Furniture and Hillenbrand Industries, with the help of good, skilled, German workers. These industries helped the city prosper. Easy access to Highway 74 has aided this Germanic city's growth.

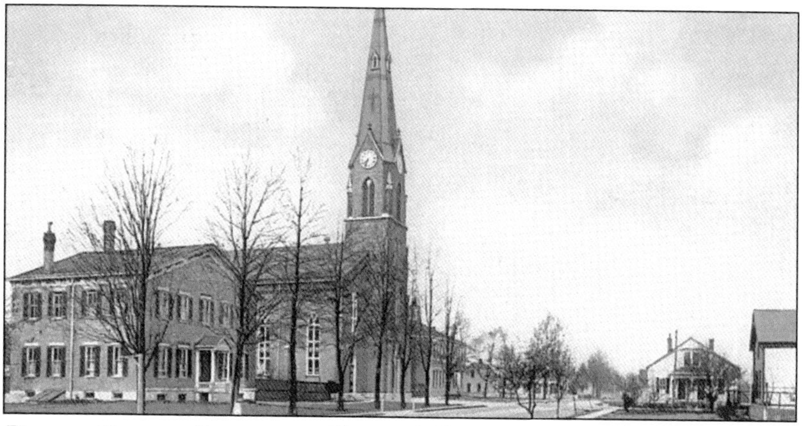

St. Louis Rectory Church, School, and Teacher's Residence. At the time of construction this was the oldest church in Batesville, started in 1868 and completed in 1870. A steeple was added in 1892. The church was named after its patron saint, St. Louis 1X, King of France. Today the parochial school, church, and rectory are well maintained, and look similar to this picture. (Card #79162, "Photostint," by Detroit Publishing Co.)

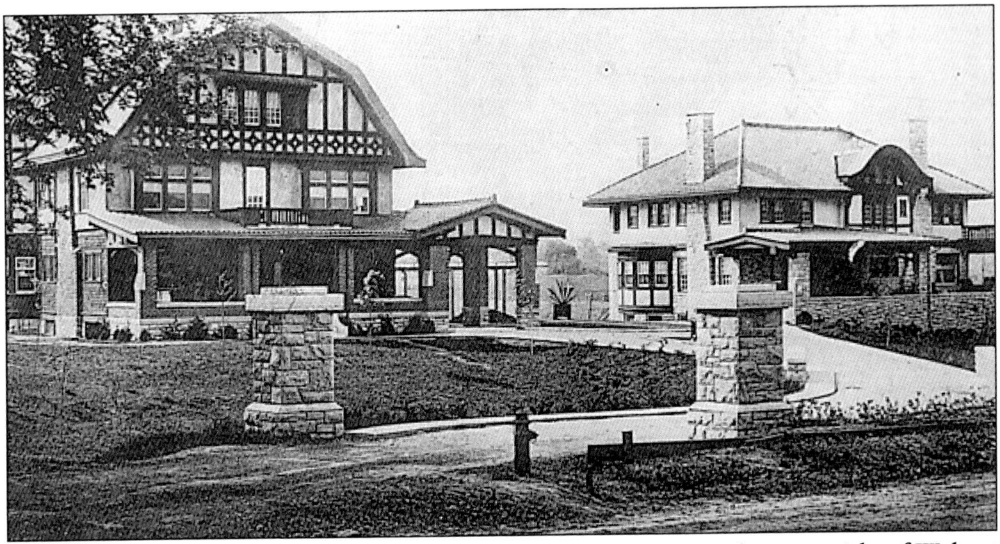

Hillcrest Homes, Batesville. These two beautiful homes are on the west side of Walnut Street, and were the homes of John A. Hillenbrand, who formerly lived in a large frame house where the new library rests today. Today, one is a residence and the other an office for attorney John Schuerman. Definitely constructed in a German style, they fit well in Batesville. (Unnumbered Kraemer Art Card Co., Cincinnati & Berlin.)

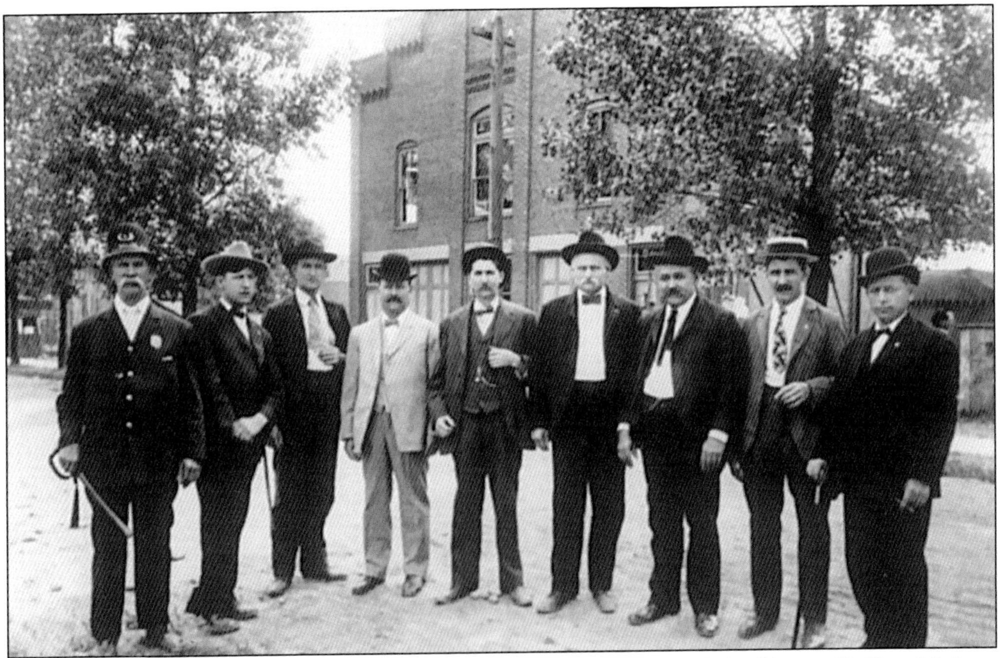

Town Officials in 1907. These gentlemen posed in front of the Town Hall, which at that time was only 20 years old. The Batesville Town Officials are, from left to right, as follows: Marshall J.H. Borgstede; attorney M.F. Bohland; Trustee 4th Ward William Wisman; Trustee 2nd Ward J.O. Kaiser; Trustee 1st Ward. Pres. Schork; Trustee 3rd Ward. William Straus; Treasurer J.P. Schwartz; and Clerk. J.F. Dresher. They are all "dudded-up" for the occasion. (Photograph by unknown photographer.)

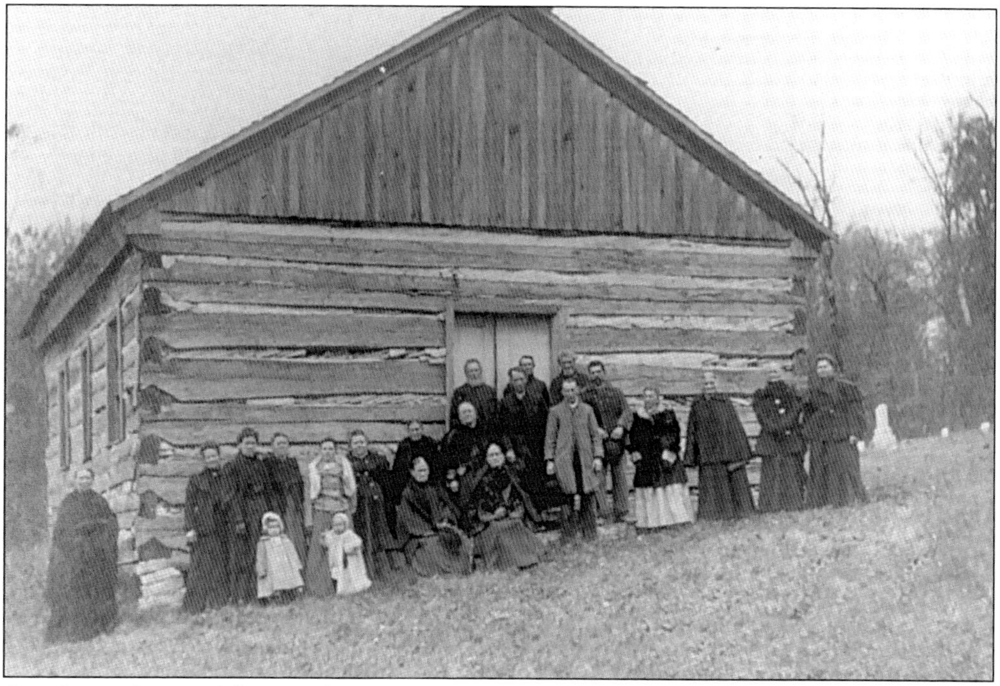

Old Salem Church. The Laughery Township Church was built of native logs in 1840. The members of the predominately female congregation are seen dressed in their long, dark dresses, the style in the 1880s, in front of the old church. A church cemetery can be seen to the right of the building. (Photograph by unknown photographer.)

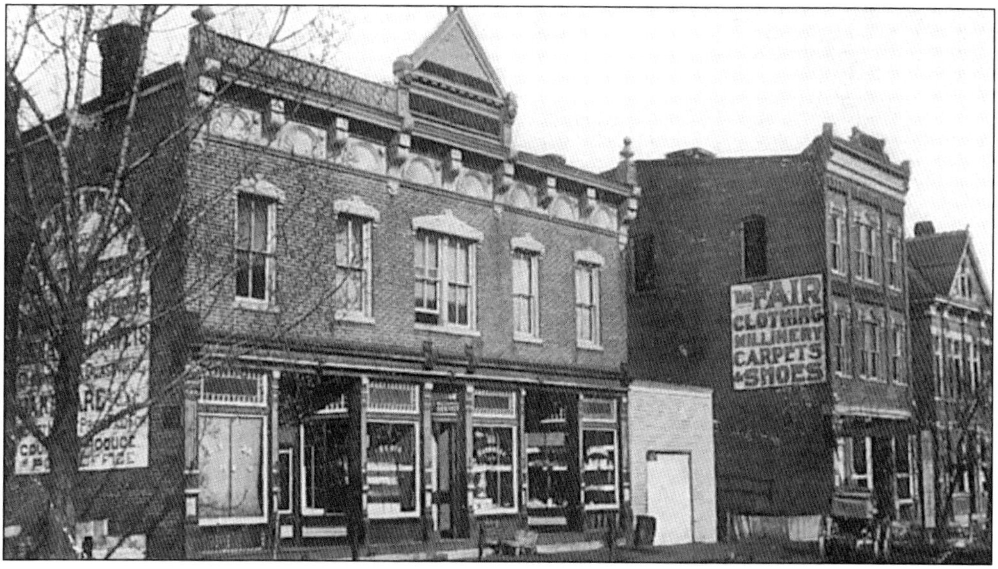

North Main Street. Geisen's Dry Goods & Grocery Store is shown on the corner of North Main Street, where Blank's and Rite Aid Drug Stores were located much later. Note the sign for the Fair Store, which sold clothing, shoes, carpeting, and millinery, prominently painted on the side of the next building. The last building seen is the old Batesville State Bank. (Unnamed card mailed in 1919.)

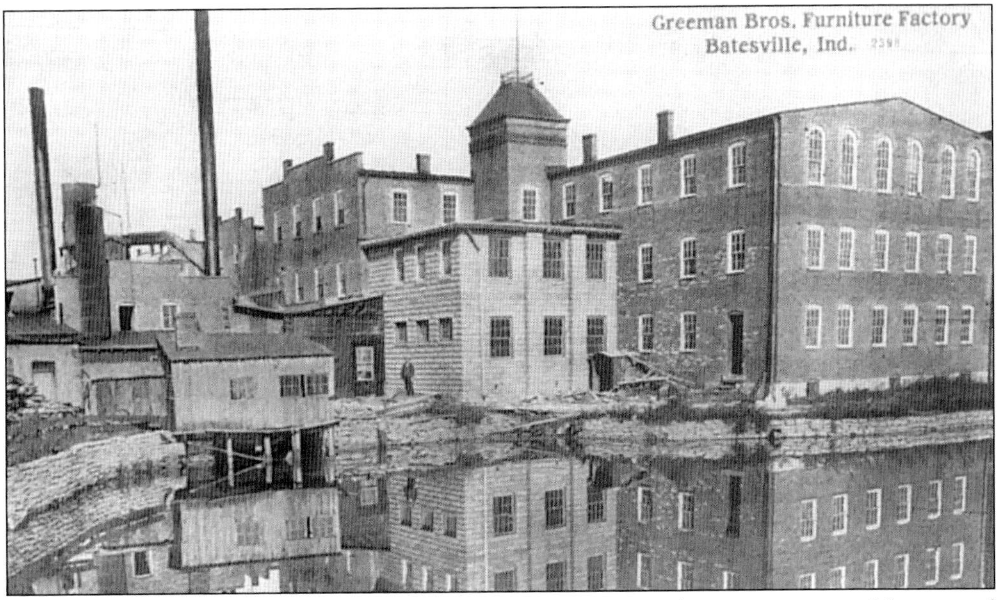

GREEMAN BROS. FURNITURE FACTORY. Theodore Greeman and Henry Borgstedde started the Batesville Carving Company in 1876. The plant, on the southeast corner of Depot and East Pearl Streets, employed 130 men. Later the plant became Greeman's Furniture Factory, which sold out to Hillenbrands in 1913. Notice the great reflection. (Photograph by unknown photographer.)

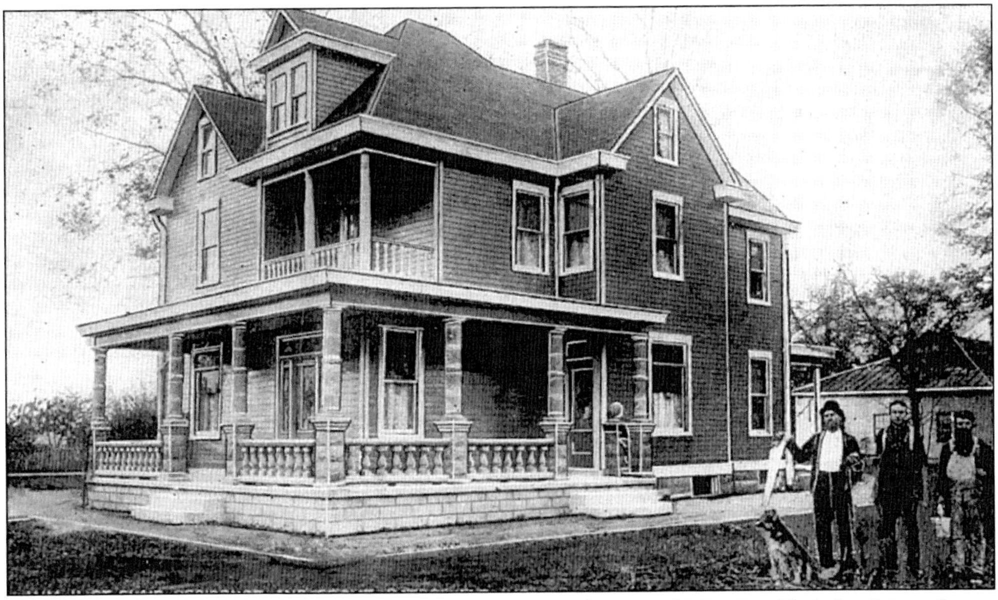

WM. M. ST. CLAIR RESIDENCE. The large, frame residence of Mr. St. Clair had just been built when this card was mailed. The faithful family dog is shown with the carpenters, one of which holds a hand saw. The other two pictured are plasterers or painters. Batesville contained many large homes of this style. The cellar has a window through which coal was shoveled down in the winter, and a large shed is seen behind the house. (Colored Card, by Norwood Souvenir, Cincinnati, Ohio.)

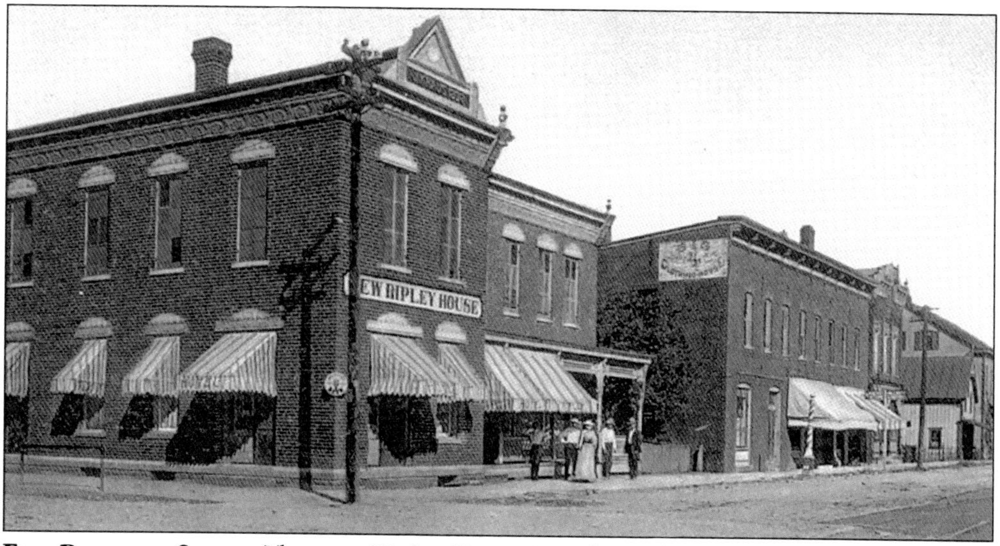

East Broadway Street. The new Ripley House Hotel stands out on the left of this card. It was summer when this photo was taken, as awnings are conspicuous. Most likely there was a bar in the hotel somewhere. Four men and one woman stand in front of the porch, while others rest languidly on the inside. Down the street is the large "Big Four Clothing House," and in front a striped barber pole grabs your attention. (#1805 Kraemer Art Co., Cincinnati & Berlin.)

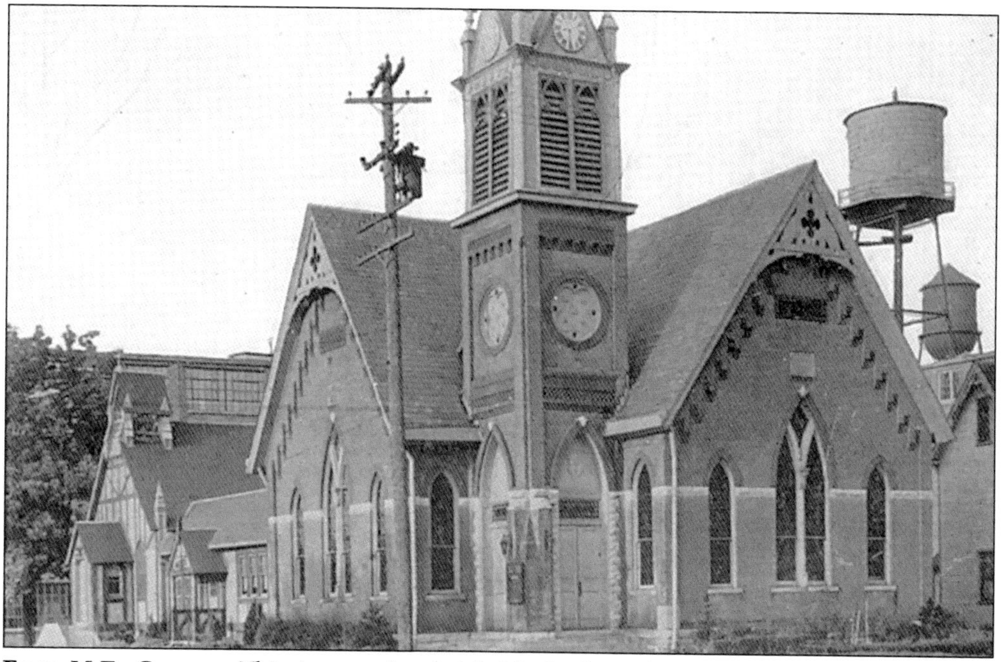

First M.E. Church. This impressive brick Methodist Church was built in 1889, and replaced the German Episcopal Church on South Mulberry Street. Services were conducted in the German language until 1918, when it became more popular to use English due to WW I. Today it is the United Methodist Church. (Eagle Postcard Co., New York, NY, Published by E.B. Schultz.)

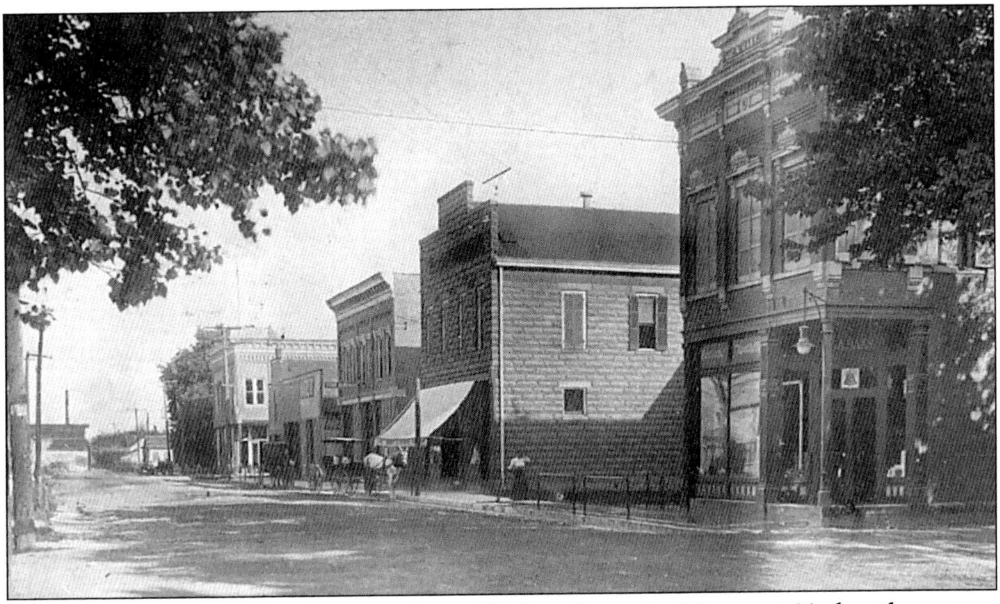

GEORGE STREET. This 1910 photograph is of Walnut Street looking east. Today, the corner building is the site of Nolte-Walsman Pharmacy. Nobbe Clothing Store was the next store down for many years. Hitch racks for tethering horses are handy for customers arriving by buggy. A buggy and one surrey liven up this street scene. (E.C. Kropp Co., Milwaukee, Wisconsin.)

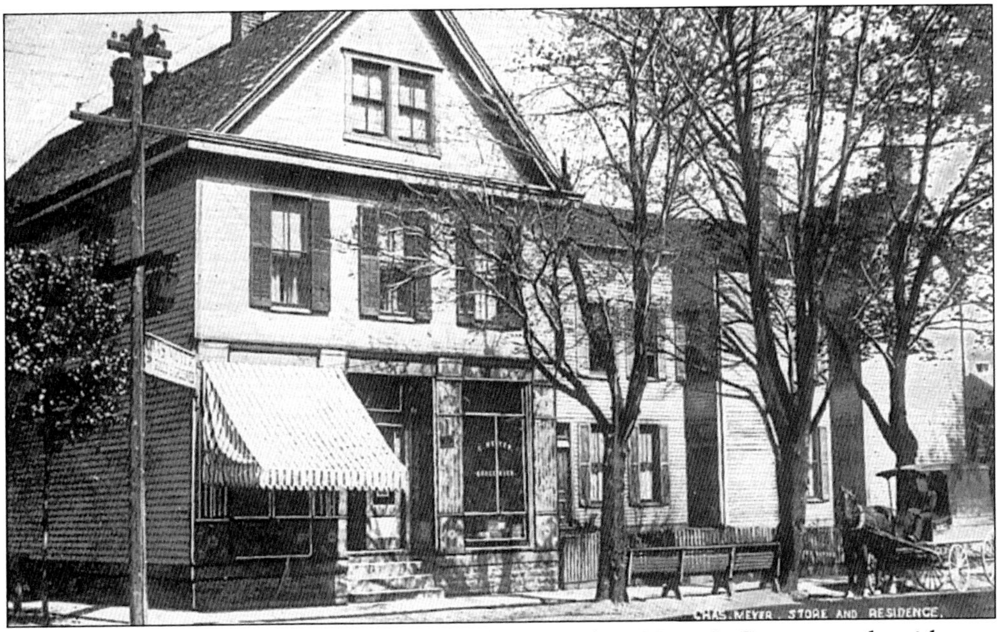

CHARLES MEYER'S STORE. This beautiful card features Chas. Meyer's Grocery and residence. Meyer's was on a corner lot with a picket fence and shutters on all windows. The large loafer's bench between shade trees looked very inviting. Charlie's delivery wagon with its ever-faithful horse pulls from the curb. (Norwood Souvenir Co., Cincinnati, Ohio.)

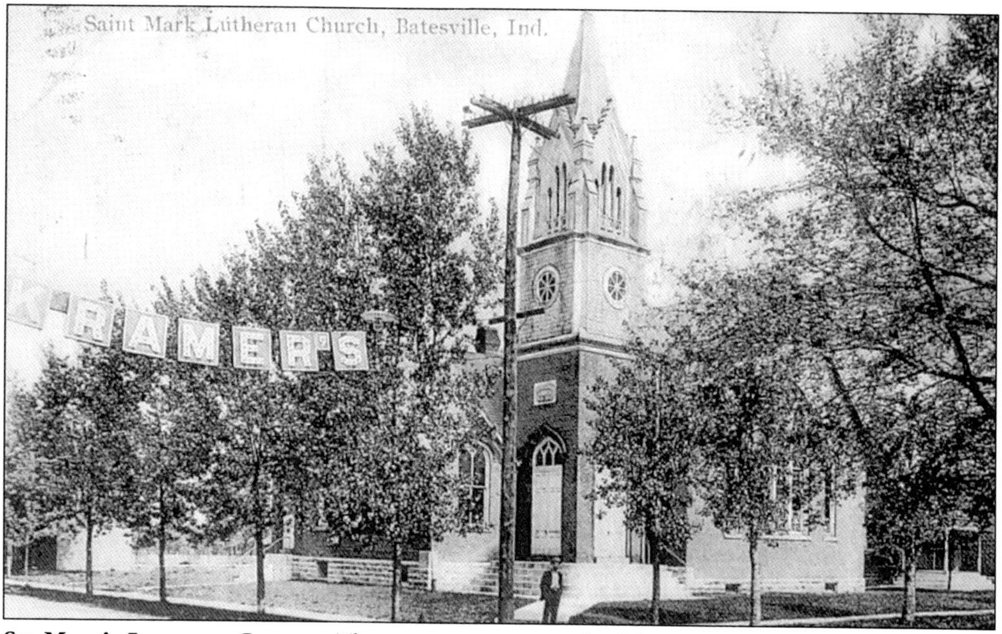

St. Mark's Lutheran Church. The cornerstone was laid for this Lutheran Church on the corner of West Pearl and Vine Streets on August 15, 1897. The cost of construction was $7,000. In 1902, a parsonage was built behind the church. Most families in Batesville were either Catholic or Lutheran, since these were the dominate churches in Germany. (1915 card by Kraemer Art Co., Cincinnati & Berlin.)

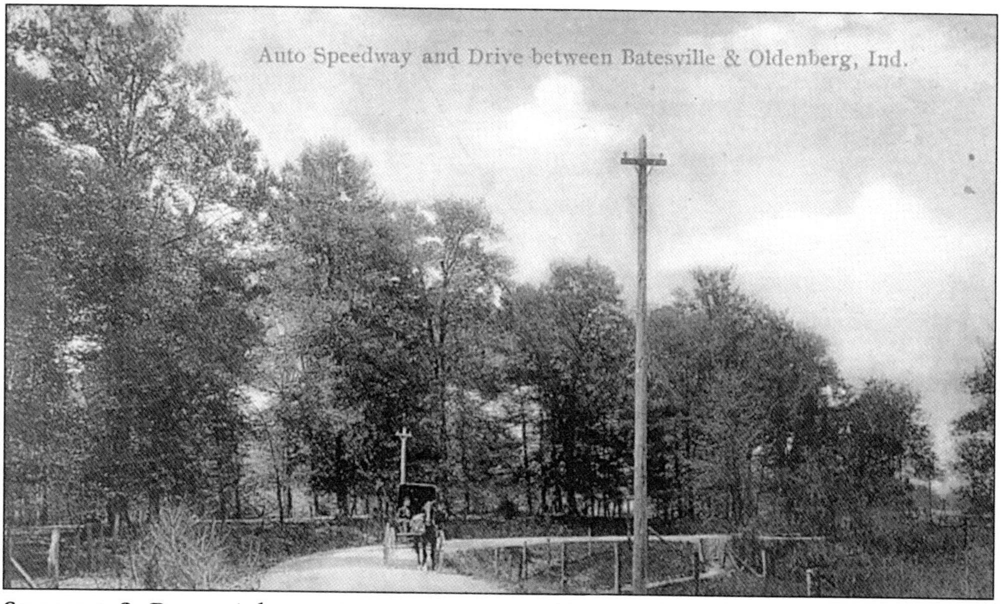

Speedway & Drive. A buggy is seen traveling this speedway between Batesville and Oldenberg. They should see it now! Glancing at this card, one would not call it a speedway; however, the road was probably the scene of many a buggy race by young wags, causing the name for this road. (Unnumbered card by Kraemer Art Co., Cincinnati & Berlin.)

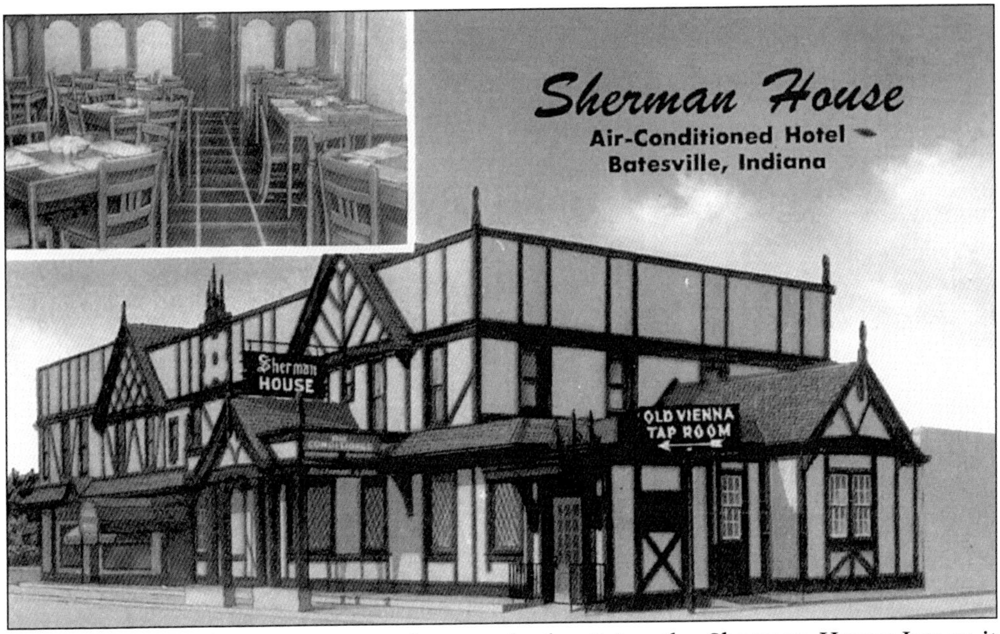

Sherman House. This is a more modern card advertising the Sherman House Inn as it looks today. The inn has large banquet rooms for weddings, business meetings, dinners, and Sunday brunches. Excellent food and service has made this a favorite haunt in the Batesville area for many, many years. (Published by Terre Haute Adv. Co., Terre Haute, Indiana.)

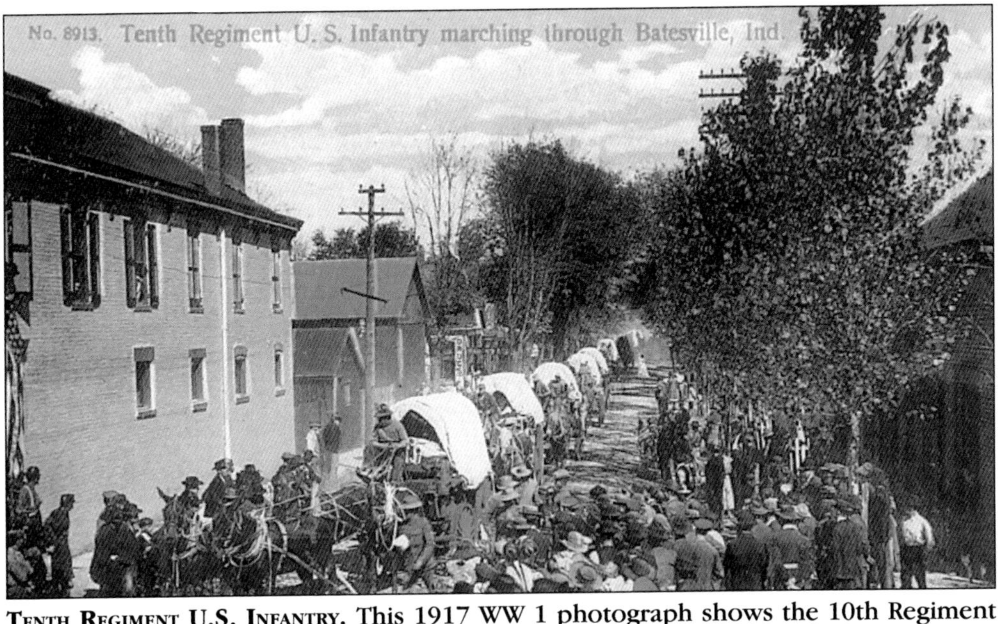

Tenth Regiment U.S. Infantry. This 1917 WW 1 photograph shows the 10th Regiment in full regalia marching down Walnut Street. Barely visible on the left looking north is Gauck's Drug Store. A large crowd of locals lined the streets to see this long line of soldiers and supply wagons. The unit bivouaced near town, probably on a "Bond Drive" through the area. (Baas & Schultz card #8913, made in Germany.)

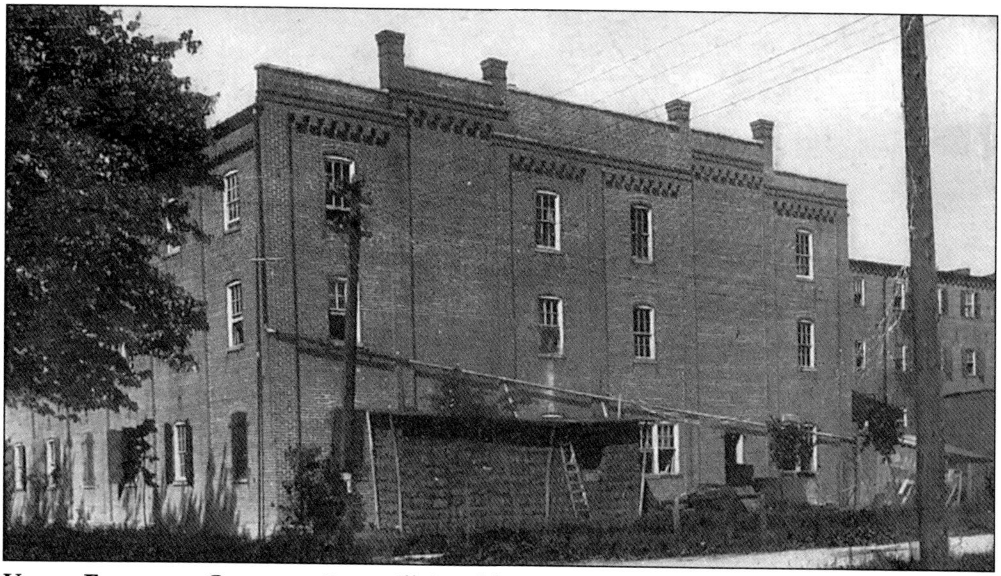

Union Furniture Company. Batesville's oldest, continuously operating company was organized in 1867, by George, Frederick, and William Schultz as a mutual stock company. The employees owned a large portion of the stock company. After a devastating fire in 1875, the plant was rebuilt. When another fire struck in 1885, it was again rebuilt. Today, the Union is a subsidiary of Jamestown Sterling Company. (Card #13825, by unnamed publisher.)

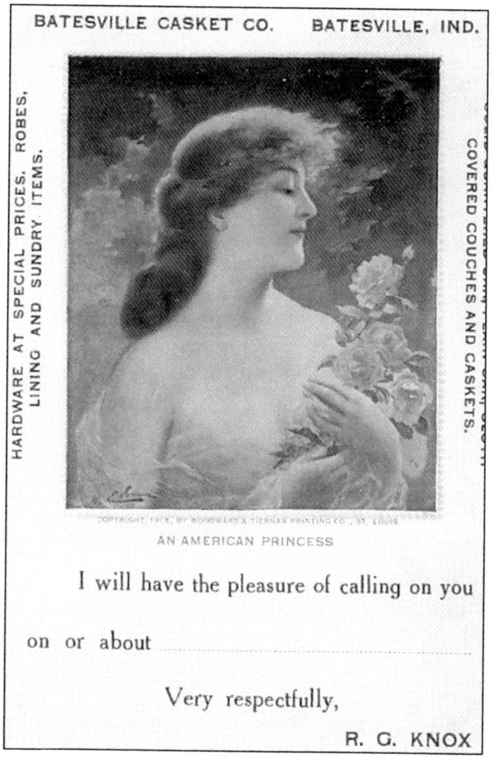

Advertising Card. Salesmen for the Batesville Casket Company mailed these pretty cards to their customers to inform them on which date they would soon be calling on them. Solid oak caskets, fancy hardware, robes, linings, and sundry items were pitched on these cards. R.G. Knox was the company rep who used this card. (Card by unsigned publisher.)

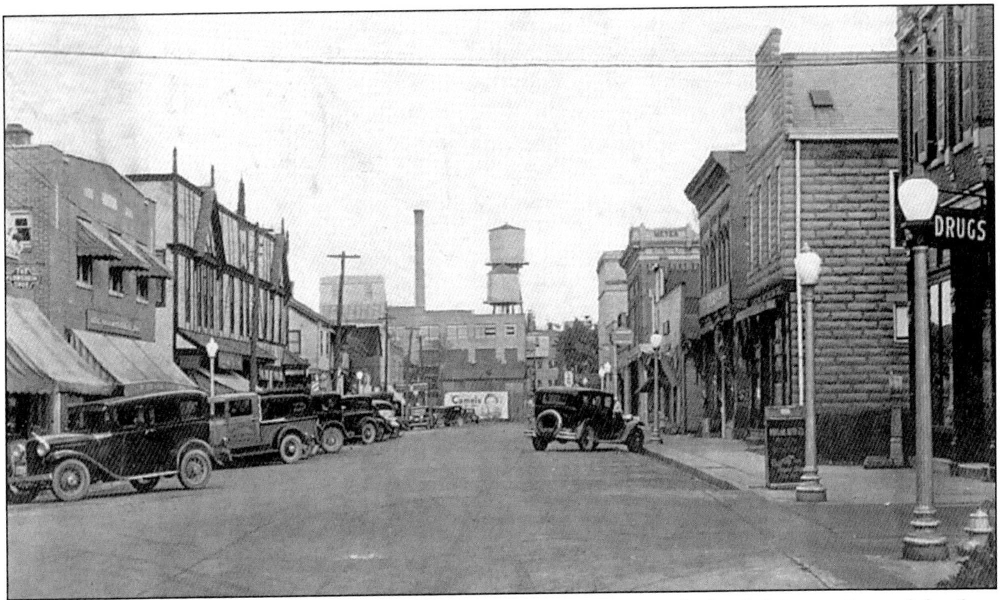

East George Street. A sign advertising shoes is seen at the left of this card, and farther down is the Sherman House corner. A drug store appears on the right, while in the center is a large sign pushing "Camel Cigarettes." Several 1930s cars and a factory are in the distance. (Eagle Post Card Co., New York, NY.)

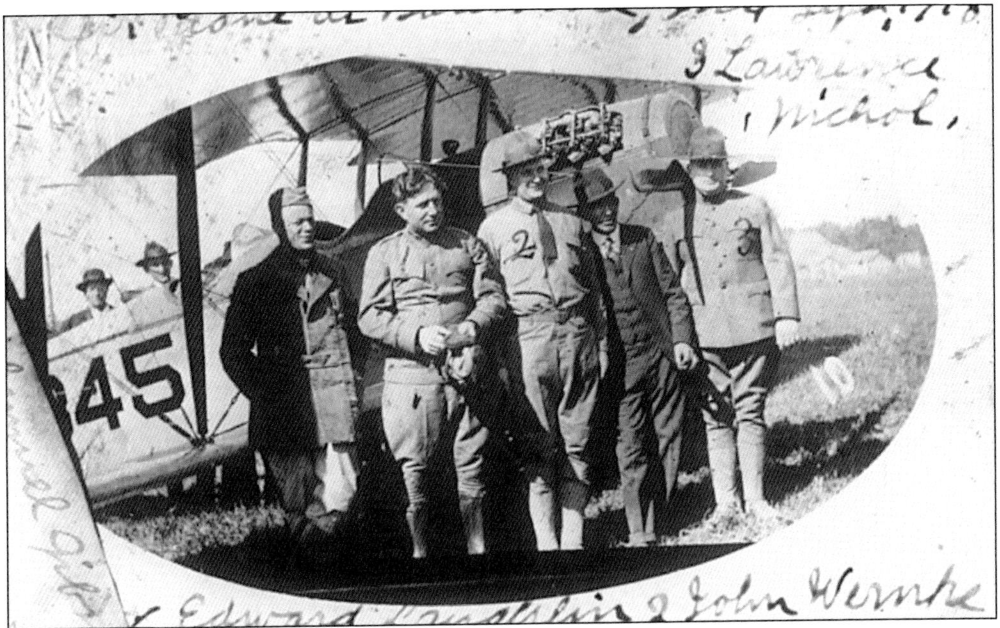

Early Airplane. This open-air cockpit airplane landed in Batesville in September 1918. The occasion for this stunt was a Bond Drive for WW 1. These drives were conducted all across the country featuring different military displays. Pilot Edward Laughlin is number one, John Wernke is second, and Lawrence Nichol is third. On the left is copilot Sam Gib. An unknown civilian also crept into the picture. (Photograph by unknown photographer.)

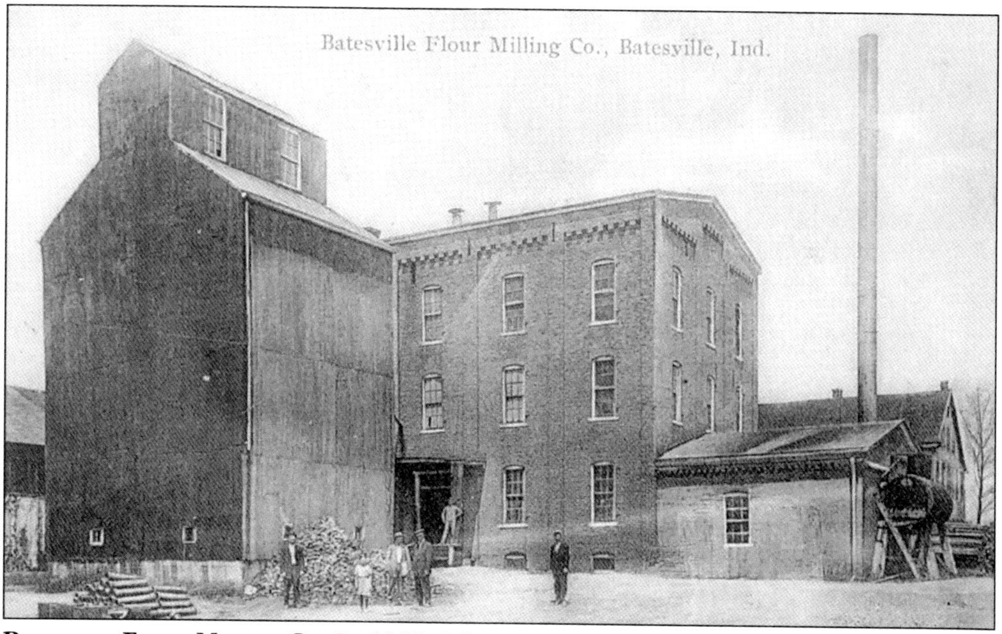

BATESVILLE FLOUR MILLING CO. In 1908, John Meyer organized a stock company to build a flour mill. The directors included John Meyer, John Hillenbrand, H. Kramer, H. Greeman, and Gus Bloemer. Lot #35 was leased from the city for a period of 99 years. Today, a parking lot occupies this lot. To the right is the large water tank used for the mill's boiler, and a stack of fuel wood can be seen behind the men and young girl. (Kraemer Art Co., Cincinnati & Berlin.)

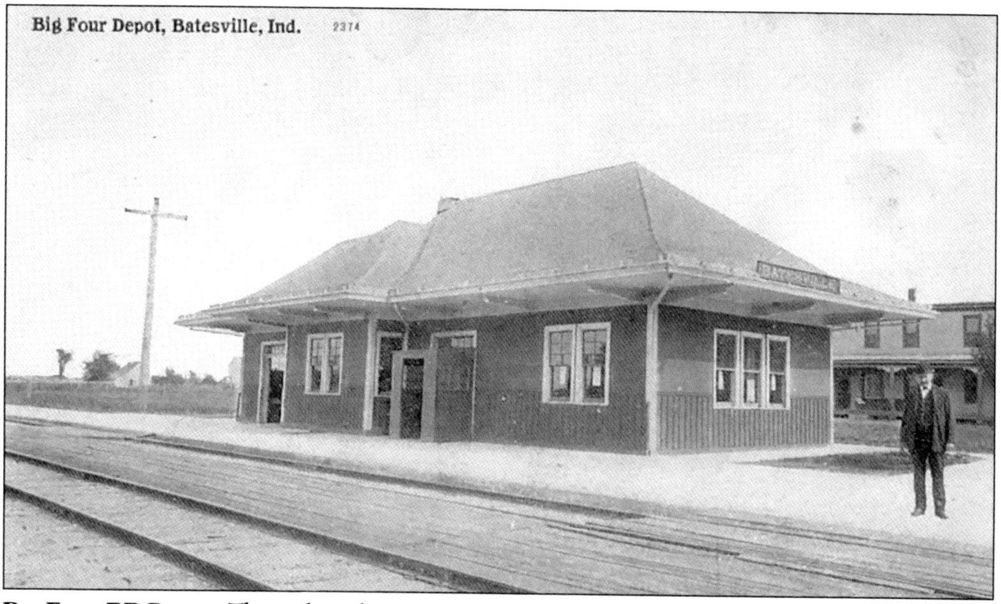

BIG FOUR RR DEPOT. The railroad rerouted from East Pearl Street to its present location in 1906. This depot was a busy hub for passenger and freight service to both Indianapolis and Cincinnati. Obviously it was a slack day when this picture was taken, for only the station agent was on hand. (Colored Card #2374, by M.A. Card Company.)

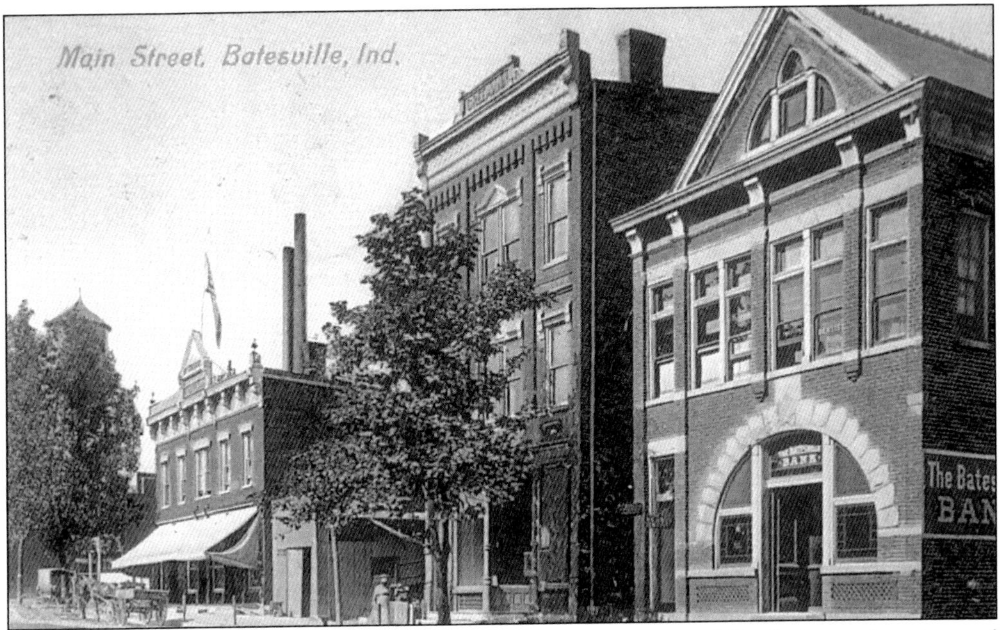

Main Street. The buildings shown on this card are on Main and Boehringer Streets, and remain standing today. The bank later moved to the northwest corner of Catherine and Main Streets, and the Fair Store is now owned by the Knights of Columbus. A wagon, buggy, and woman in a long skirt date this card to 1908. (Card #1808, Baas & Schultz, Kraemer Art Co.)

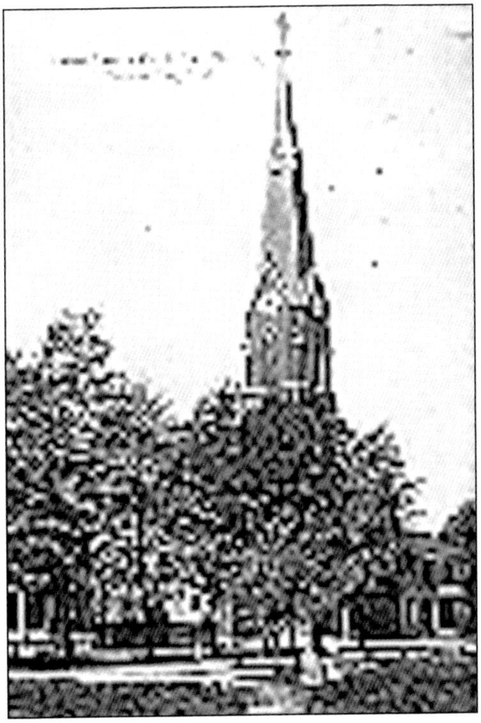

St. Louis Catholic Church. Two little girls are seen walking away from the church on this green colored card, mailed in 1913. Today, if one looks directly south from Highway 46, it appears you could drive into the center of St. Louis Catholic Church. (Unnumbered Kraemer Art Co. card.)

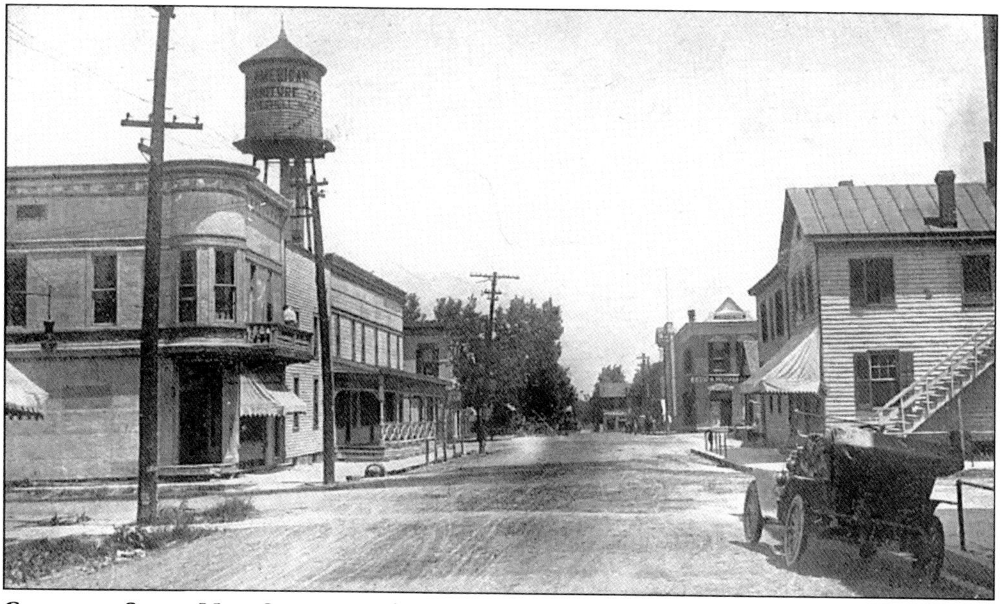

Corner of South Main Street. Looking north from the intersection of Main and George Streets, one can see the Sherman House on the left and the water tower belonging to the American Furniture Company. On the right, standing on the site of the Old Batesville Hotel, is Burkart's Saloon. Further down is the early depot. Across the street is the new Ripley House. The roadster is from an earlier time than this 1912 card. (Card by E.C. Knopp Co., Milwaukee, Wisconsin.)

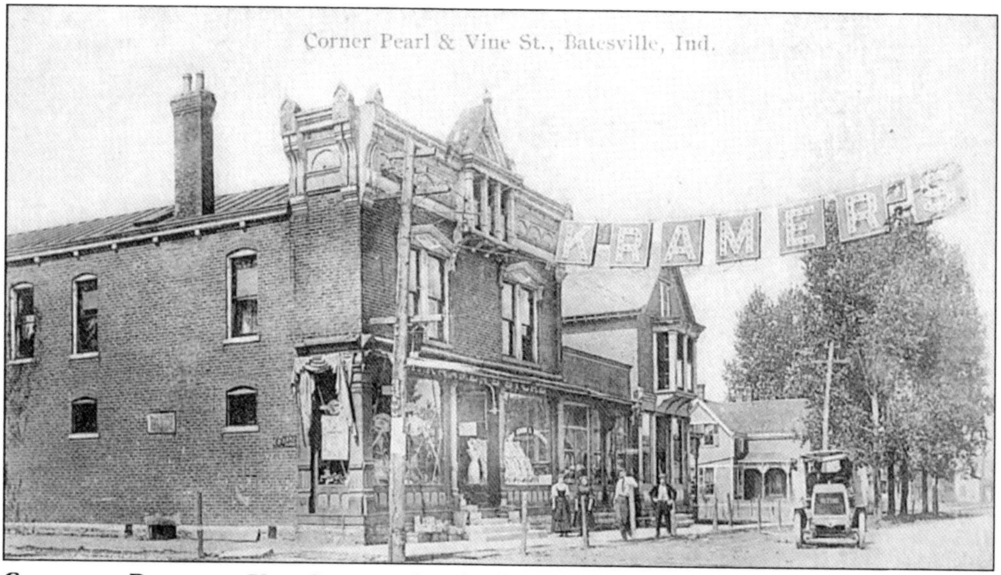

Corner of Pearl and Vine Streets. On the banner above the street, Kramer's Store is boldly displayed. Kramer's was on the southeast corner of Pearl and Vine Streets before 1876. John H. Bosse was the owner. Bosse later sold the store to B. Bertram, whose daughter Anna married H. Kramer. Anna lived in this building for 60 years until 1940. Notice the car and dresses in the front windows. (Green-tinted card by Kraemer Art Co., Cincinnati & Berlin.)

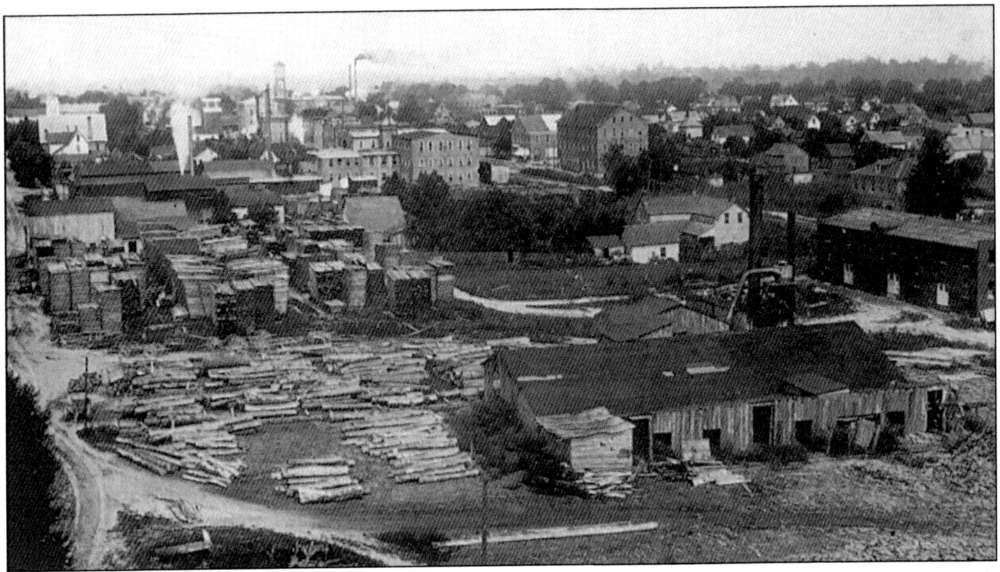

Bird's-Eye View. The Hillenbrand Sawmill and Lumber Yard was located between South Street and the old railroad tracks on East Pearl Street. This photograph was taken from the water tower near what is now the City Maintenance Building. (Baas & Schultz card.)

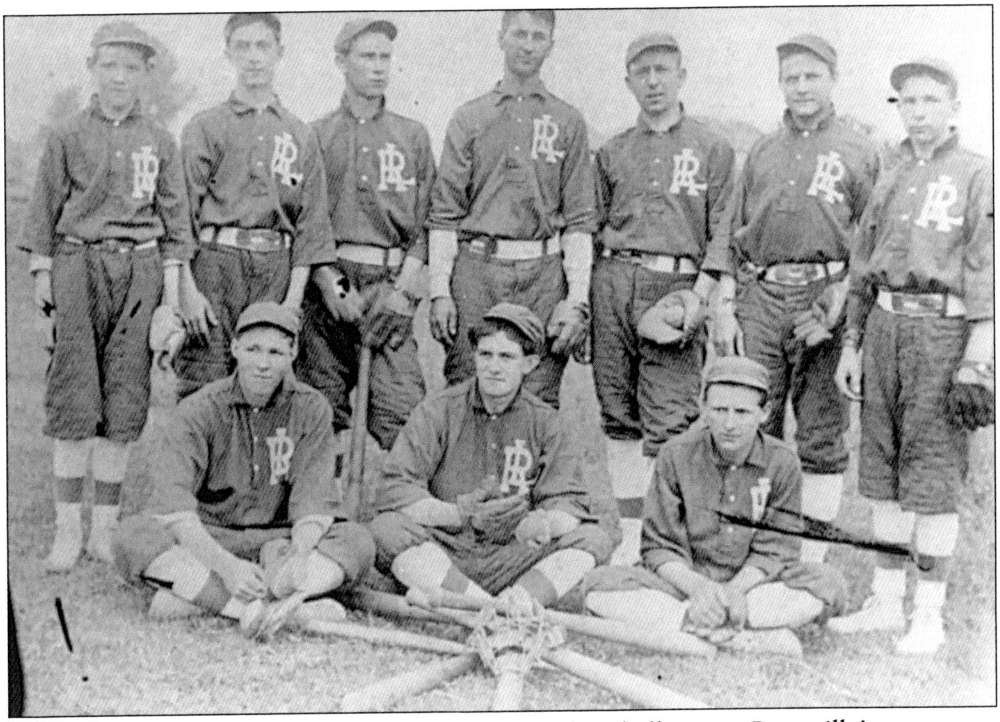

The Leroys Baseball Team. At the height of the baseball craze, Batesville's team was named "The Leroys." In 1907, the players were, from left to right, as follows: (front row) Matt Weigle, Francis Blank, and George Obermeyer; (back row) Frosty Weigle, Otto Fritsch, Dale Parsons, Otto G. "Blackie" Roell Charles "Sticker" Benz, Joe Wintz, and Dan Foley. (Photograph by unknown photographer.)

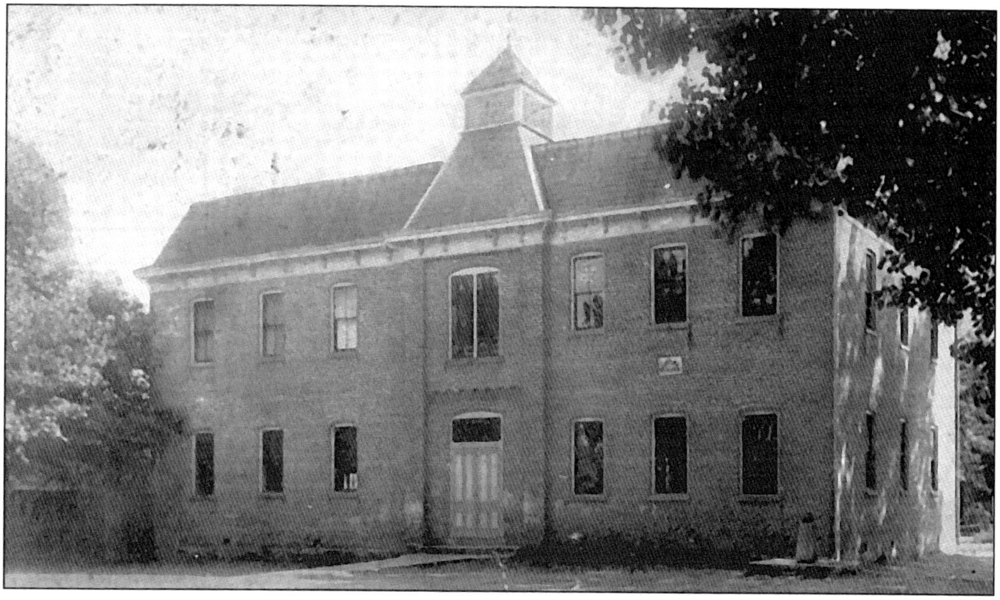

Old Batesvile Public School. In early years, Batesville students went to church-supported schools. Later, township schools were established. In 1875, the building on this card was built. It was a four-room, brick schoolhouse with a large upper and lower hallway. The school was called "Old South Street School." Because of over-crowding, a new building was constructed at the corner of Mullberry and Pearl Streets in 1895. (Card #13820, dated 1912, by unknown.)

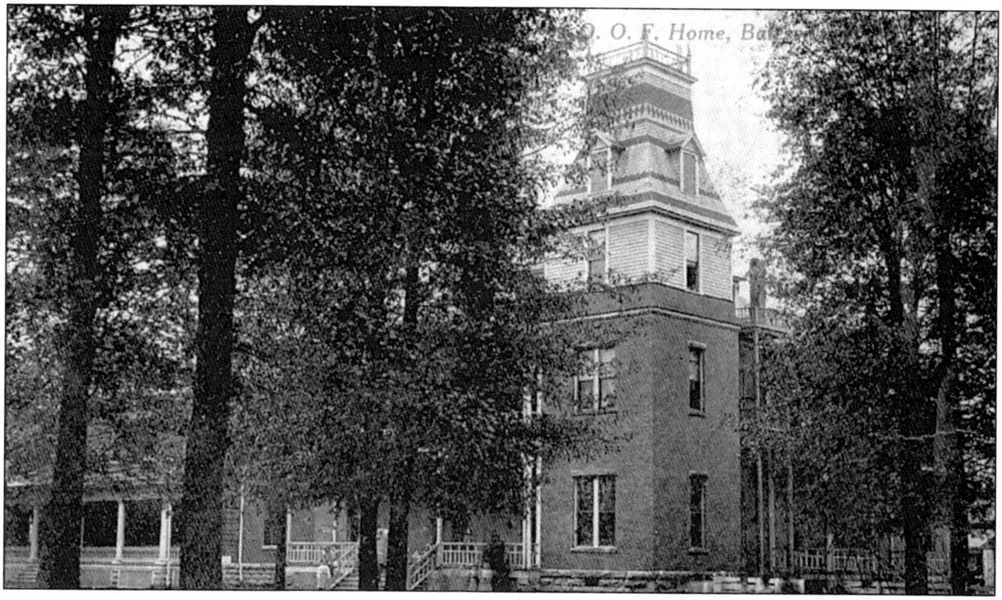

O.O.F. Home. This large, brick home, with a three-story tower in its corner and porches on each side, was the home of the "Odd Fellows Lodge." Lodges were very popular in the early 1900s, and this is the reason for such a large, imposing structure. An I.O.O.F. home for aged lodge members is at the edge of Greensburg, Indiana. (Card by unknown publisher.)

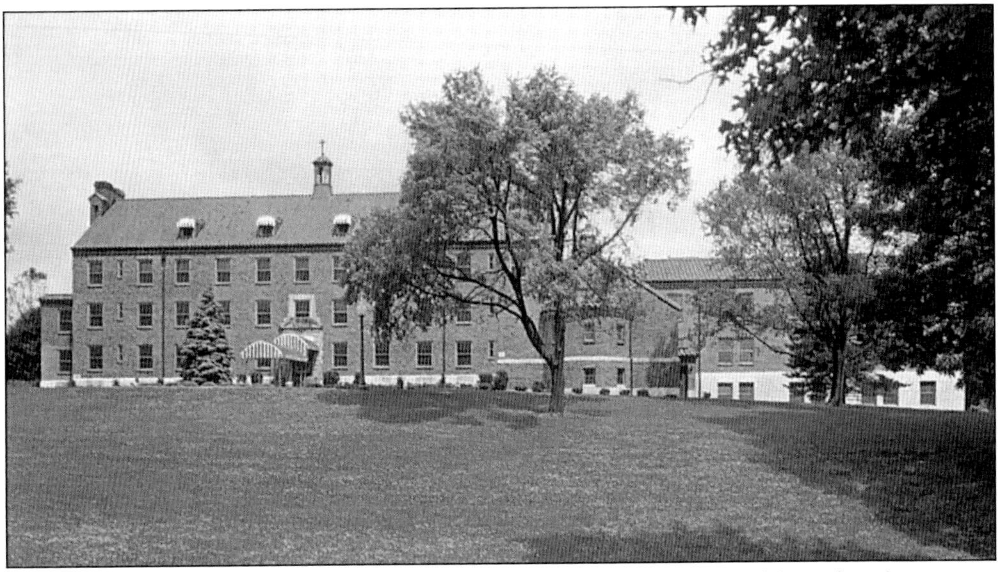

Margaret Mary Hospital. Named after Margaret Hillenbrand and her daughter Mary Mitchell, this 50-bed facility opened its doors on October 29, 1932. The Hillenbrands donated this greatly needed hospital to the "Sisters of The Poor." As years sped by, many additions have been added to Margaret Mary. At present, a 15-member board of directors governs the hospital, and it includes acute care, home care, extended care, an emergency room, and many other health care specialties. (Chrome Card by Curteichcolor, 3-D Reproduction.)

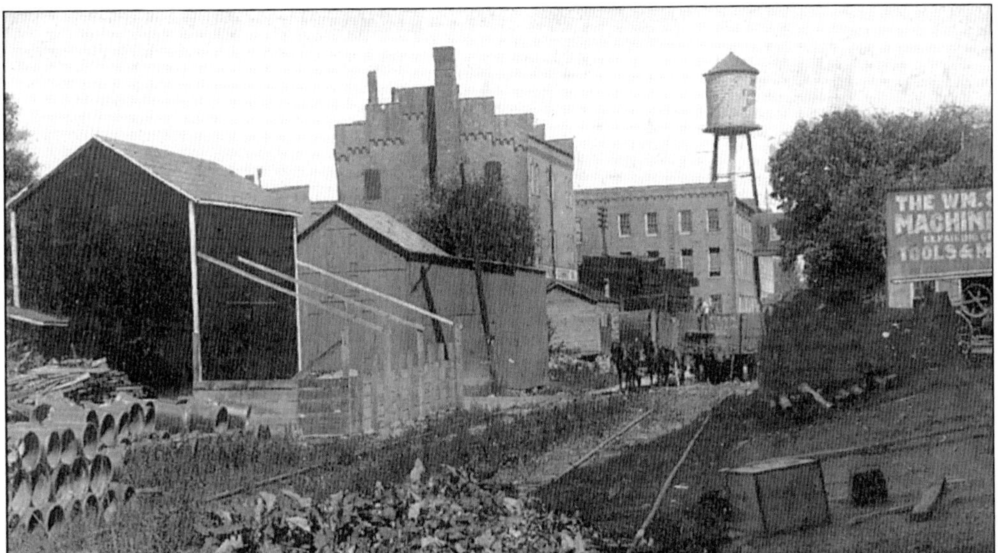

Casket and Furniture Factories. This is an unusual photograph of the backs, not front views, of two of Batesville's factories. To the right is William Schultz's Machine Shop, with his large painted sign. The railroad tracks were used to load and unload spurs for both these factories. Wagons of freight await loading onto cars, and stacks of various materials line the tracks. (Card #13829, by unknown publisher.)

Two

Jackson Township

In May 1822, previous township lines were obliterated, and eight new townships were formed in the county. Jackson, named for Andrew Jackson, was one of the eight. This small township in the northwest corner of the county includes 27 full and 7 fractional sections. Waterways in Jackson include Muscatatuck, Sugar, and Otter Creeks. The 1880 census lists a population of 1,482 in the township. The only town remaining today is Napoleon.

Napoleon. This was the second town to be platted in Ripley County. William Wilson founded the new village on the Lawrenceburg to Indianapolis Stage Line in 1820. Soon, taverns and hotels were built to accommodate the stage coach travelers. In 1970, Napoleon staged a very successful Sesqui-Centennial, and the village is now awaiting the year 2020.

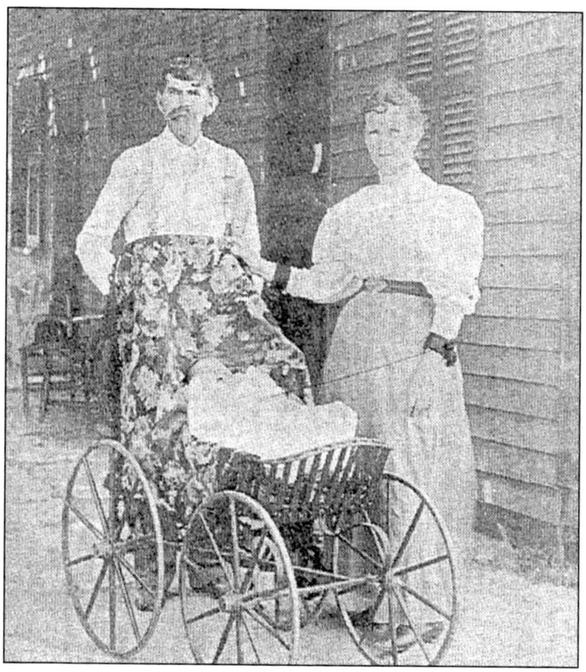

Albert and Emma Griffith and Son in Baby Carriage. Napoleon's post office is in the background. (Photograph by unknown photographer.)

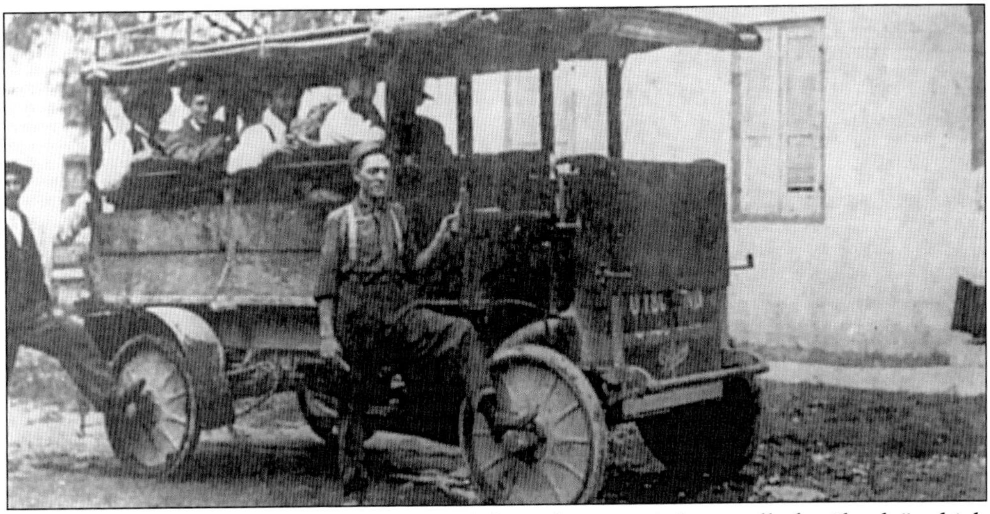

Early Motor-Driven Hack. Notice this solid-tired, open-air bus, called a "hack," which served as Napoleon's transportation. A luggage rack on top, canvas side curtains, and a small light adorn this chain-driven, unknown vehicle. The proud driver and full load of passengers indicate some special event. (Photograph by unknown photographer.)

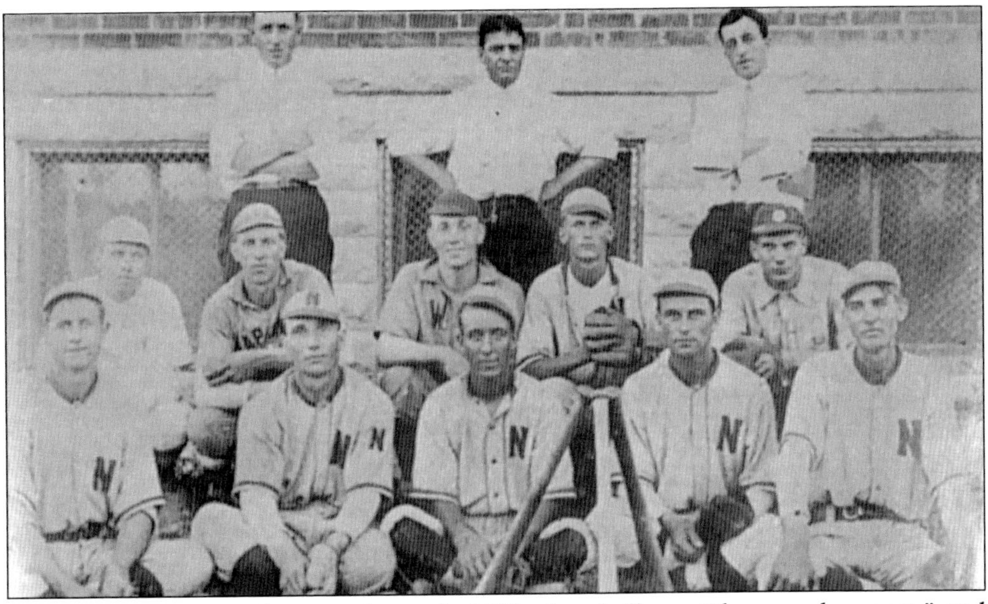

1914 Men's Baseball Team. In the early 1900s, baseball was "the popular sport," and every village, small and large, had its local team that played before large crowds every weekend. Many towns paid pitchers to bolster their teams when playing an arch-rival. In this picture the players are named, and each has the big "N" on his uniform. (Photograph by unknown photographer.)

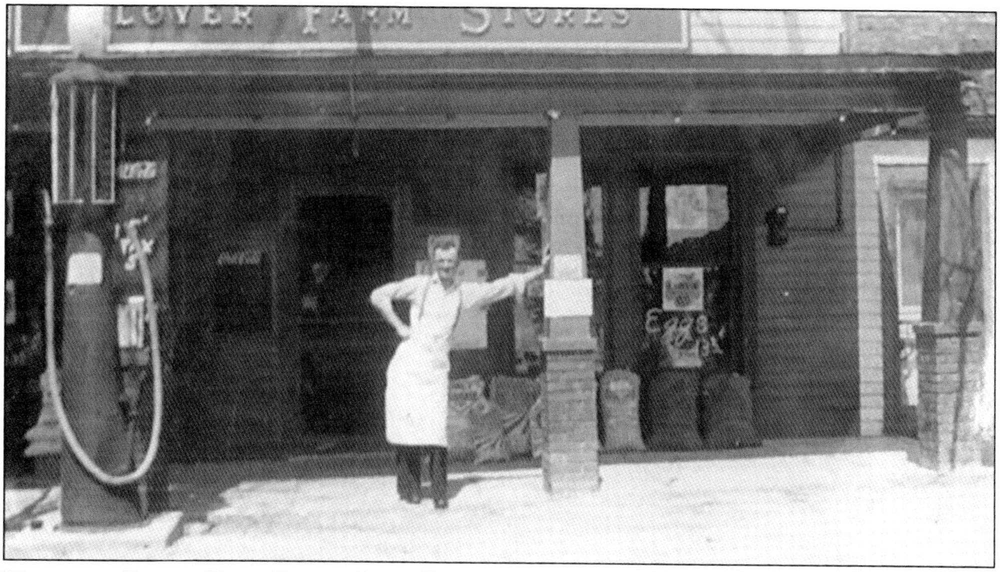

NAPOLEON CLOVER FARM STORE. Russell Griner is standing in front of his Clover Farm Agency Store in this 1930s photograph. Clover Farms were agency grocery stores, popular from the 1930s through the 1950s. Griner operated the store from 1932 to 1958. He also sold gasoline from this very tall gas pump. The white apron was common for butchers and clerks. (Real photograph by Griner Family.)

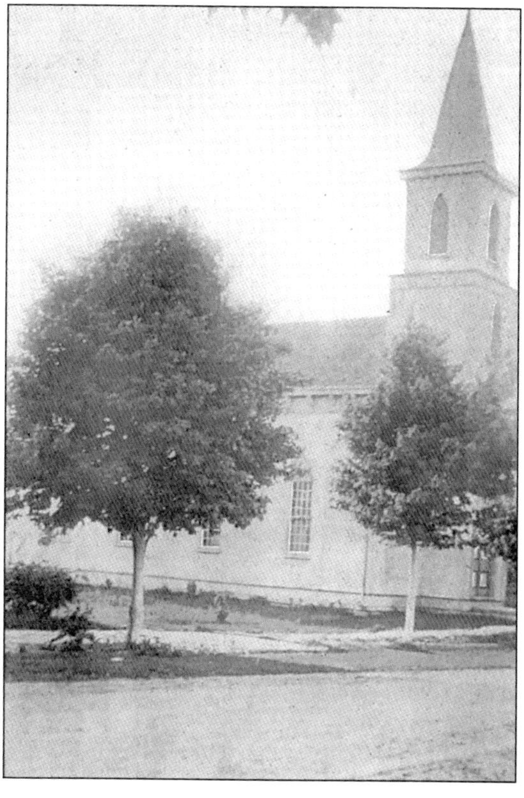

ST. JOHN'S LUTHERAN CHURCH. People living in the area around Napoleon were of predominately German descent, so a large percent were either Catholic or Lutheran. This 1912 card depicts St. John's Lutheran at the time. Today, St. John's continues as a house of worship in Napoleon. (Card by E.C. Knopp Co., Milwaukee, Wisconsin.)

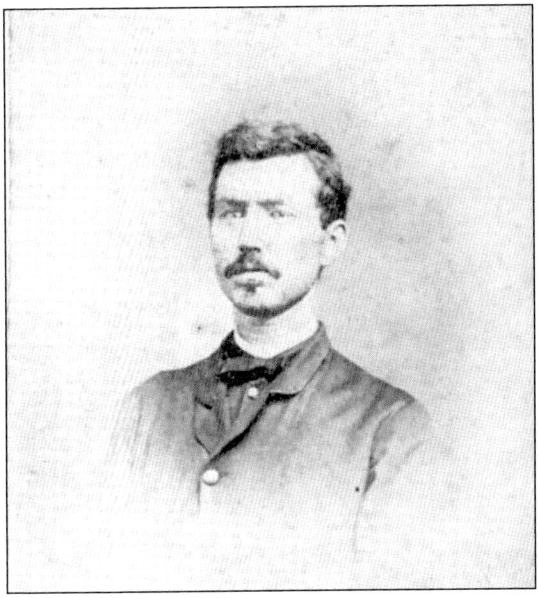

Captain John Hicks. Physician John Hicks served in Company F, 68th Ind. Volunteers during the Civil War. Hicks was a popular Napoleon physician until his death in 1915. His descendants reside today in the Napoleon area. (Photograph by unknown photographer.)

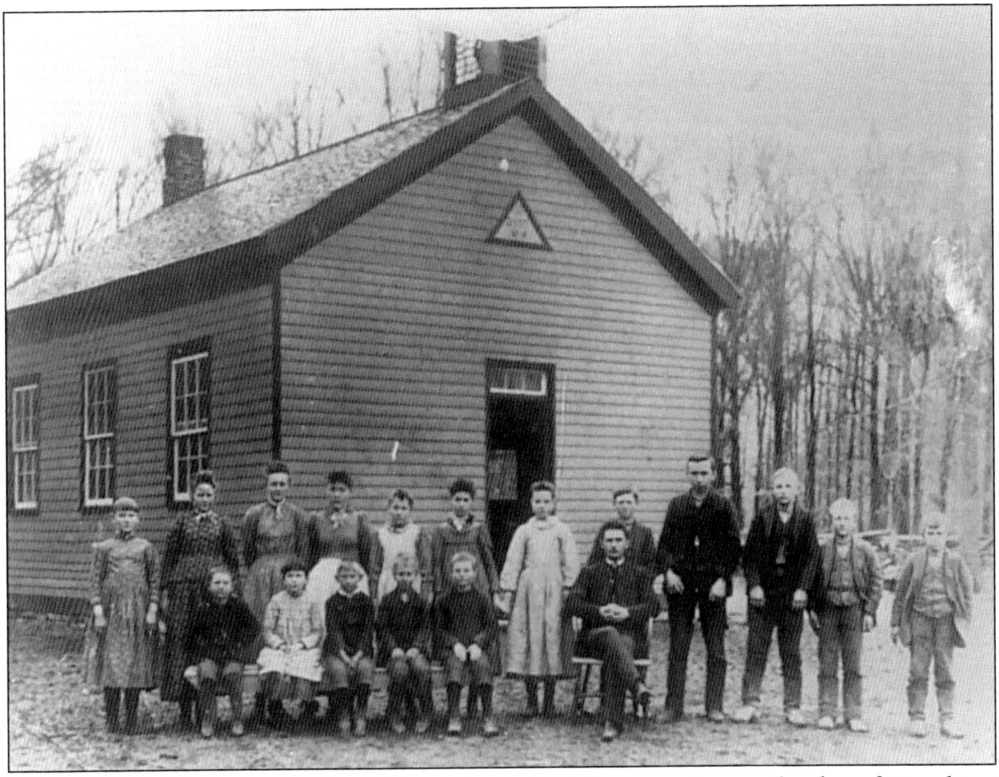

Van Kirk School House. A Jackson Township school house at the north edge of Napoleon was called Van Kirk's School after the Van Kirk family. This 1910 photograph features the teacher seated in his chair, surrounded by the students of all ages. All 17 students were taught by the one teacher, who you can bet had complete control. The first student in the second row is Marie Eaton. (Photograph by unknown photographer.)

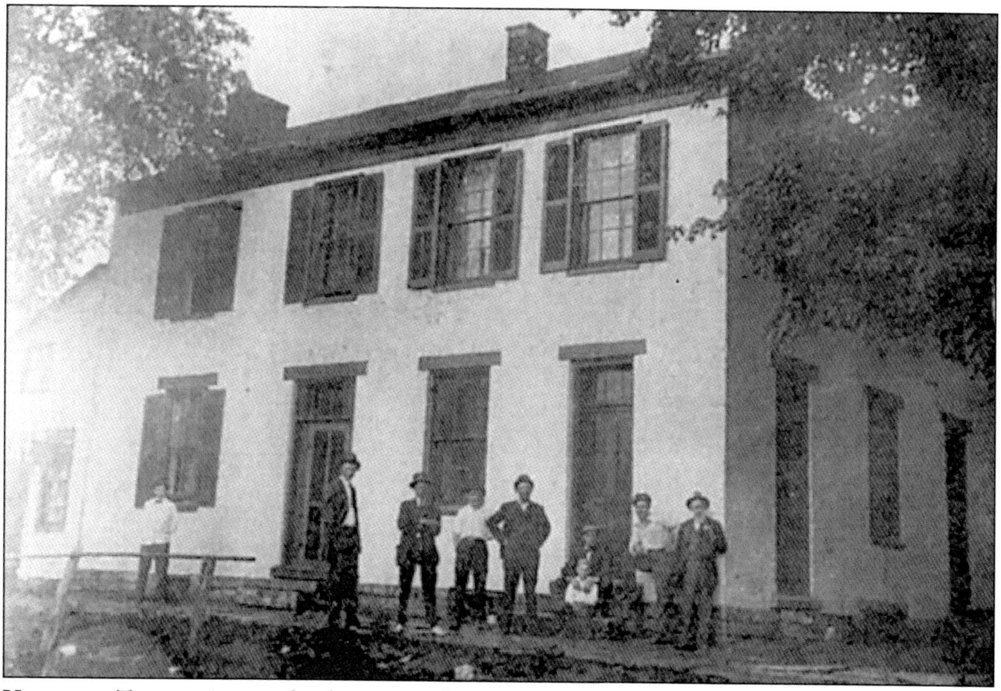

Napoleon Tavern. A popular hang-out for years in Napoleon, this tavern and restaurant was operated by Irvin Morrison. It was the hub of Napoleon. Those in the picture are listed by name from left to right. The building is of historic old brick. (Photograph by unknown photographer.)

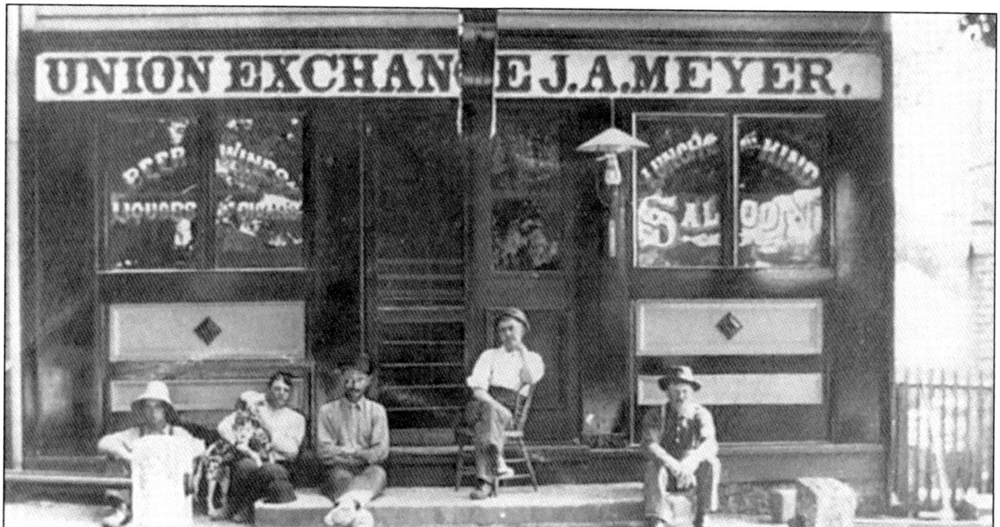

Union Exchange. This saloon was originally built in 1860, and was later owned by William Graff in 1877. Located southeast of the bank, the saloon was managed by Andrew Meyer. In this picture Fritz Meyer is seen holding a dog, while the others seem intent on watching whatever goes by. The windows feature beer, liquor, and lunch of all kinds. (Photograph by unknown photographer.)

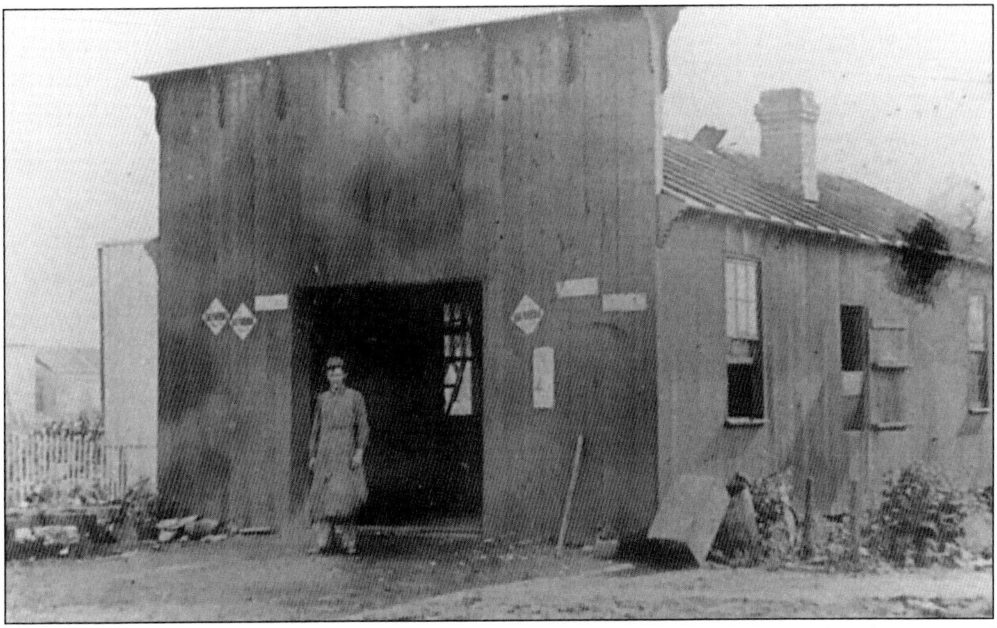

George Adams's Blacksmith Shop. George Adams is seen standing in the doorway of his shop clad in his leather apron. The apron was for his protection while he shod horses for his many customers. Before welding became available, the local blacksmiths heated, hammered, molded, and hardened all kinds of metal materials for farmers and townsmen. The shops were also a favorite hangout for loafers. (Photograph by unknown photographer.)

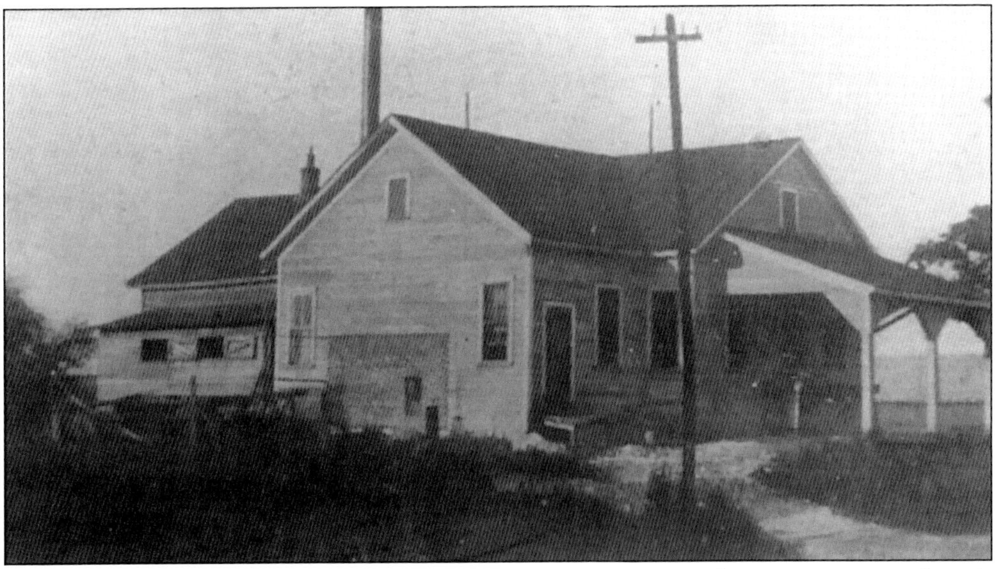

Napoleon Creamery. This large creamery was an important business to Napoleon's farm community. The creamery purchased milk, cream, butter, and eggs from area farmers, then shipped them to city markets. This was a profitable business for all concerned. Pre-packaged food products finally changed this trade. (Photograph by unknown photographer.)

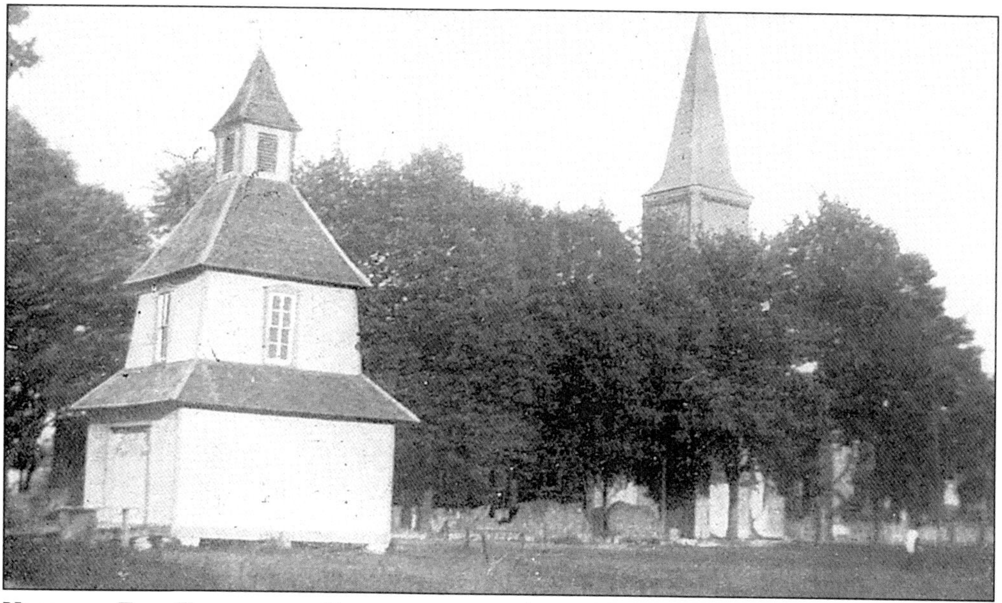

Napoleon Fire Department. For many years this odd little building was the home of the Napoleon Fire Department. The pumper was a hand-pulled water pumper, or a chemical-type apparatus stored in this building. In the background behind the trees, the steeple of the Catholic church towers over the greenery. (Card by E.C. Knopp, Milwaukee, Wisconsin.)

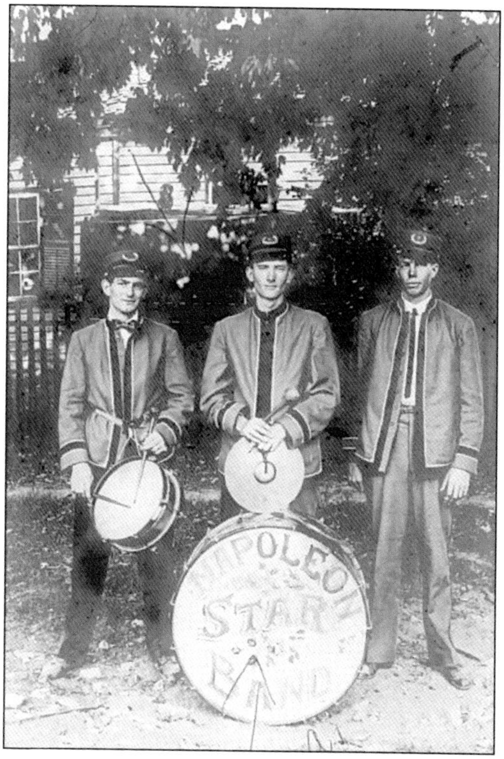

Napoleon's Star Band. The Napoleon Band members are, from left to right, as follows: Albert Narwold, Monford Alexander, and Edward Stegemoller. During the early 1900s, almost all towns sported a men's band. The bands performed at all local functions in their fancy uniforms. Many large towns had salaried bandmasters. (Card by unknown publisher.)

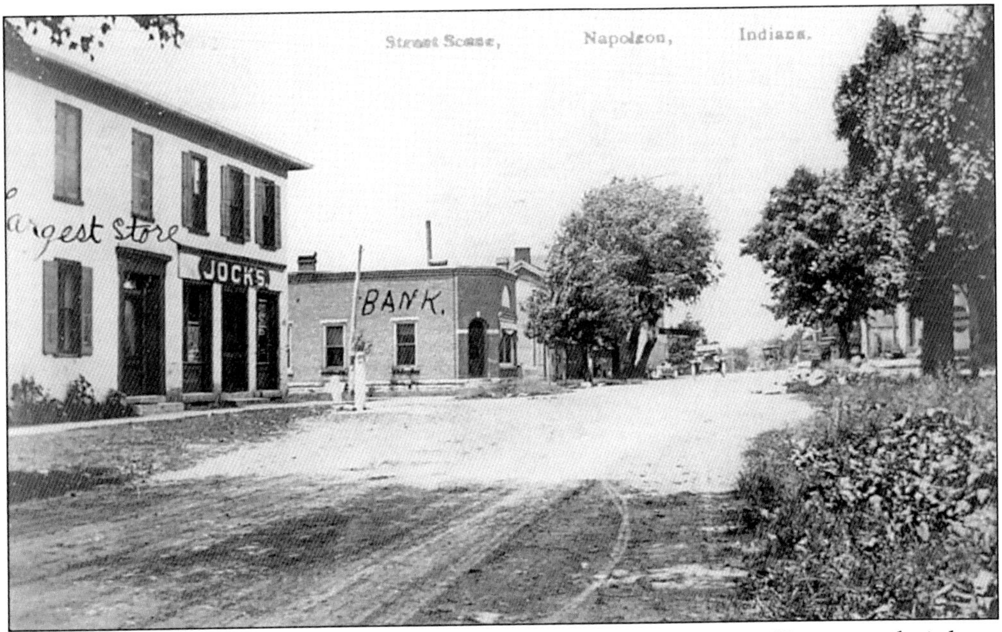

Napoleon's Main Street. In 1914, Napoleon's Main Street was still unpaved. A lone motor car is shown going south, and trees line the main drag through town. Jock's Store, and the brick bank building stand out in the picture. Notice the window flower boxes on the bank, and the classic wooden shutters on the large store building. (Card by unknown printer.)

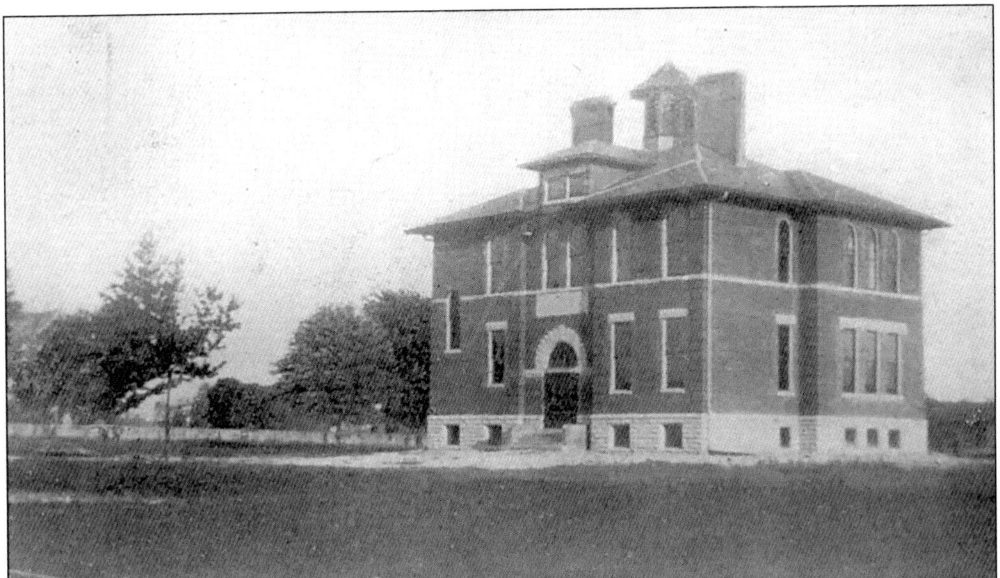

Napoleon Public School. Built in 1910, this two-story brick school building had four rooms on each floor and a full basement. The school graduated its first class in 1911, with 14 members. (Card by E.C. Knopp Co., Milwaukee, Wisconsin.)

Three

Center Township

Center Township was carved out of parts of Otter Creek, Jackson, Delaware, and Johnson Townships in June 1852. Center has 32 whole and 4 half sections, which include the towns of Osgood, Otter Village, and Vine Springs. Osgood is the principal town.

Osgood was named in honor of A.L. Osgood, who was chief civil engineer for the O&M Railroad which built through town in 1853. Before this time the area was known as "Clay Town." Mr. Osgood named the streets after the type of trees grown locally; hence the names Buckeye, Sycamore, Walnut, Cherry, Elm, and Maple Streets. As a result of the railroad, stone quarries, dairy farming, and other industries, the town prospered. Last year the town received a very generous gift from the Gilmore & Goldie Reynolds family, who left more than $20 million in a foundation for the benefit of the town.

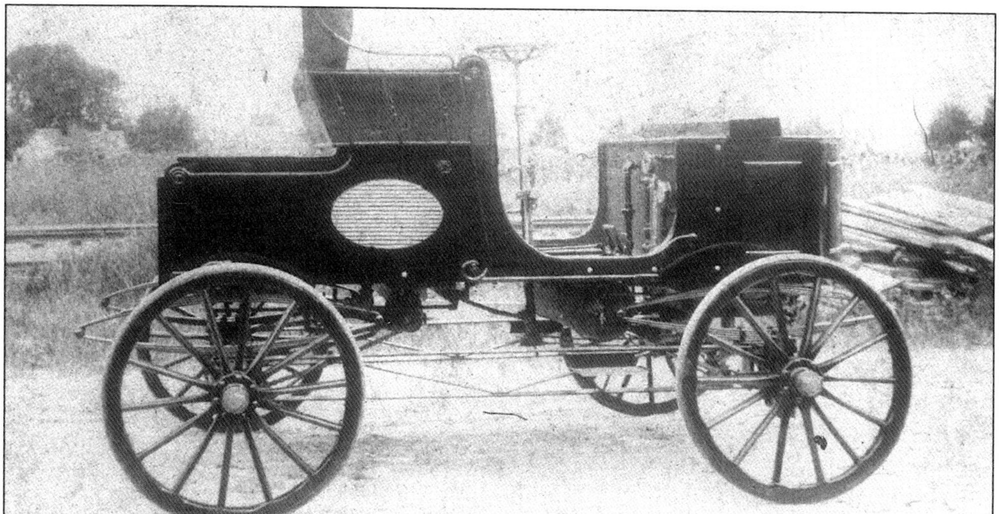

King Steam Car. In 1897, Henry P. King and his helper, James Humphrey, planned to build a car. King owned the Osgood Foundry & Machine Shop and furnished all the metal parts, while The Huber Buggy Co. of Cincinnati made the body. In 1898, the car was running back and forth to Benham, Indiana. The car was registered with the State of Indiana in 1904, the first year registration was required. The Kings were master machinists who solved all kinds of knotty problems in their shop. The car runs on compressed air today. (Photograph by unknown photographer.)

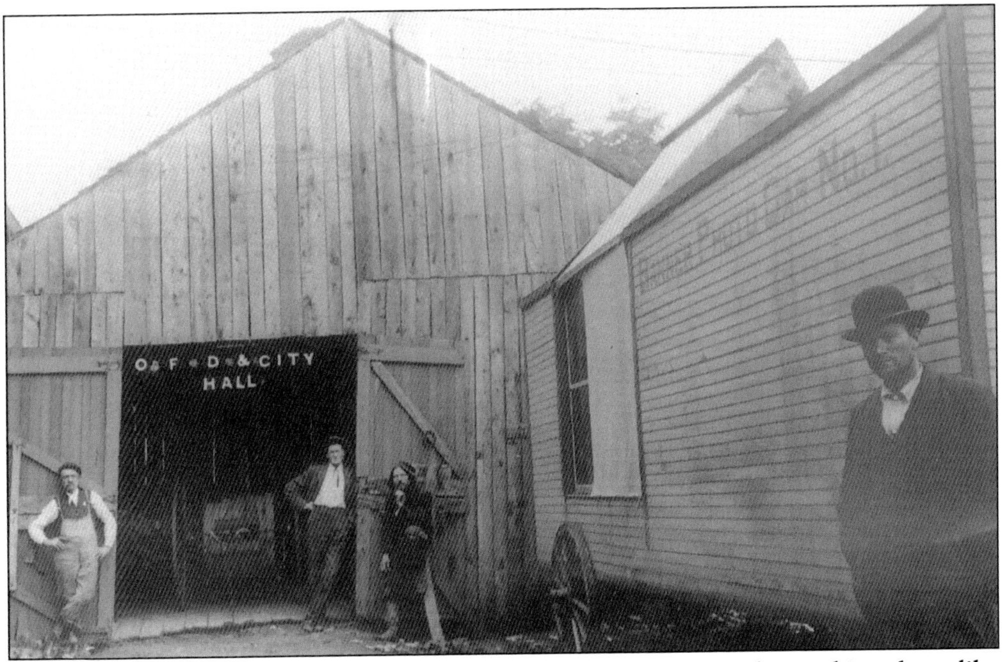

Osgood Fire Department and City Hall. The fire department was housed in a barn-like structure in the main part of town. The engine was a chemical apparatus pulled by the townsmen. Before more modern firefighting equipment was available, this type snuffed out many a fire. On the right is "Robert's Banner Photo," a portable photo laboratory. (Banner Photo.)

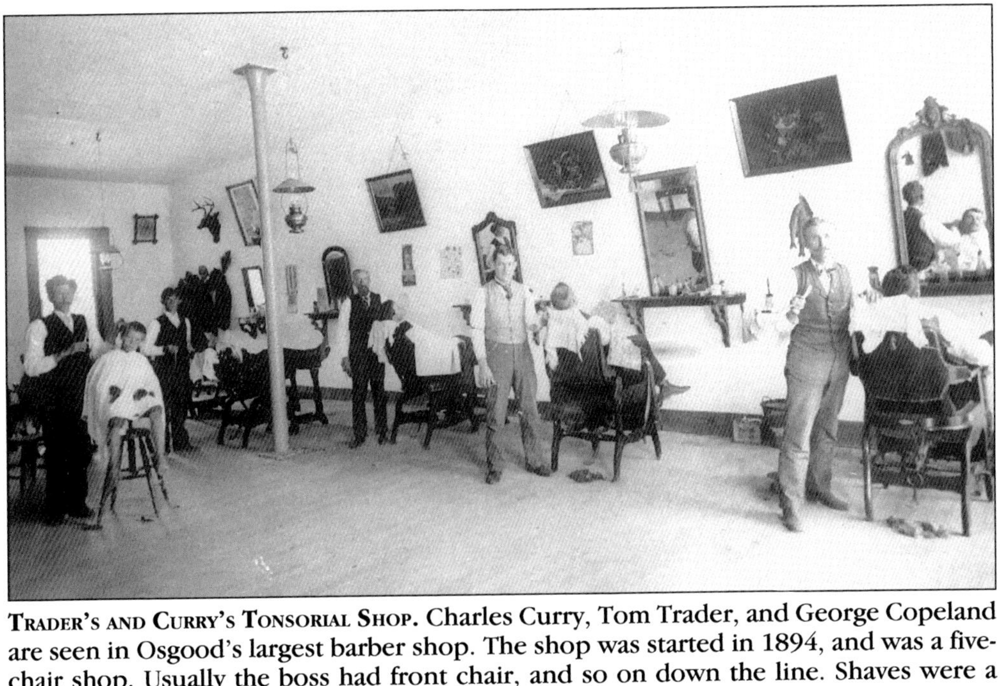

Trader's and Curry's Tonsorial Shop. Charles Curry, Tom Trader, and George Copeland are seen in Osgood's largest barber shop. The shop was started in 1894, and was a five-chair shop. Usually the boss had front chair, and so on down the line. Shaves were a major part of the old time barber's business. (Photograph by unknown photographer.)

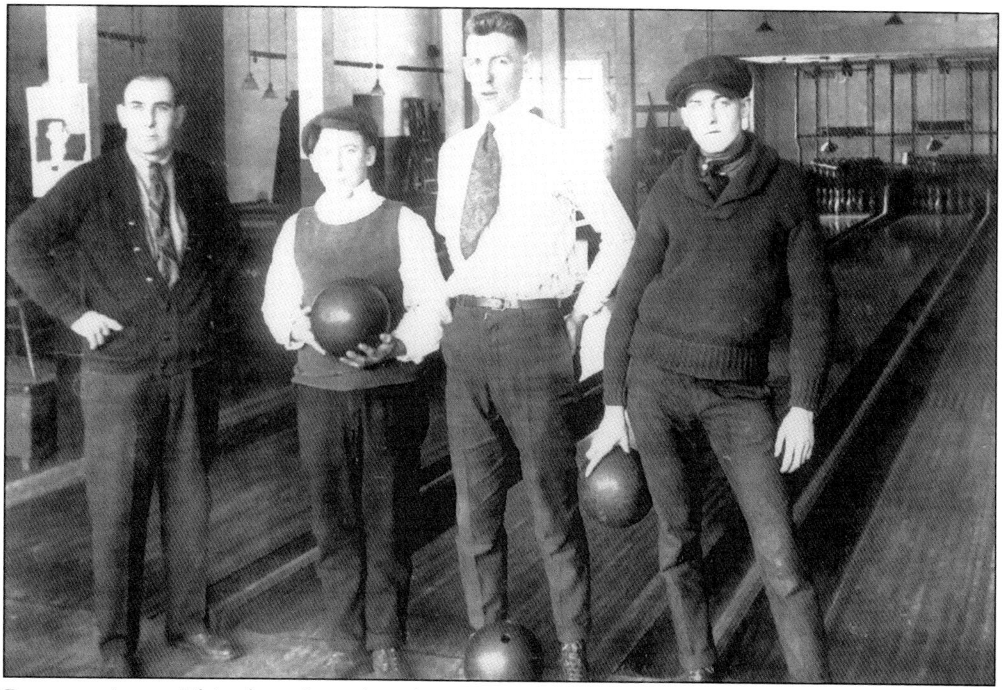

Bowling Alley. This three-lane bowling alley was upstairs in a large brick building on Buckeye Street, and was once owned by Humphrey's Garage, a Chevrolet agency. Today, a new medical building occupies the site. Hand setters, usually young boys, set the pins. This was a dangerous job at times. (Photograph by unknown photographer.)

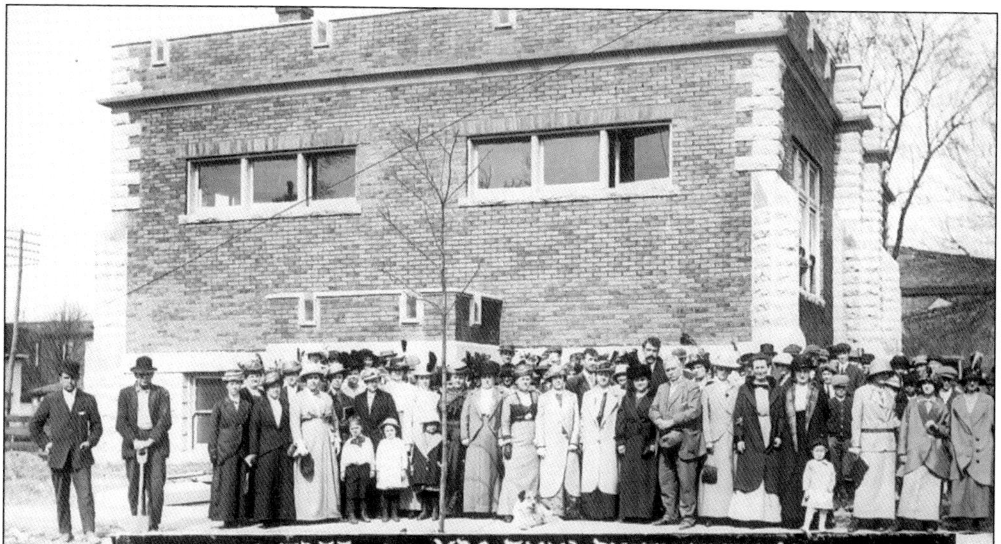

Memorial Tree at Library. On April 17, 1914, the Entre Nous Club of Osgood planted a tree in memory of Mrs. Emma Pusey Freeman. The club was organized in 1909, and belonged to the Indiana Federation of Clubs. Many good works were performed by these women. (Photograph by unknown photographer.)

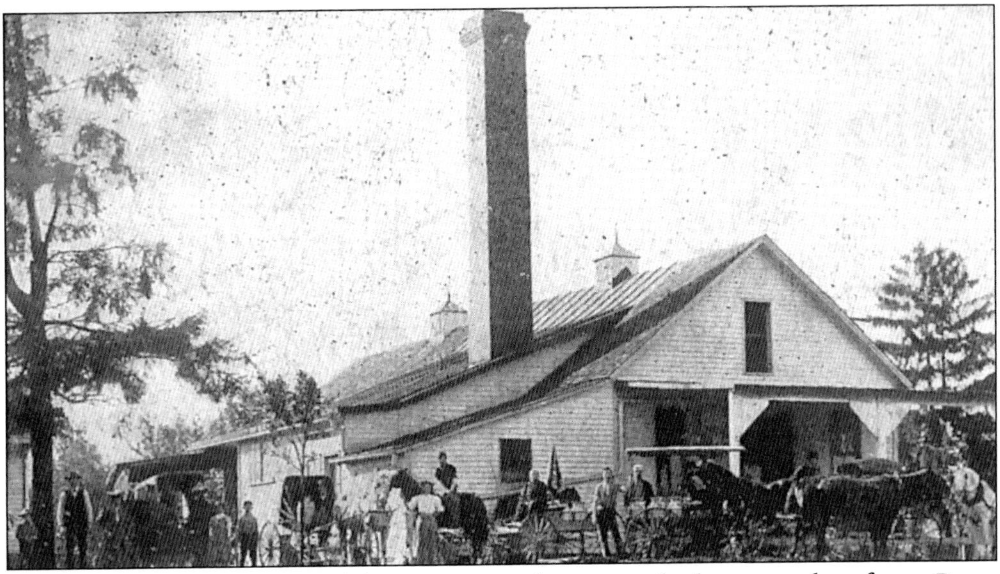

The Herman Creamery. Gottleb Herman, a butter and cheese maker from Bern, Switzerland, opened a creamery in 1904 on lot #242, on the southeast corner of Walnut and Jefferson Streets. Herman also had creameries in Pierceville, Napoleon, North Vernon, and Look-out. A very busy day is depicted on this 1908 card. (Unsigned card.)

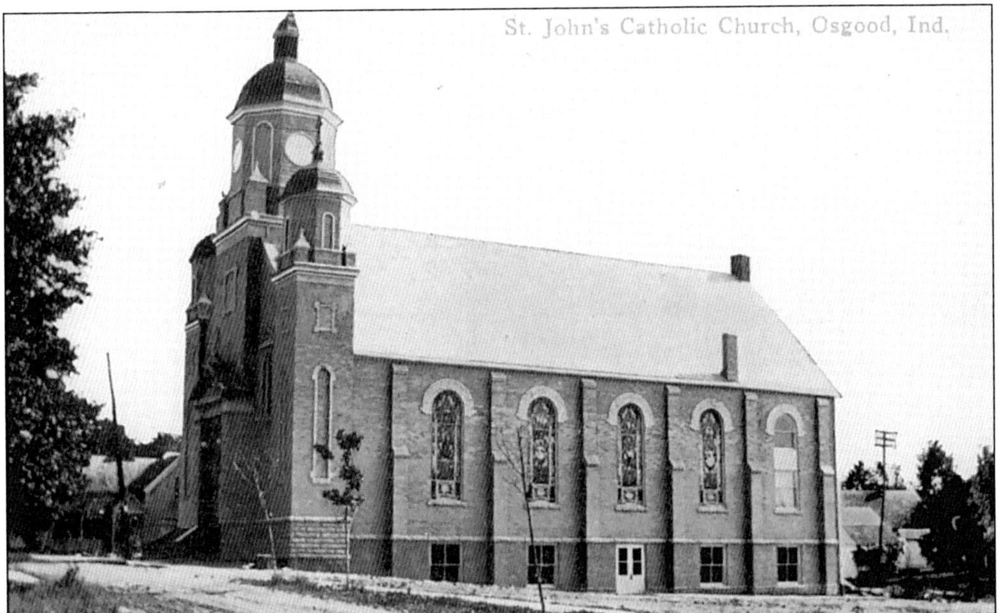

St. John's Catholic Church. A crowd of two thousand attended the cornerstone laying and dedication of this second Catholic Church in Osgood on August 23, 1913. St. John's is easily seen on the west side of Highway 421 (Buckeye Street.) (Card #40131 by unknown publisher.)

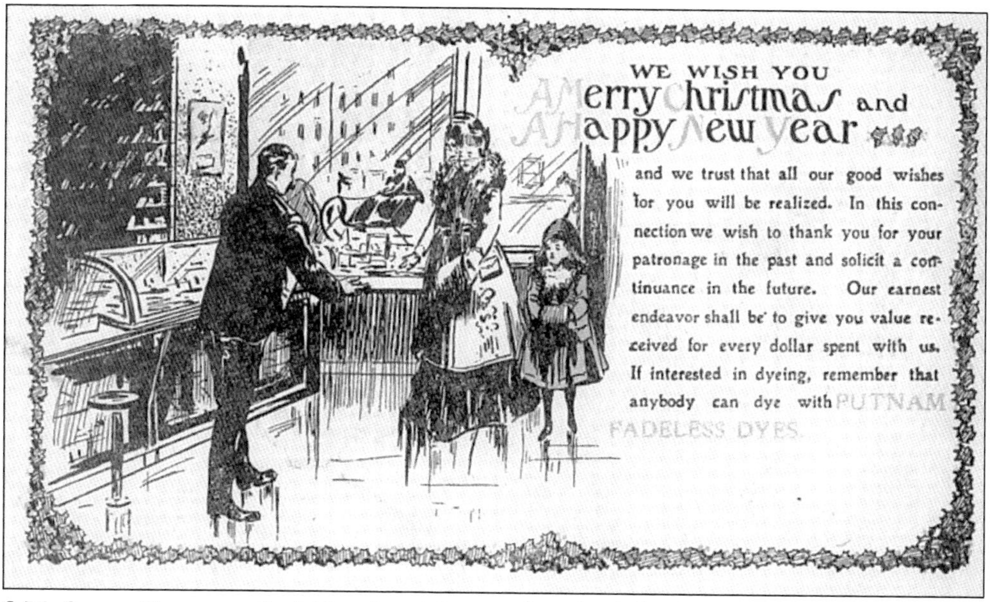

S.M. SMITH, DRUGGIST. Smith's advertising card wished the lucky receiver a very Merry Christmas, and a Happy New Year. This was Smith's method of thanking his old customers for past patronage, and plugging "Putman's Dyes." Smith's store was located on the east side of Buckeye Street. (Card by unknown publisher.)

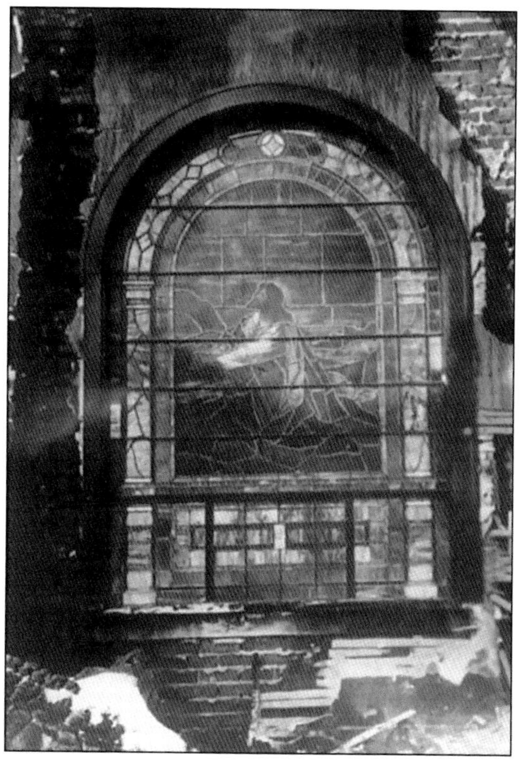

M.E. CHURCH WINDOW. The Gethesemane stained-glass window was a gift honoring the memory of Dr. William Kemper, Osgood pharmacist and physician. On February 24, 1934, the church suffered a devastating fire. The $10,000 fire between the plaster and brick walls doomed the building. To the amazement of all who saw it, the window survived without a scratch or crack—a near miracle. The words: "Lo, I am with you always" written on the window gave members the will to rebuild. (Photograph by unknown photographer.)

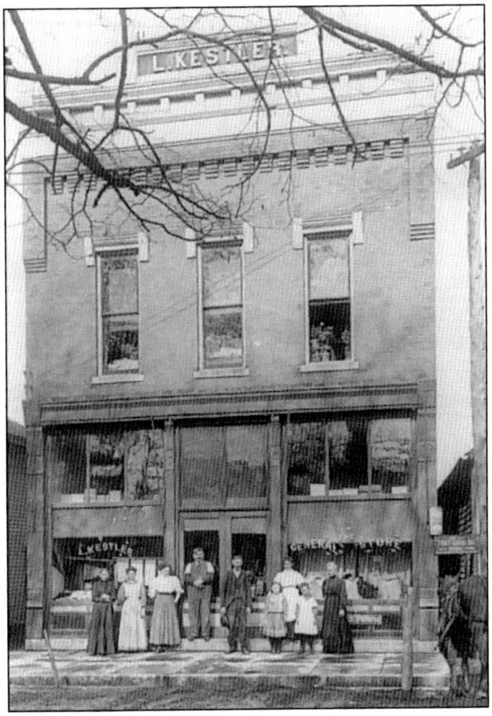

L. Kestler's Big Store. In 1901, Lawrence Kestler built this two-story brick "House of Quality Store." In his Buckeye Street store, Kestler sold dry goods, notions, groceries, and general merchandise. In front of the store are Lawrence Kestler with his wife, children, and one horse. (Photograph by unknown photographer.)

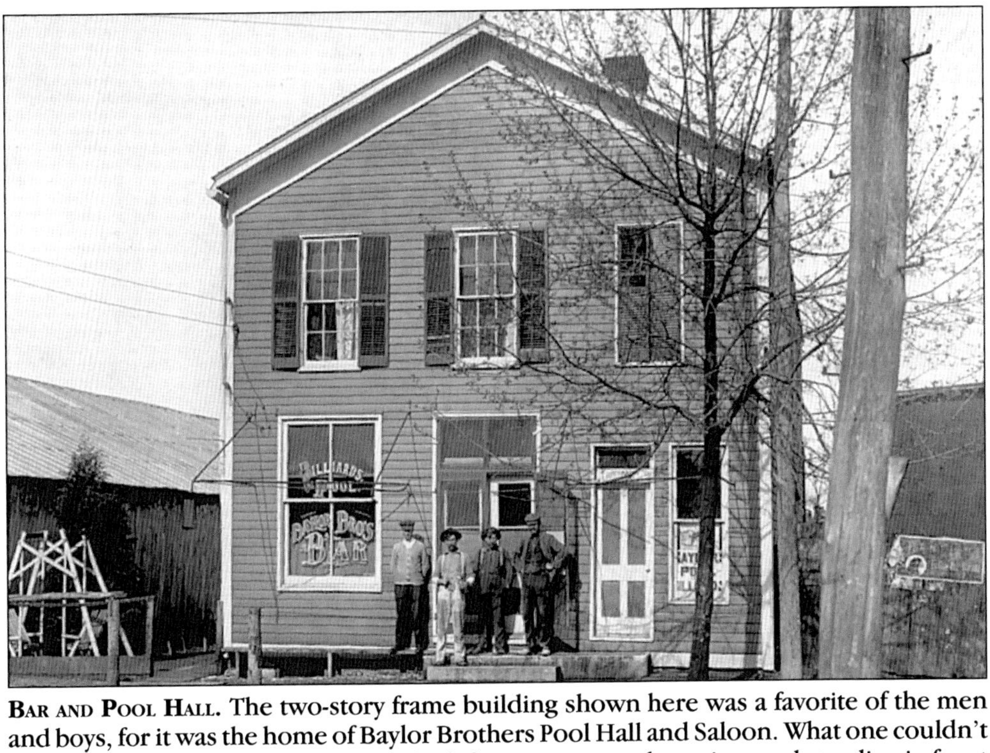

Bar and Pool Hall. The two-story frame building shown here was a favorite of the men and boys, for it was the home of Baylor Brothers Pool Hall and Saloon. What one couldn't learn here wasn't worth learning. At the left is a once popular swing, and standing in front are a few of the bar's happy customers. (Photograph by unknown photographer.)

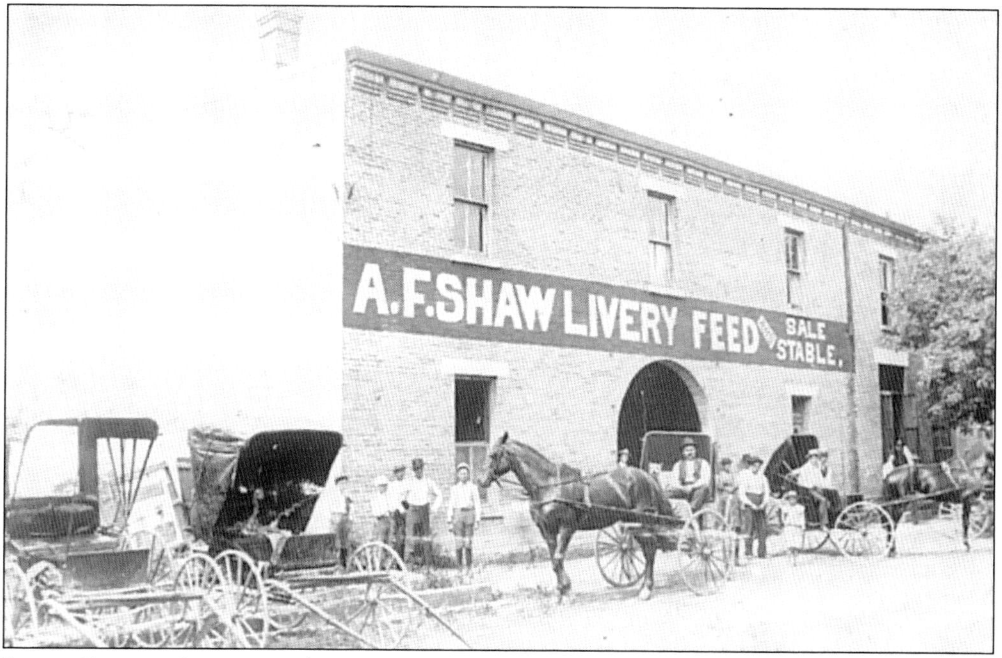

Livery Stable. Constructed in 1891, this large brick building was on the site of two earlier liveries that burned. Albert Shaw came to Osgood in 1898, and purchased the livery and feed business. With the advent of the automobile, the livery was forced to close. Later, Beer and Herman remodeled the building into the Columbia Theatre, a forerunner to the Dam Theatre. (Photograph by unknown photographer.)

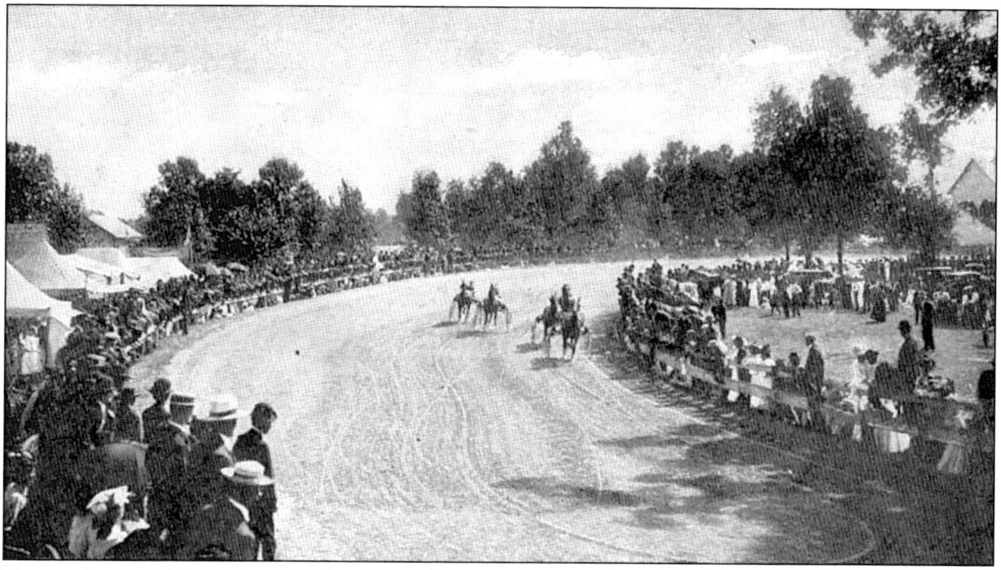

Ripley County Fair. A nice, big woods on the edge of Osgood was selected as Ripley County's Fairgrounds. The trotting and running horse races drew crowds, with a lot of side betting. Oddly enough, Thursdays were considered "the day" to go to the fair. In 1911, President John Eckert and Secretary G.R. Kemper were the promoters. (Card #3021, Fair Publishing, Norwood, Ohio.)

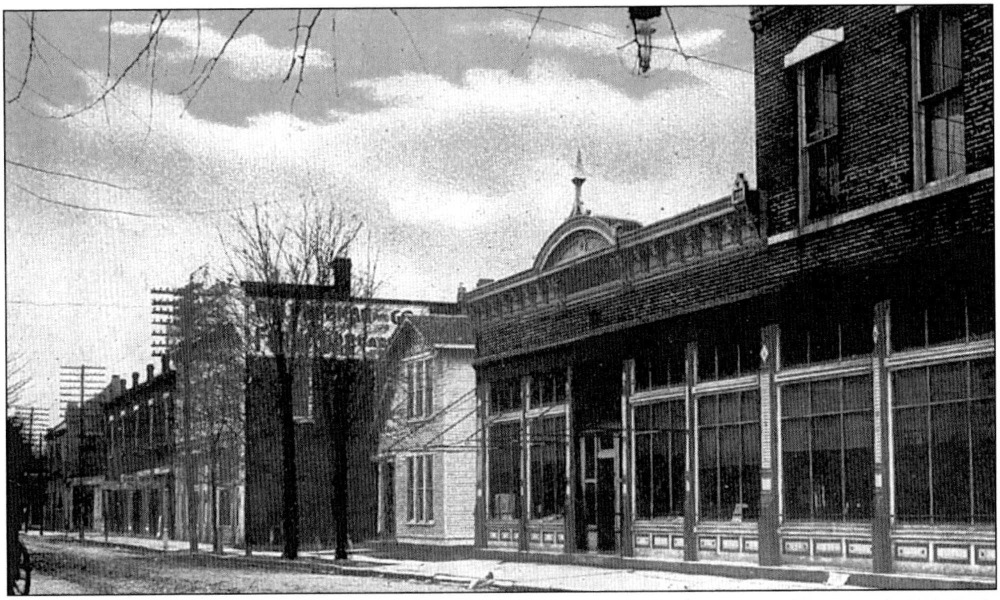

Ripley Street. At the corner of Ripley and Walnut Streets, Ashman & Glascow held their store's grand opening in 1890. Henry Stork ordered 100,000 bricks to build this $10,000 building. Many a business has operated in this building since Ashman & Glascow. (Card by unknown publisher.)

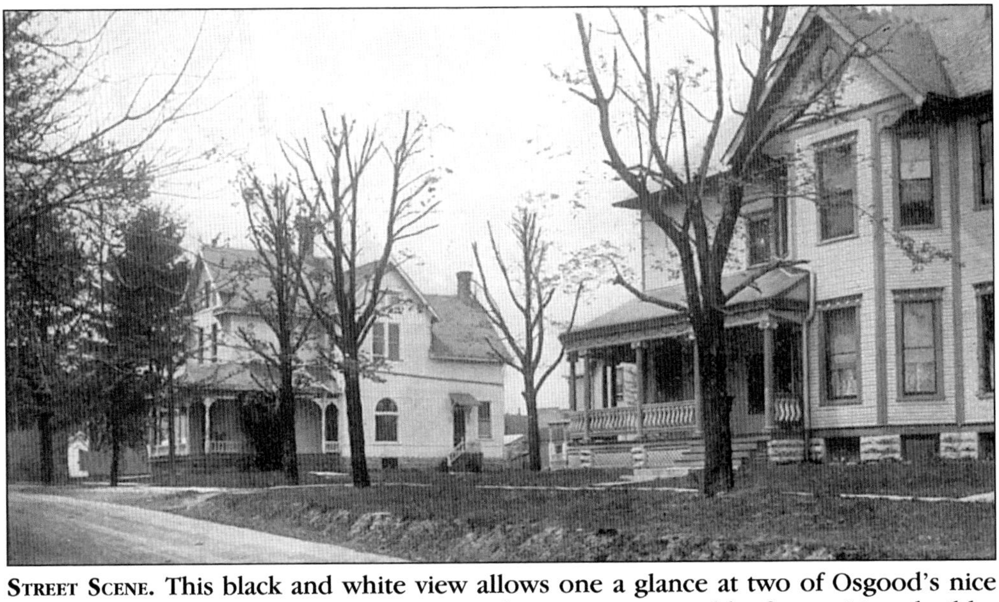

Street Scene. This black and white view allows one a glance at two of Osgood's nice homes. Many times, successful farmers or businessmen would, after retiring, build a pretentious home in town. These are that type of home. (Batavia Card Co., Batavia, Ohio, for Van Dewall Music Co.)

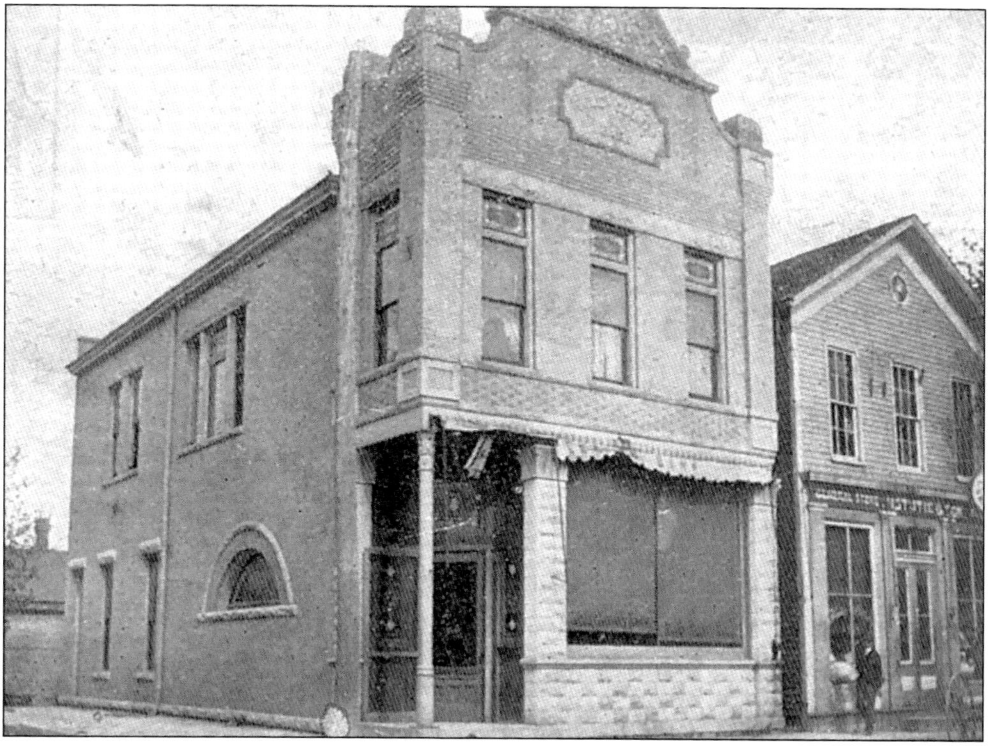

Osgood Bank. The Ripley County Bank was organized in 1887. The pictured building was erected in 1902. *The Journal* office was moved to a lot farther south to allow space for the new bank. In 1977, the bank moved into a new modern facility at Buckeye and Eckert Streets. (Card by unknown publisher.)

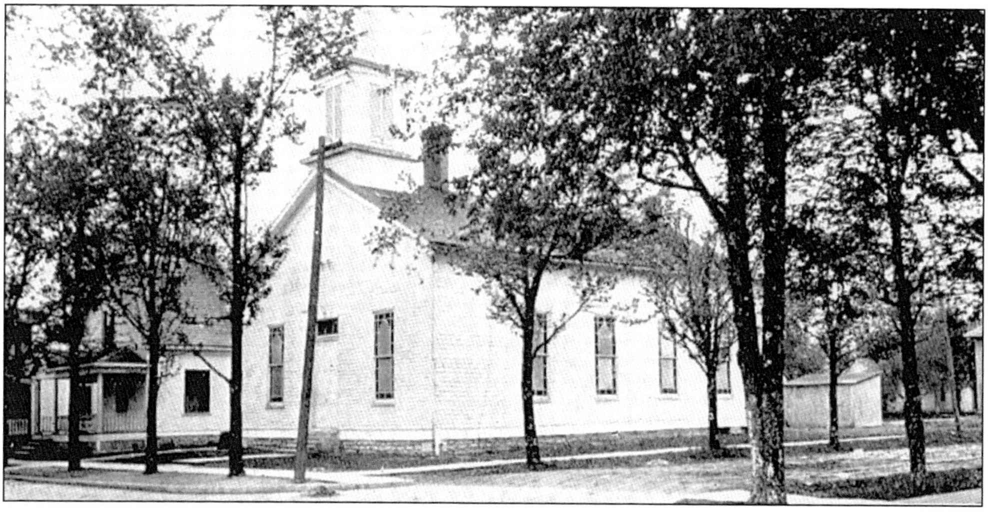

Methodist Church. The United Methodist Church was completed in 1862, on lots #41 and 42. The first public service in the new church was a political address by Governor Oliver P. Morton. In 1922, the church was raised to its present height, and a basement with a furnace was installed. In 1933, the walls were brick veneered. (Card published by G.A. Triplett, Osgood, Indiana.)

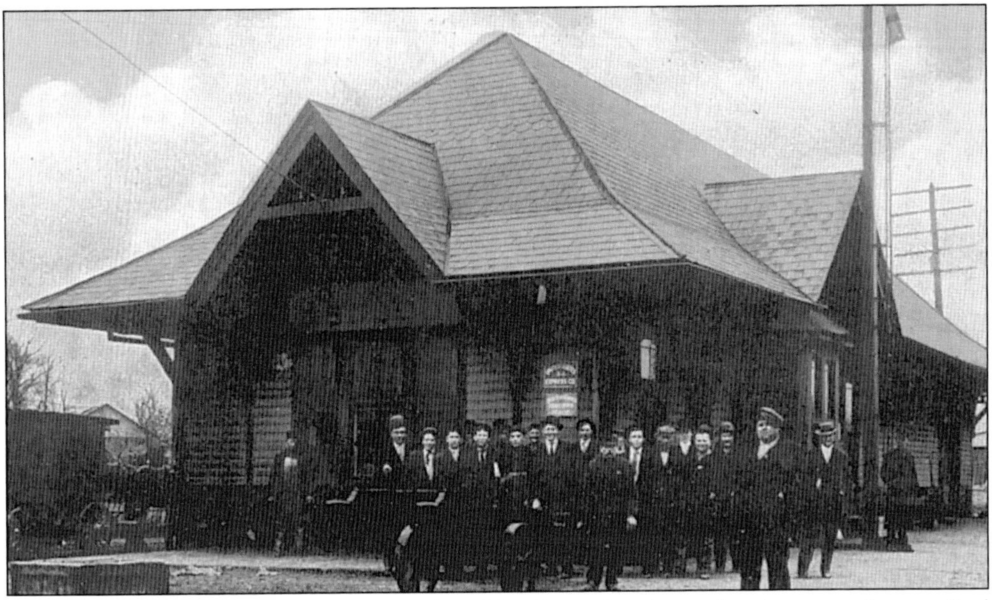

B&O Railroad Depot. The O&M Railroad built tracks through what was then called "Clay Town" in 1852. The head surveyor and engineer was a Mr. A.L. Osgood, and it was in his honor that the town received the name "Osgood." The Baltimore & Ohio Railroad Company purchased the O&M, and operated for many years. On the left of this picture is a switch siding, and to the right is the modern depot. (Photograph by unknown photographer.)

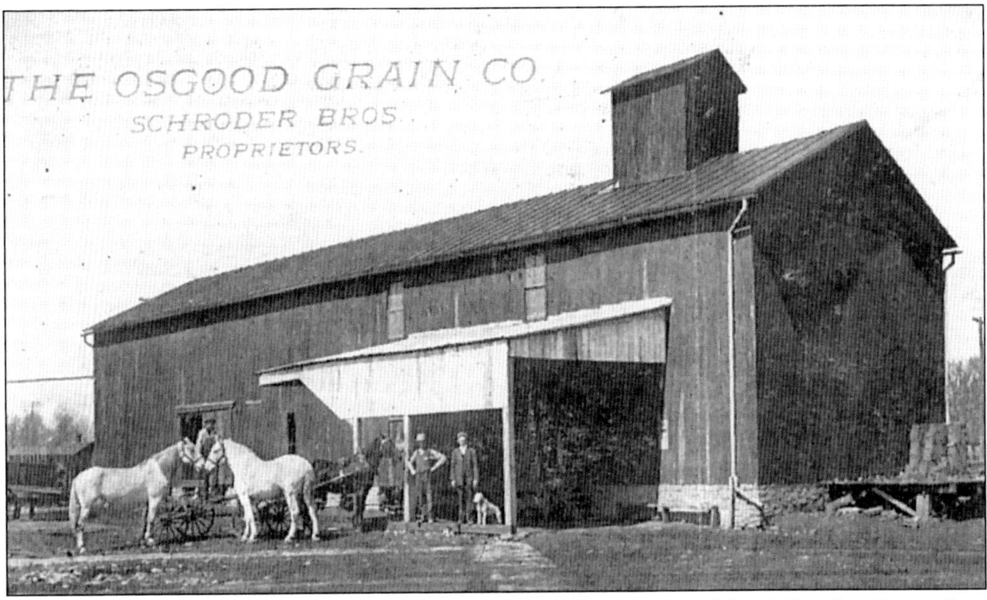

Osgood Grain Company. The grain company was first operated by Schroder Bros., but in 1916 it became the Osgood Grain Company. Pillsbury's Best was advertised on the end of the large barn-type building. The Schroder brothers and their dog are seen at the center, and two white horses are visible at the left of the picture. In 1931, Texaco Feed Co. became the new owner. (Card by unknown publisher.)

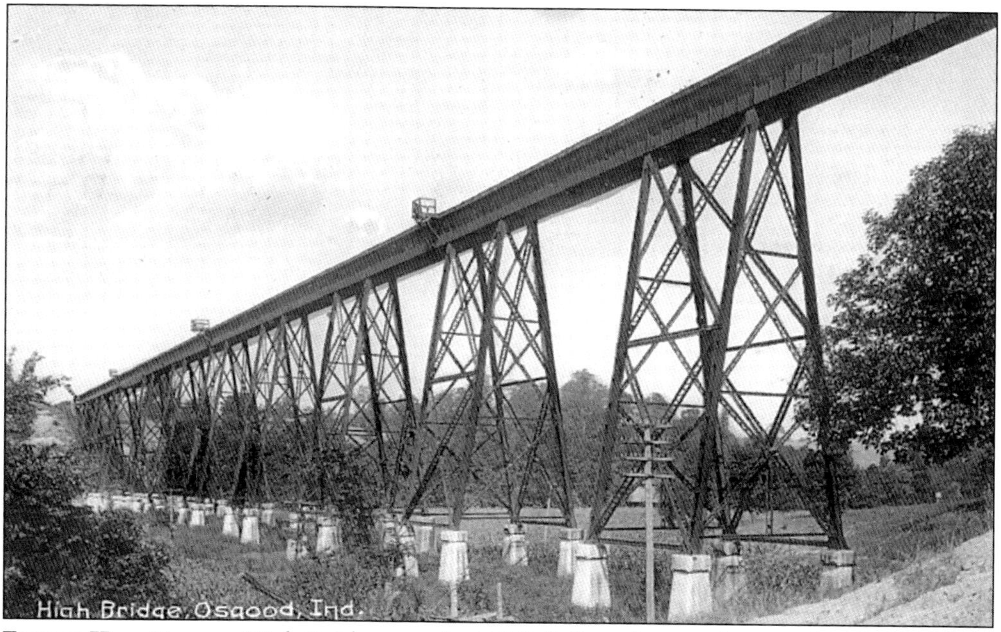

Famous High Bridge. High Bridge, on the B&O Railroad east of Osgood, was 1,080 feet long and 112 feet high. One of the largest bridges on the railroad, it had a guard at each end during WW II to prevent sabotage. The bridge is still in use today. (Card #3218, by Kraemer Art Co., Cincinnati & Berlin.)

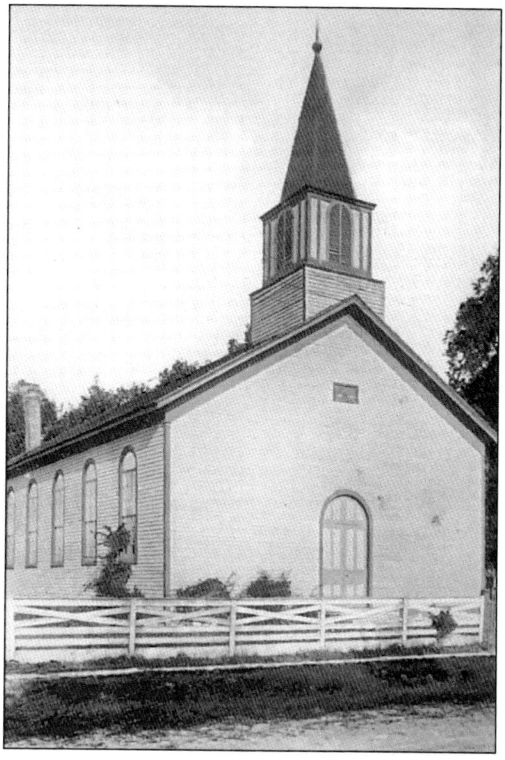

St. John's Catholic Church. Initially a mission church of St. Maurice in Napoleon, this frame structure was built in 1867 at a cost of $800. It was on the corner of North Sycamore and Western Avenues, on the west end of town. Two masses were held, at 10 a.m., on the first and third Sundays of each month. (Card #3221, Kraemer Art Co., Cincinnati & Berlin.)

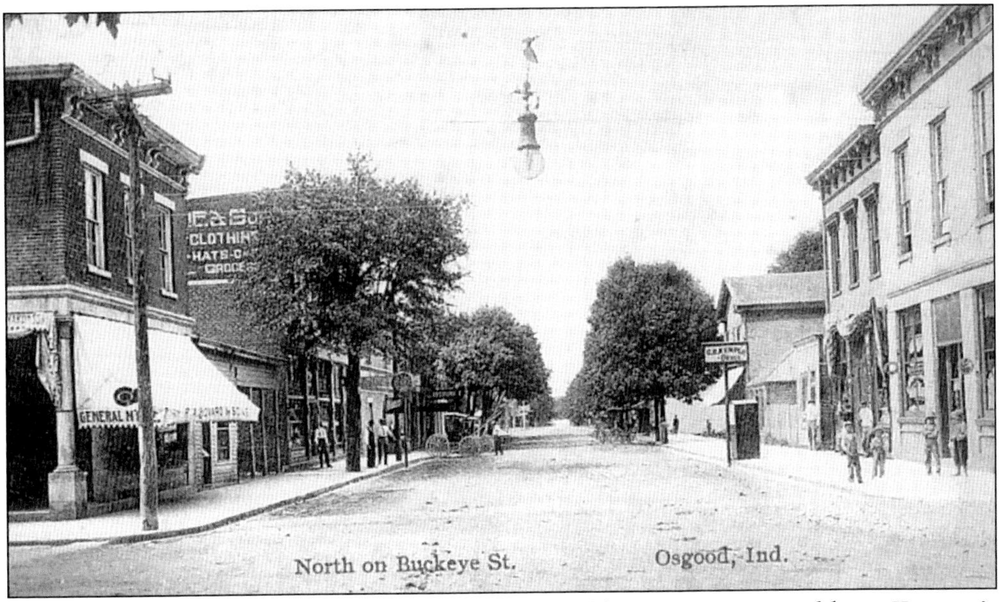

North on Buckeye Street. Looking north from Franklin Street, one could see Kemper's Drug Store sign, as well as four boys and two adults on the sidewalk. Across the street on Buckeye is R.A. Bovard & Sons general store, and next, a clothing store. A lone buggy and a strange-looking street light are in plain view. (Kraemer Art Co., card by G.R. Kemper.)

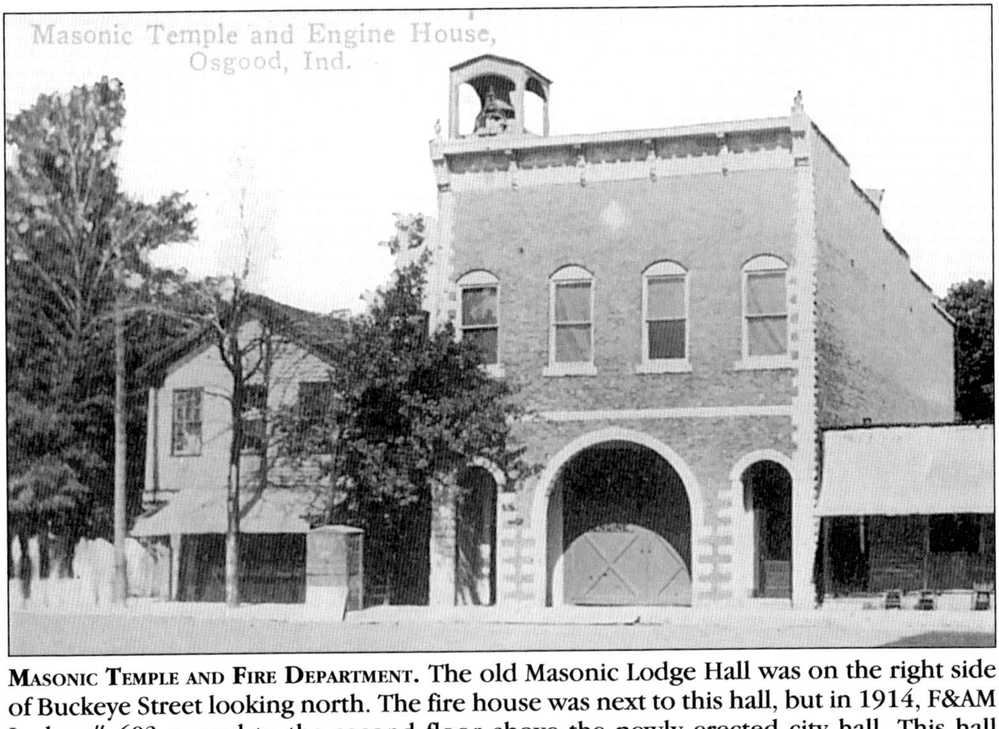

Masonic Temple and Fire Department. The old Masonic Lodge Hall was on the right side of Buckeye Street looking north. The fire house was next to this hall, but in 1914, F&AM Lodge # 603 moved to the second floor above the newly erected city hall. This hall cost $3,400. In 1984, the hall was remolded and a chair lift installed. (Card #40132 by unknown publisher.)

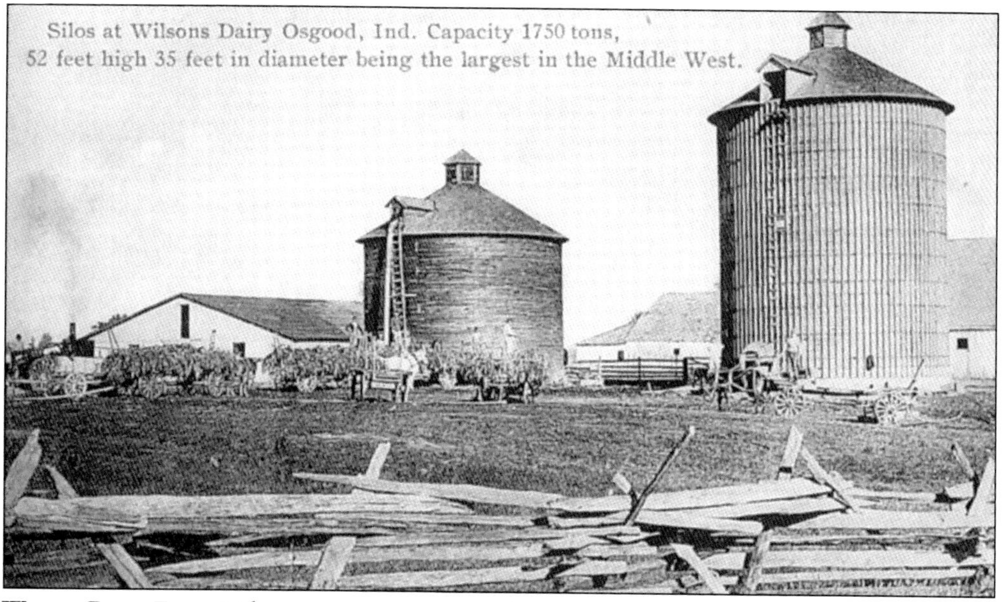

Wilson Dairy Farm. Wilson's Dairy Farm was, for a while, the largest dairy farm in Indiana. Many different view cards were published showing this famous farm. The two silos were the largest in the Midwest. Wilson hired many milkers, feeders, and farm workers to aid in shipping milk by the B&O Railroad to Cincinnati and other points. (Kraemer card, by unknown publisher.)

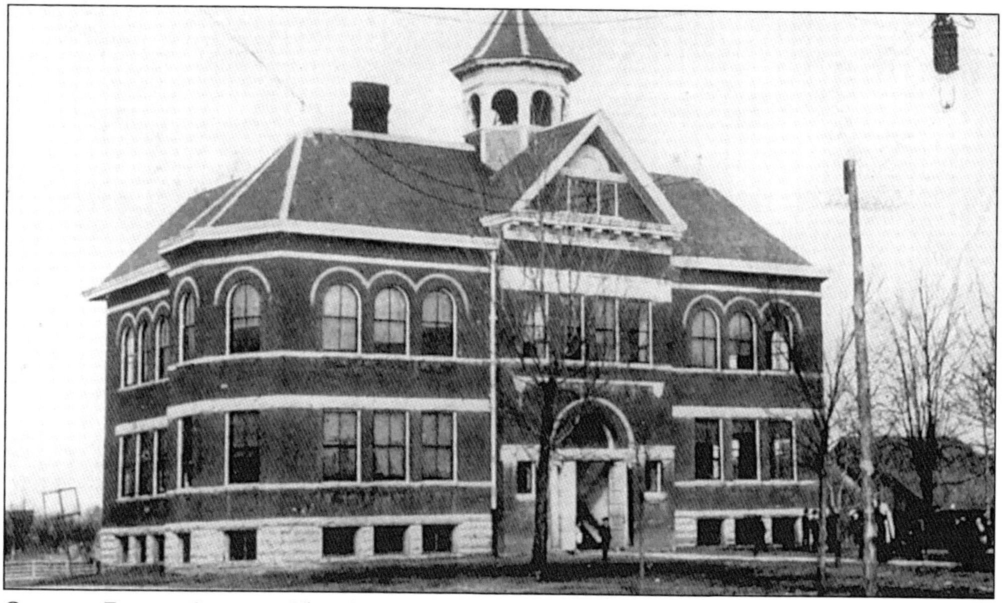

Osgood Public School. This large, two-story brick school house was built in 1886 at the corner of Cravens and Maple Streets. At first it was a six room affair, then in 1908, two more rooms were added to the north wing. In 1930, this school became the high school for all of Center Township, because of the closing of many small rural schools. This building later became Osgood's Grade School. (Card by Kraemer Art Co., Cincinnati, Ohio.)

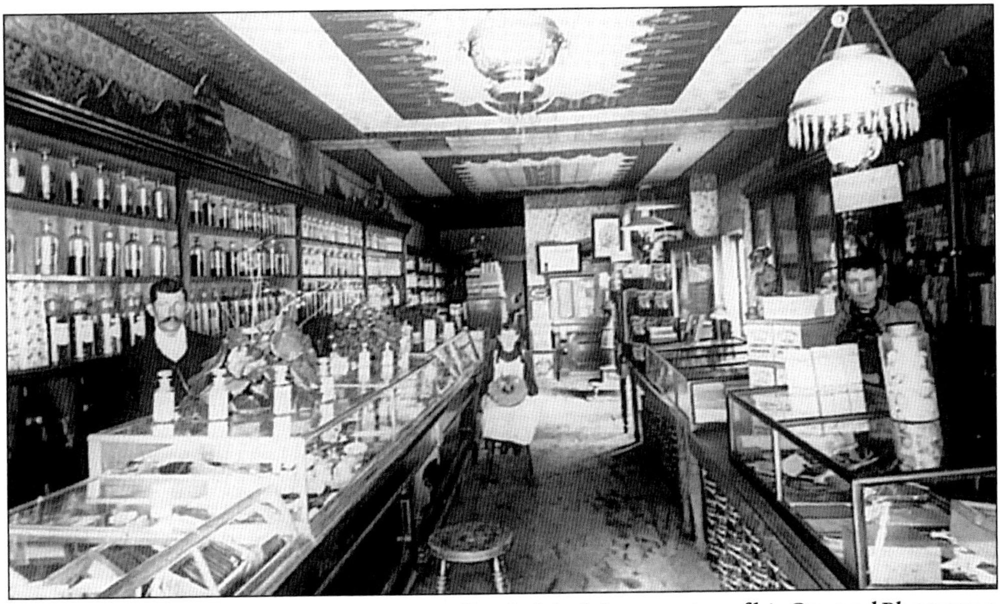

Brenton's Pharmacy. T.M. Brenton is standing behind the counter of his Osgood Pharmacy. Seated in the aisle is his daughter Mollie, and Mrs. Brenton is visible under the fancy lamp to the right. The metal ceilings, glass-covered show cases, and glass, labeled jars on the shelves were all popular at that time. (Photograph by unknown photographer.)

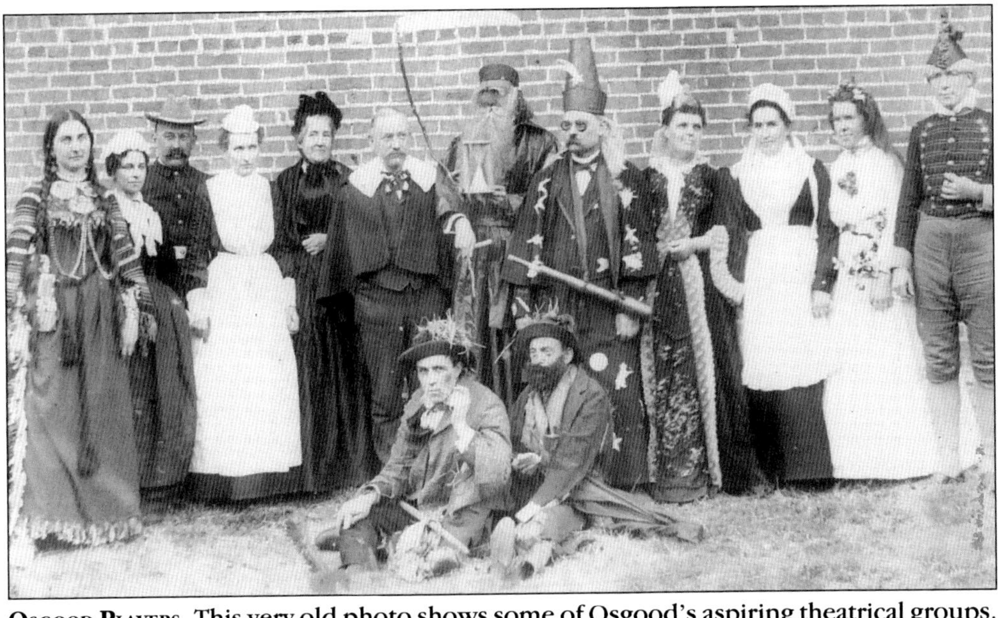

Osgood Players. This very old photo shows some of Osgood's aspiring theatrical groups. Some of the players were, in unknown order: Mrs. Wagner, Beven Glendenning, ? Smith, Ollie ?, Dr. Freeman, Gallergher, E. McCoy, Mort McCoy, Jone Freeman, Jim McCoy, Clara Jones, Harland Adams, Gutherie Glasclow, and Sadie Shook Hicks. It's hard to tell the theme of the play by the assortment of characters. (Photograph by unknown photographer.)

Four

Brown Township

In March 1822, a small portion of Switzerland County, which previously extended as far north as Olean, was added to Ripley County. The new township was named "Brown" after Benjamin Brown. Benjamin Chambers and Stephen Ludlow surveyed this area from 1798 to 1799. Brown Township is in the southeast corner of Ripley County, and it is made up of 51 whole and 6 fractional sections. Included in these are the villages of Olean, Benham, Dewberry, and Cross Plains.

Benham was named after James Benham, who first settled in this area in 1816. The village was first called "Middlefork," because Indian–Kentucky Creek had three forks feeding it, and the settlement was at its center. During the 1860s it was called "Lincolnville" in honor of President Abraham Lincoln, but after finding there was already a post office in Indiana by that name, Benham again became its final moniker. For many years the town had a mill, post office, school, saloon, shingle factory, and stores. Today it is primarily a town for private, comfortable living.

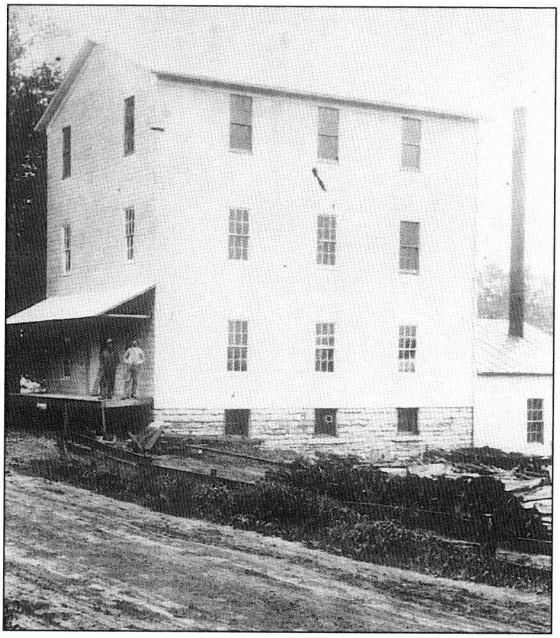

Benham's Mill. A large, three-story mill was built in Benham in 1901, but soon burned, was rebuilt, then burned again. In 1910, the mill was rebuilt. On this card can be seen a small back engine room where steam power was generated. A tall chimney stands out from this room. Mills eventually lost their small farmer customers and were forced to close. Benham's was no exception. In the 1960s, the mill burned for the last time. (Photograph by unknown photographer.)

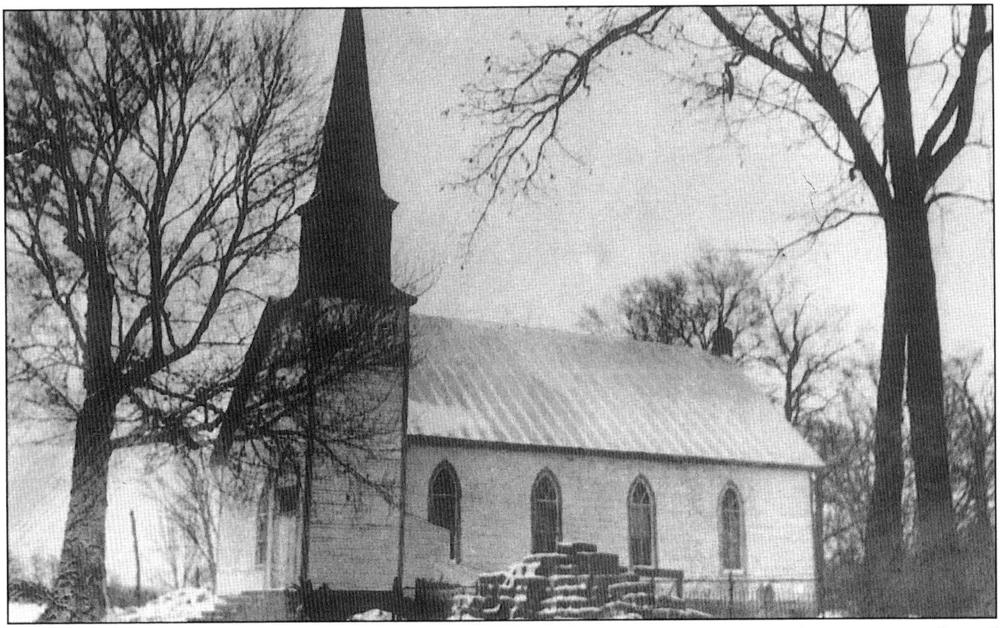

Benham M.E. Church. In 1820, a log church was erected in Benham, then was replaced in 1830 by a new frame structure. In 1889, the present church building became the third M.E. Church. This last church stands directly across from the original structures. In 1947, the congregation voted to renovate their house of worship, and today the church is very active in the Benham community. (Photograph by unknown photographer.)

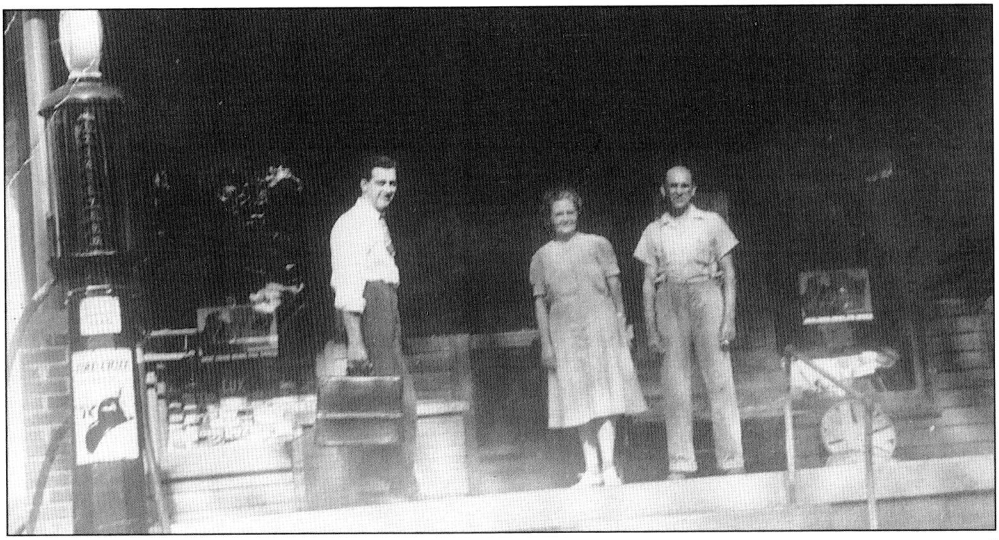

Benham's Clover Farm Store. Standing in front of their grocery store are Preston and Opal Ferguson, who operated this store for many years. A chain of small grocery stores, once very popular, were named "Clover Farm Stores," and Ferguson's was an agency store. George Staley is the salesman with the briefcase. Notice the very tall gas pump (we liked to buy from tall attendants, not the shorties who saw the arrow on the pump too soon and gave you less gas). (Photograph by unknown photographer.)

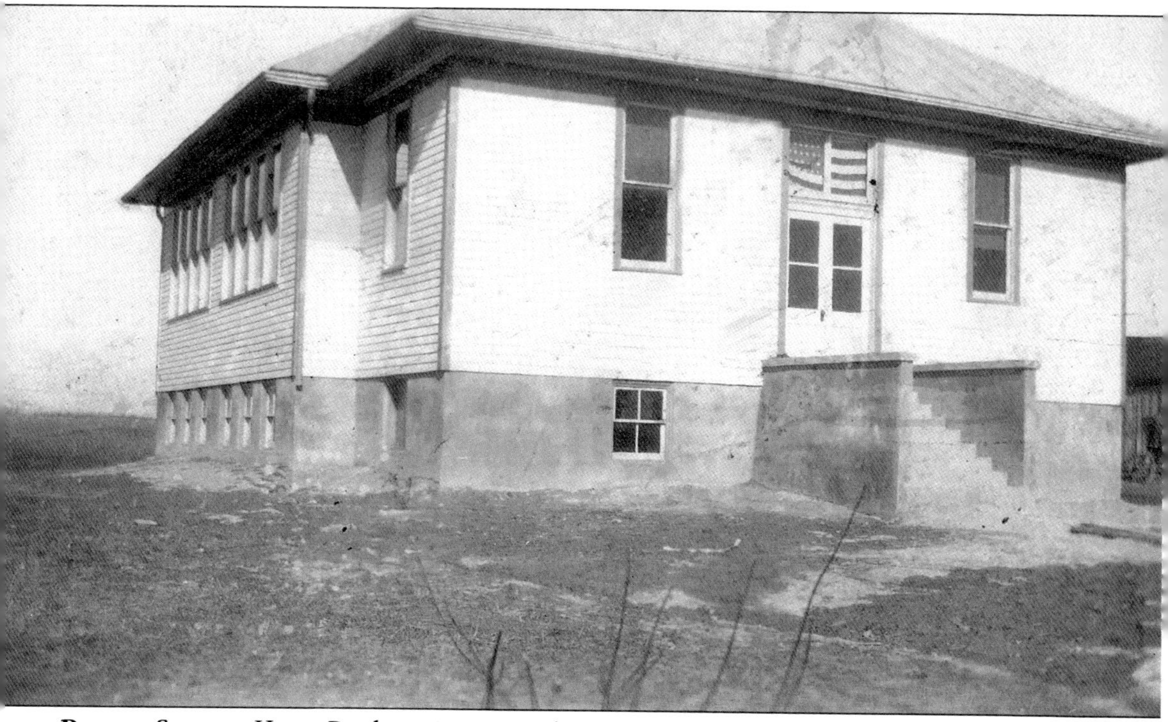

Benham School. Here, Benham is pictured in 1920. A bell post was erected in front of the school's window with an X mark. Teachers Raymond McCoy and Dova McCoy Maxwell put up the bell. Benham School is still standing but is no longer a school. (Photograph by unknown photographer.)

In 1850, John H. Smith, John Whitaker, C.F. Thum, Robert Twilbeck, and others platted 62 lots and formed the town of Olean. Lot #1 is on the northeast corner of Highways 129 and Olean-Friendship Road. A two-story brick house, once a saloon ran by the author's great-grandfather, occupies this # 1 lot. Olean has two cemeteries (St. Paul's and St. Peter's) and one Lutheran Church (St. Paul's). Olean derived its name from Olean, New York. In earlier days, Olean had several business establishments, but these are now long gone.

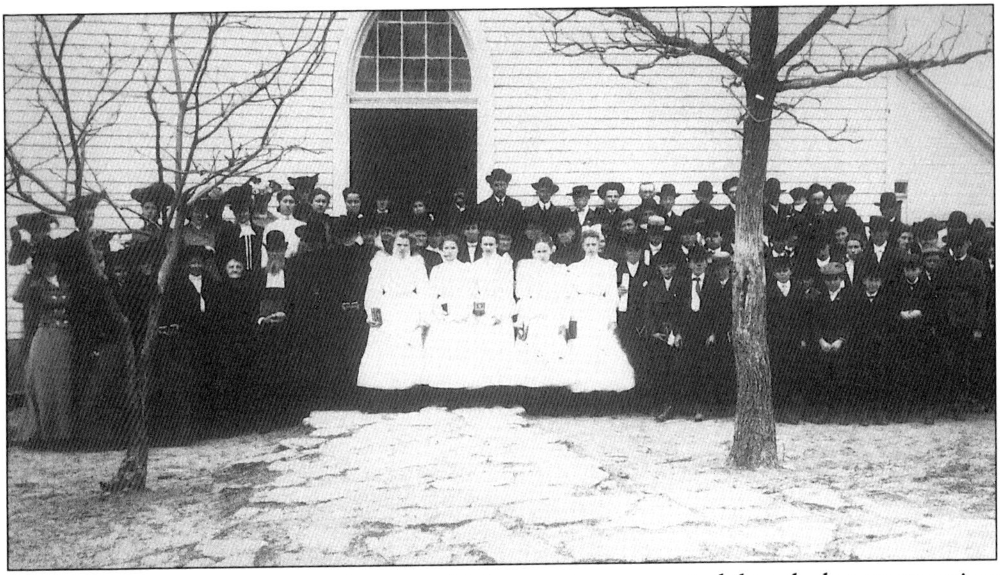

Religious Celebration. It is not known which occasion prompted the whole congregation of St. Paul's Lutheran Church to pose in front of the church on this obviously special day. Many are dressed in white, common at confirmations, but everyone seems to have showed up for the picture-taking. St. Paul's was the social center for Olean. (Photograph by unknown photographer.)

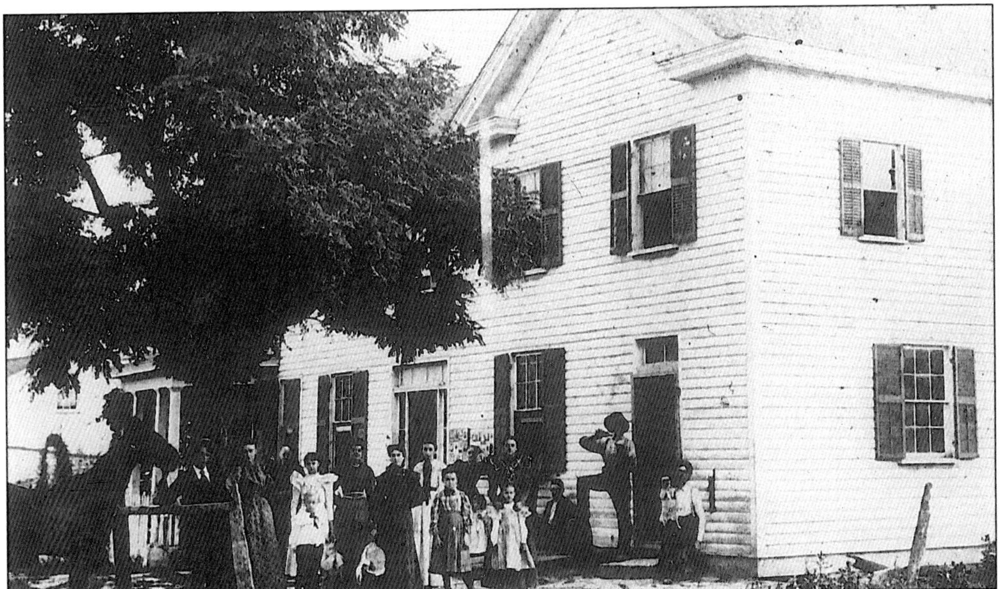

Olean Saloon and Dance Hall. This large-frame, two-story building on the west side of Highway 129 in Olean housed William's Saloon. Upstairs, over the home and bar, was the popular dance hall. For many years, the saloon was the "Gathering Place" for dancing and socials. The old frame was torn down in the late 1940s. (Photograph by Hallie Williams Miller.)

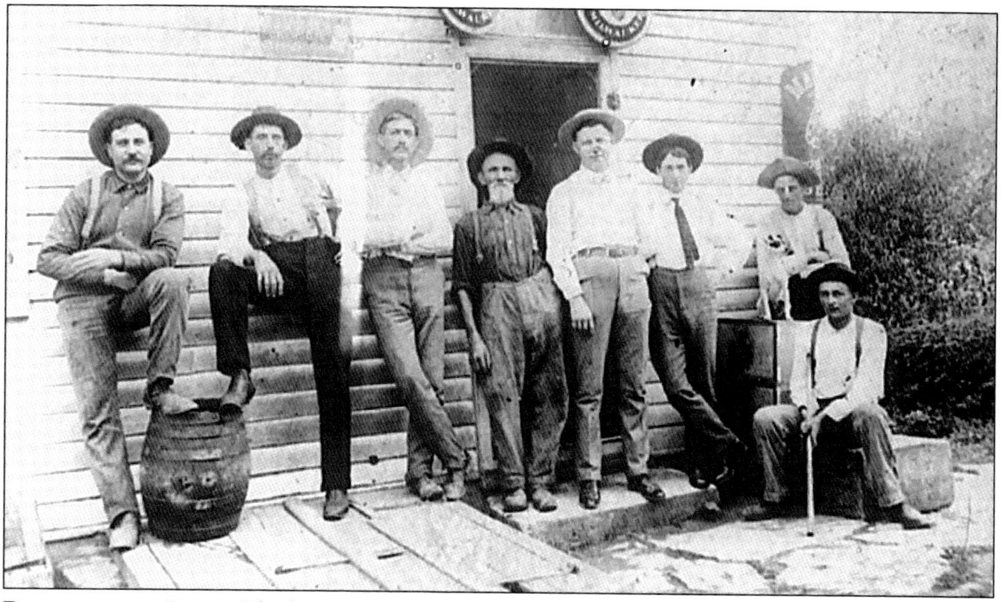

Prohibition in Olean. The boys are not smiling, because the barrels are empty at William's Saloon. Prohibition has set in. Pictured here are some of Olean's young men, with their dog, who are suffering the effects of what was long, dry spell. The names of a few of the men in the picture are: Kroeger, Obendorf, Barth, and Williams. The rest are unknown. (Photograph by Hallie Williams Miller.)

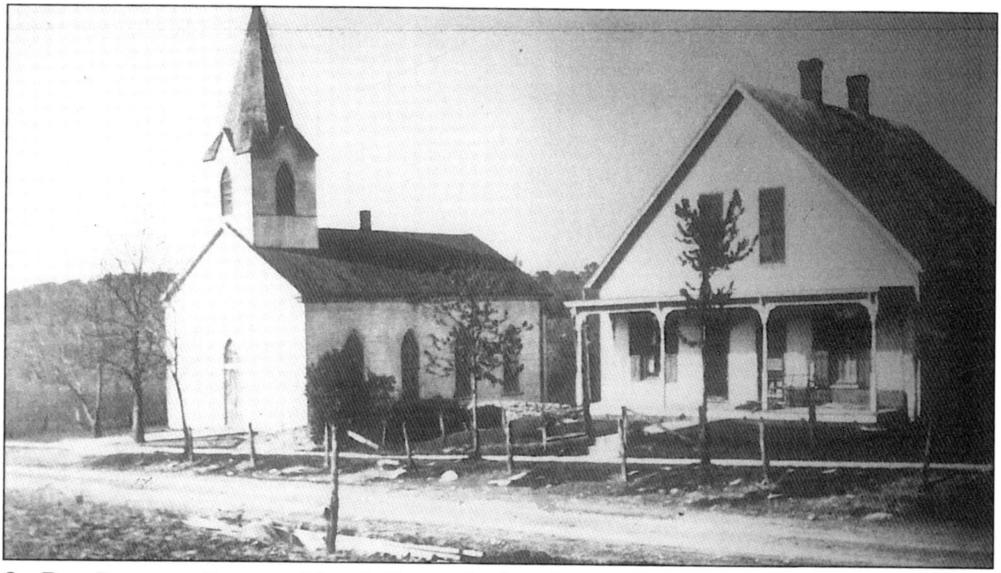

St. Paul Lutheran Church. Olean's Evangelical Lutheran Church had its beginning in 1858, and their pastors gave their sermons in the German language until well into the 1900s. The Olean neighborhood was made up of German immigrants, and they spoke mostly German in their homes and in school. The parsonage is visible to the right of the church. In 1922, a new church was erected on the same site as this frame church. In 1979, a large addition was added behind the church. (Photograph by unknown photographer.)

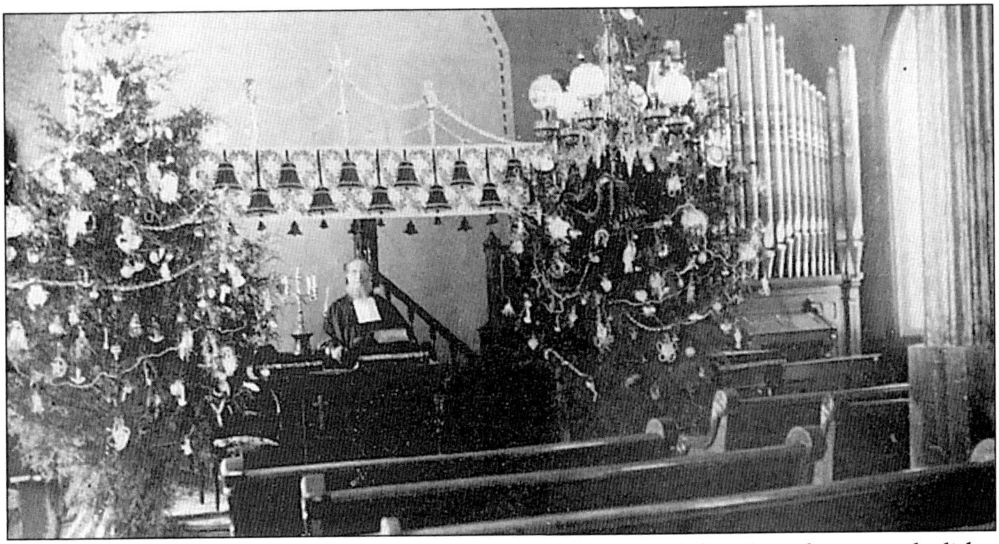

Church Interior. St. Paul Lutheran Church has decorated for the Christmas holiday season in this picture. The old-time chandelier is decorated with tinsel and wreaths, and the heavily decorated tree to the left adds to the festive occasion. Above the pastor are Christmas bells and crosses, for at one time, students wrote their lessons inside a cross drawn on their papers, causing many to write in very small print. (Photograph by unknown photographer.)

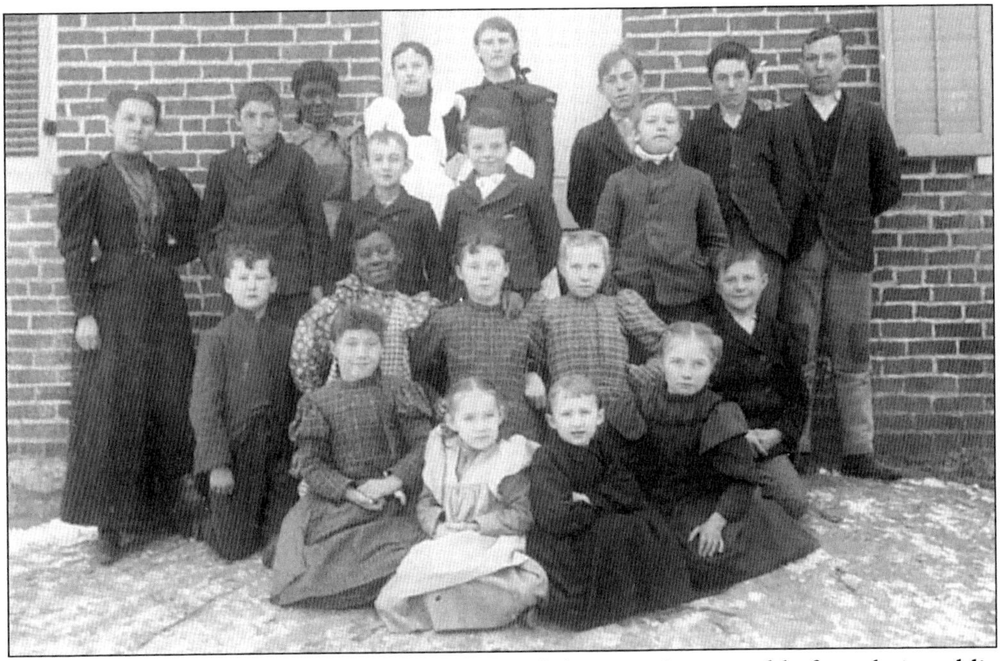

Olean School Students. Nineteen students and their teacher stand before their public school in Olean. Only the two African-American girls are identified. Their last name was Parker, and they were members of a well-respected family in the Olean neighborhood. The Parker family later moved to Detroit. (Photograph by unknown photographer.)

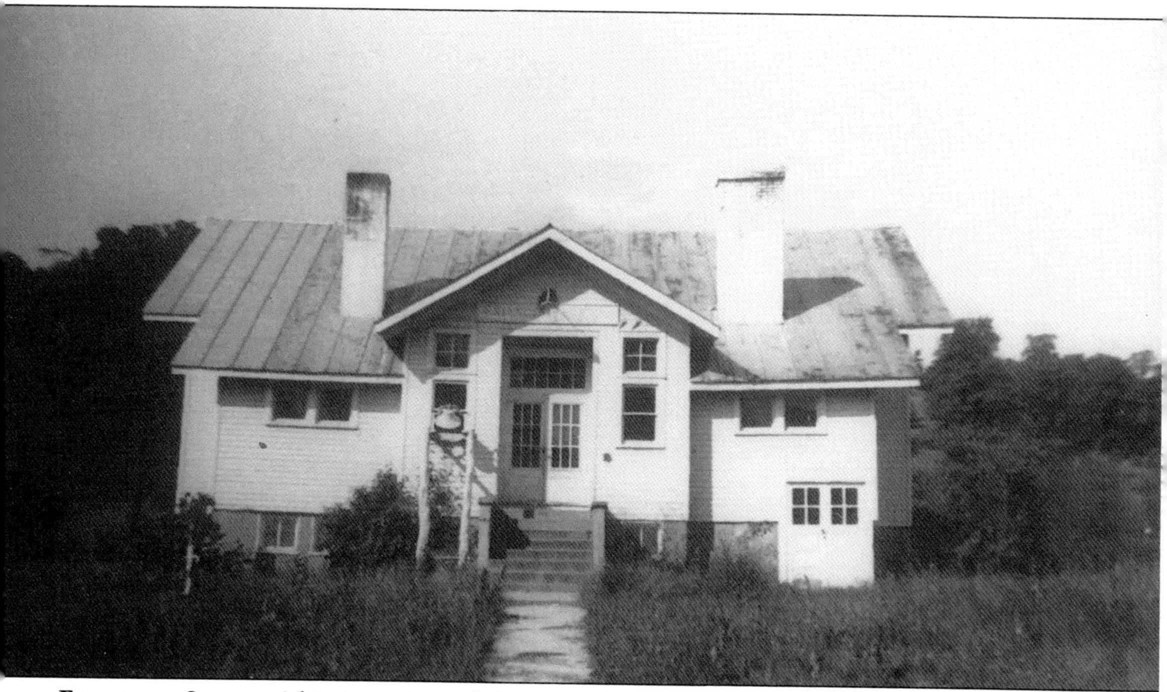

Friendship School. This is a view of the last school building in Friendship. Earlier, a small brick building at the east end of Friendship's Main Street served as a school. This now is a private residence. The author's great-uncle, Chas. Smith, built this frame school. Both Cross Plains and Benham's schools were of the same plan. Across from the school, the mill race meanders into town from the west.

FRIENDSHIP

A picturesque village in a valley on Laughery Creek, Friendship has had three different names: it was first called "Hart's Mills" after early settlers named Hart; then "Paul's Town" after an early postmaster named Paul; and finally, because these two names sounded too much like other post offices, the name was changed to "Friendship." The Masonic Lodge in town was named the "Friendship Chapter," and this name stuck. A flour mill, several stores, a bank, a blacksmith shop, a church, and a school once flourished in Friendship. Sixty years ago the National Muzzle Loaders Association held their shoots in Friendship, and it is the home of the association's National Headquarters.

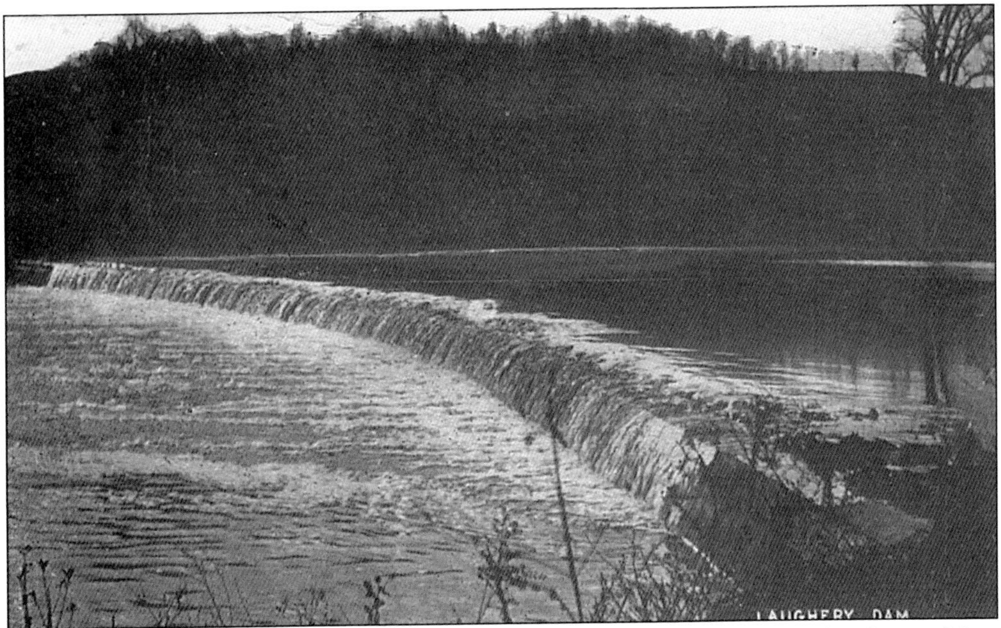

Laughery Creek Dam. A short distance up Laughery Creek from the west side of Friendship was the site of this dam. The purpose of the dam was to control the water in the mill race for Friendship's Mill. The mill's paddle wheel was powered by the water from this dam. This was a favorite spot for picnics, which is the reason for this card. (1910 card by unknown publisher.)

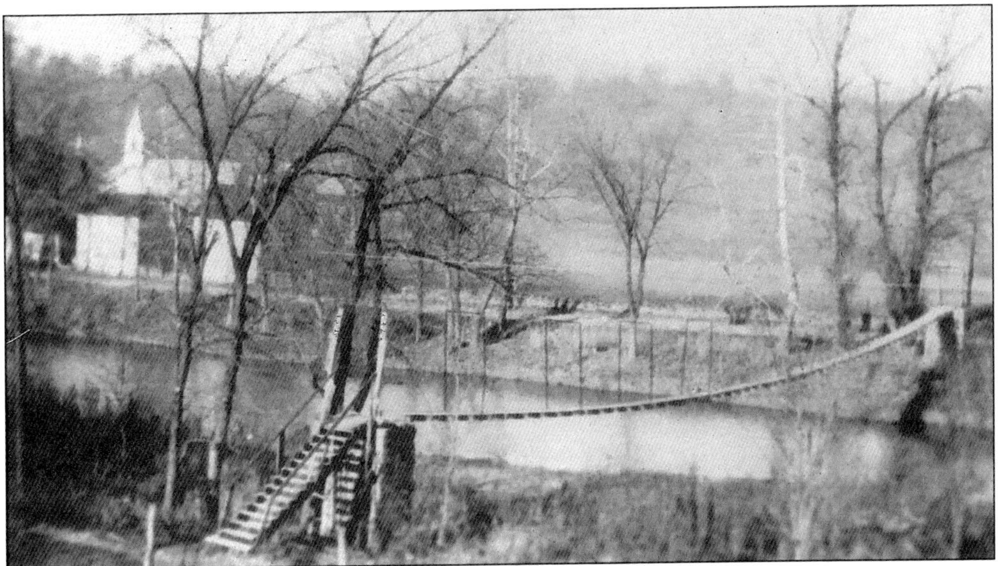

Very Nice Swinging Bridge. This is a side view of Friendship's swinging bridge. To the left is the town of Friendship. A large stone abutment at each end of the bridge raised the floor above any high water mark. Cables supported this bridge, and although it would swing and sway, it was fun to cross. This was the only way to cross Laughery until a new concrete bridge was built. One stone abutment remains today. (Photograph by unknown photographer.)

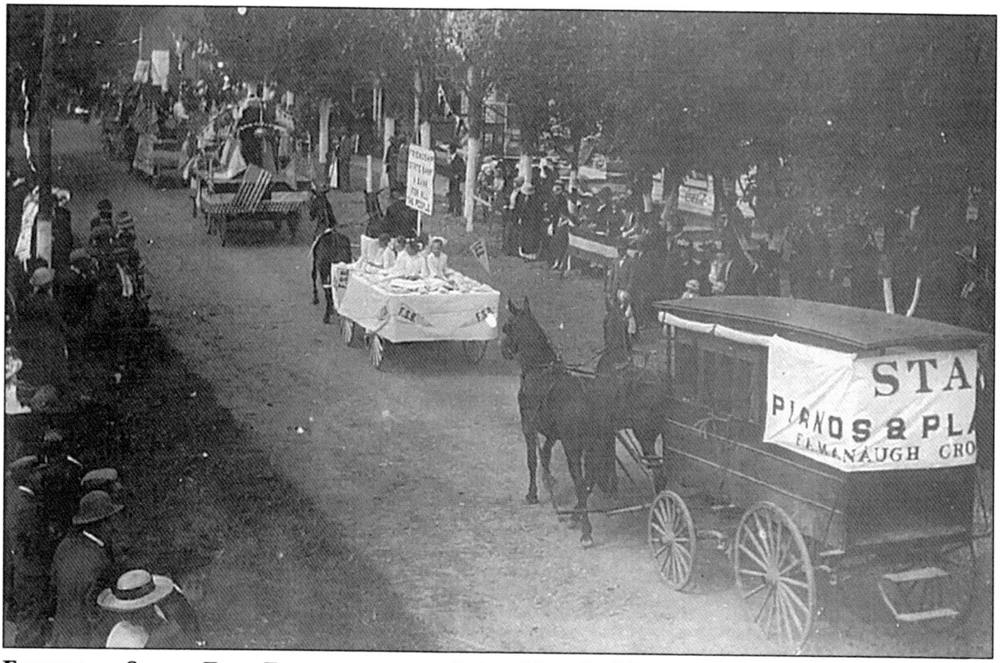

Friendship Street Fair. For many years, Friendship held an annual street fair that attracted large crowds. Blue and red ribbons were awarded for cooking, baking, livestock, produce, singing, and unusual contests. A big dance was held on Saturday night, which left many with a dry mouth on Sunday morning. (Photograph by unknown photographer.)

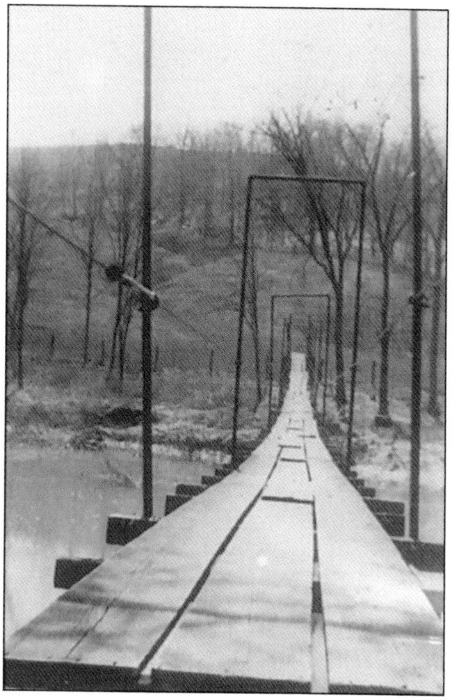

Swinging Bridge. The hills south of Friendship can be seen by crossing this swinging bridge. Handrails made of steel cables comforted nervous pedestrians who could see water through cracks in the wooden floor. (Photograph by unknown photographer.)

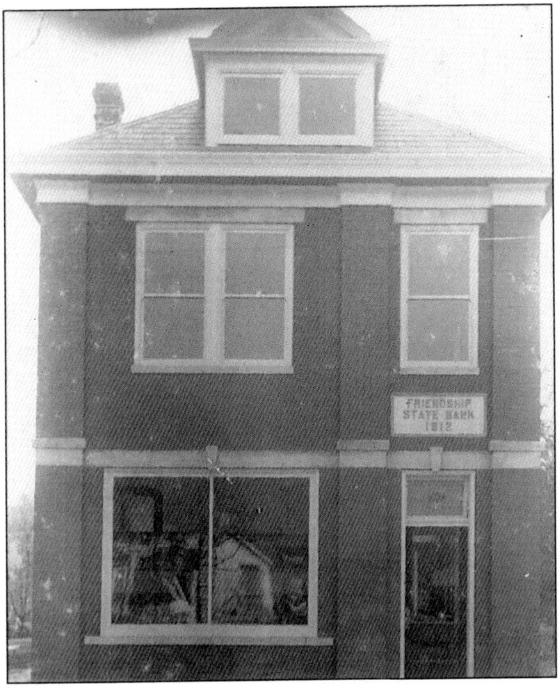

Friendship State Bank. Built in 1912, the State Bank has been one of Friendship's oldest and most important businesses. Additions were added to the bank in 1948, 1961, and 1999. In the last ten years, the bank has built new branches in Dillsboro, Rising Sun, Cross Plains, and Versailles. Wilkie Lemon, his son James, and grandsons James and Tracy have managed the bank. (Photograph by unknown photographer.)

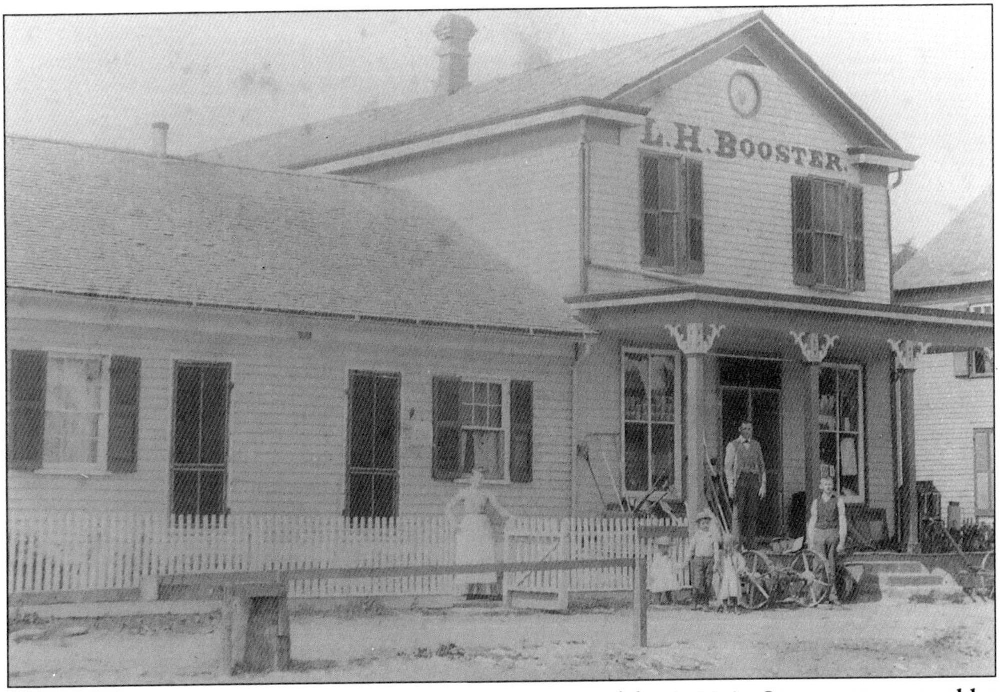

H. Booster's Store. This large general store on Friendship's Main Street was owned by Louis H. and Lisa Booster. Pictured in front of the store are Jesse, Clifford, and Howard Booster, as well as an unidentified man. In the 1880s, Boosters carried groceries, shoes, dry goods, and hardware. The building, although vacant, remains in town today. (Photograph by unknown photographer.)

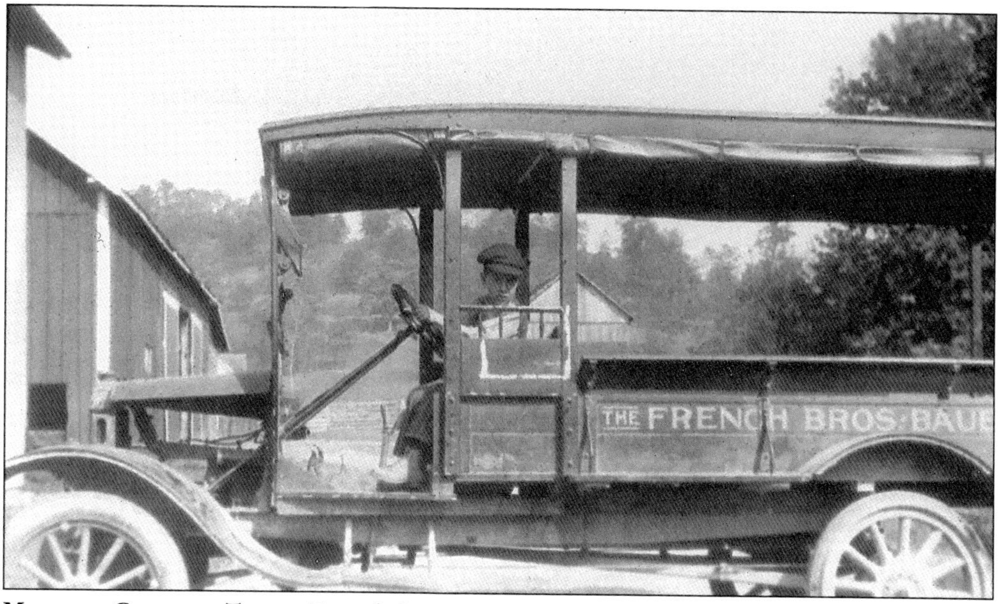

Milk and Creamery Truck. French Bros. Bauer was a large Cincinnati creamery which purchased milk and cream from a wide area. Mr. Rosengarn drove this solid-tired, open-air truck to Cincinnati twice a week. Canvas side curtains are rolled up in this picture. (Photograph by Evelyn Rosengarn Libbert.)

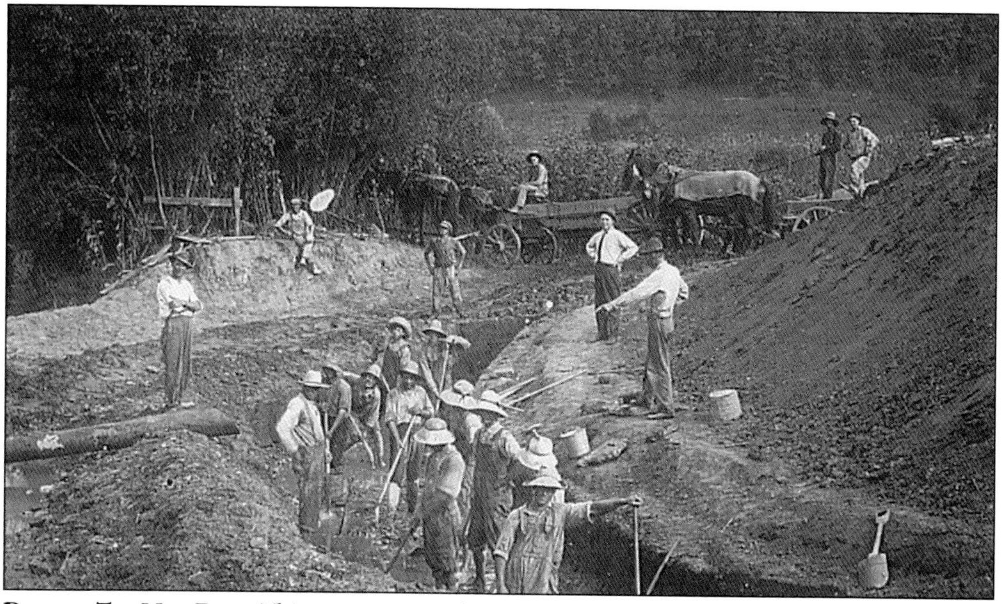

Digging The Mill Race. This rare picture shows how the men dug the race for Friendship's Flour Mill. Shovels, picks, slip-scoops, and wagons were used to dig the long waterway. Today, the remains of the race can be seen alongside the road on the west side of town. (Photograph by the Rost family.)

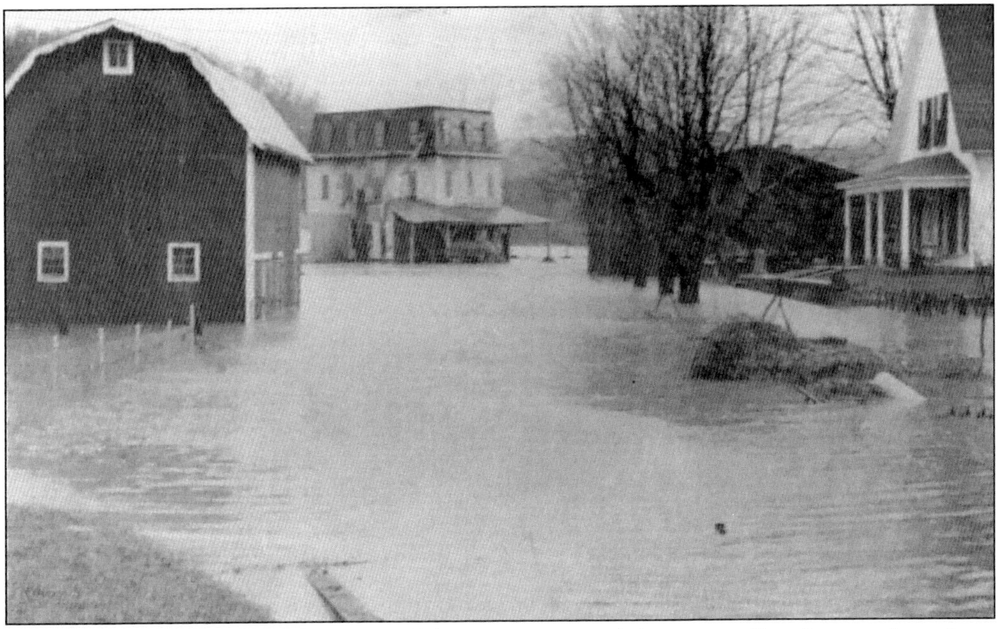

FRIENDSHIP'S FLOOD. In 1959, Friendship experienced its worst flood ever. Laughery Creek rose higher than ever recorded, according to the local citizens. Caesar Creek and Raccoon Creek added to the problem, and water surrounded the downtown area. Water was platform-deep at the mill. (Photograph by unknown photographer.)

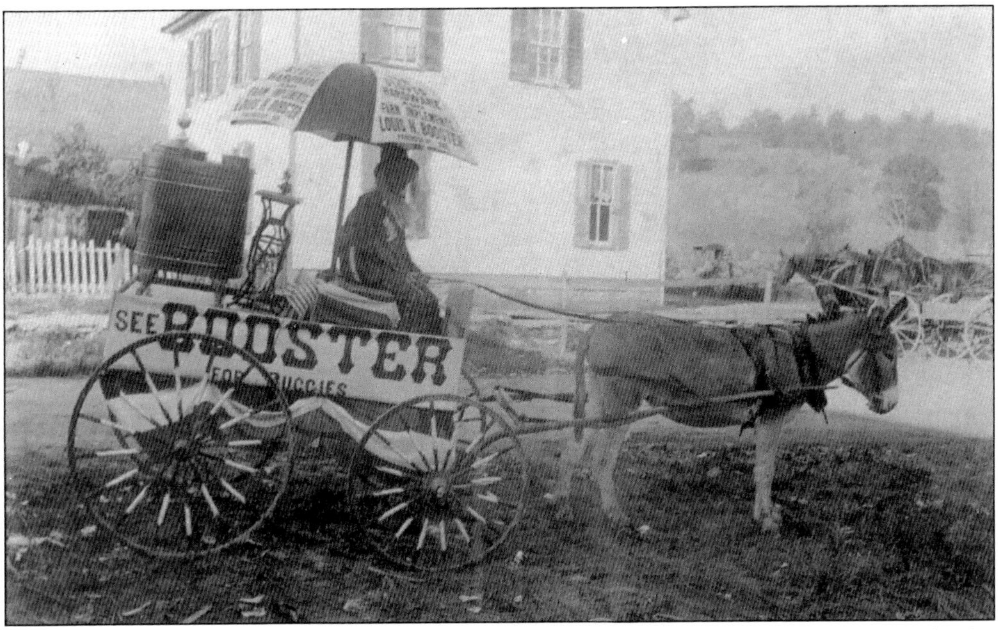

STREET FAIR PARADE FLOAT. Merchant L.H. Booster's parade float features a large umbrella with his name emblazoned in large letters. "See Booster For Buggies" appears on the sides of a small wagon. The burro looks a little dejected, but the driver is pert. A "Drum Stove & Sewing Machine" are displayed on the wagon. Even the wheel spokes are decorated. (Photograph by unknown photographer.)

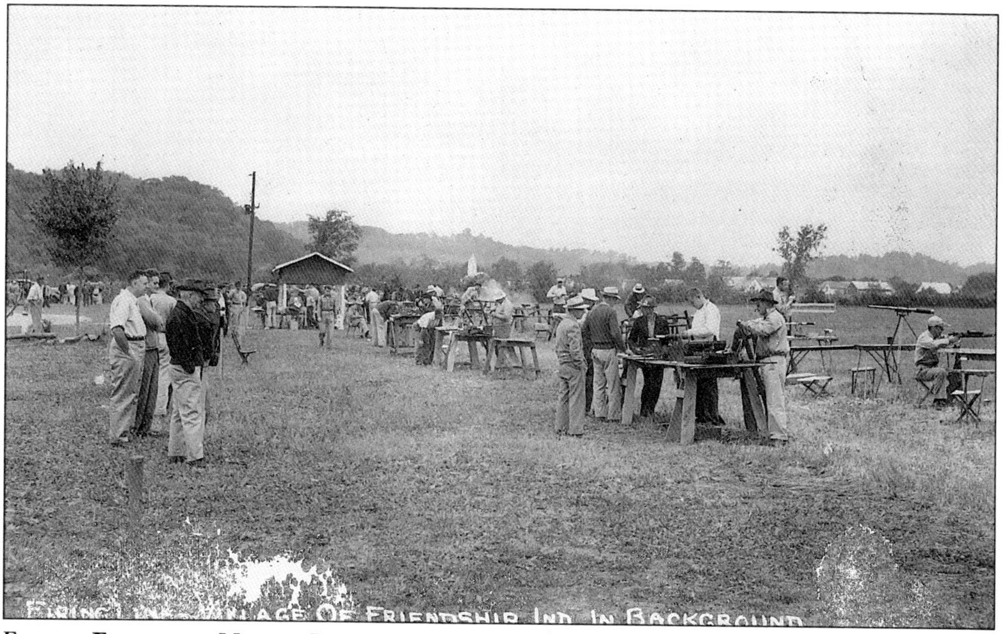

Famous Friendship Muzzle Loaders. For some 60 years, spring and fall muzzle loader shoots have been held at Friendship, Indiana. The Association has a permanent, year-round office, trading booths, target ranges, and a primitive camping area at the east end of Friendship. Shooters from every state in the union attend these shoots. This card shows part of the firing range. (Card by unknown publisher.)

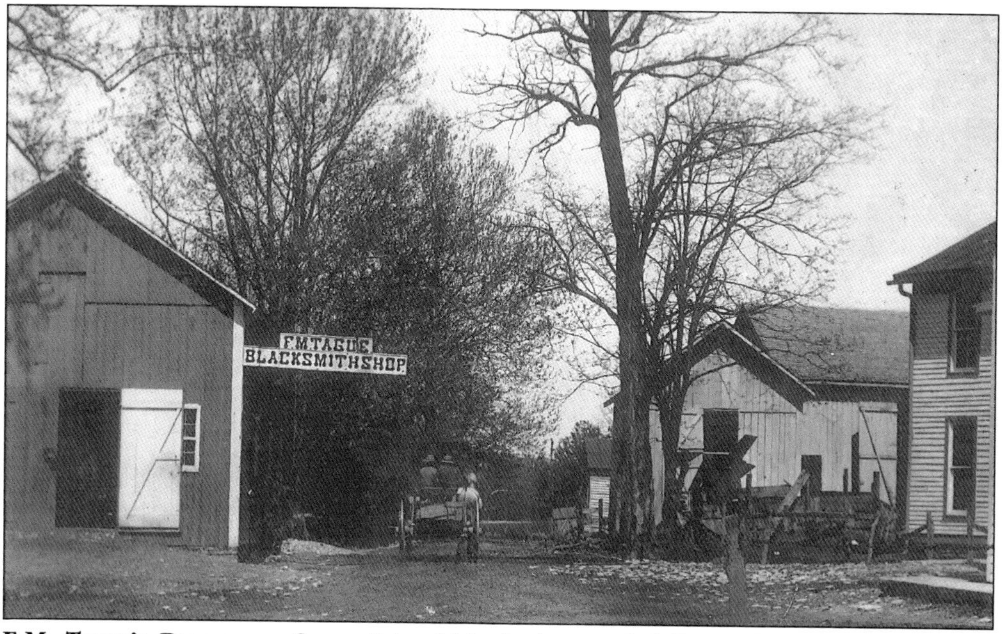

F.M. Tague's Blacksmith Shop. Friendship had several different blacksmiths over the years, but this is the only photograph of one of the shops. F.M. Tague was one of the more popular smithies. A lone wagon with three passengers pulls away from the shop on the unpaved street. (Photograph by unknown photographer.)

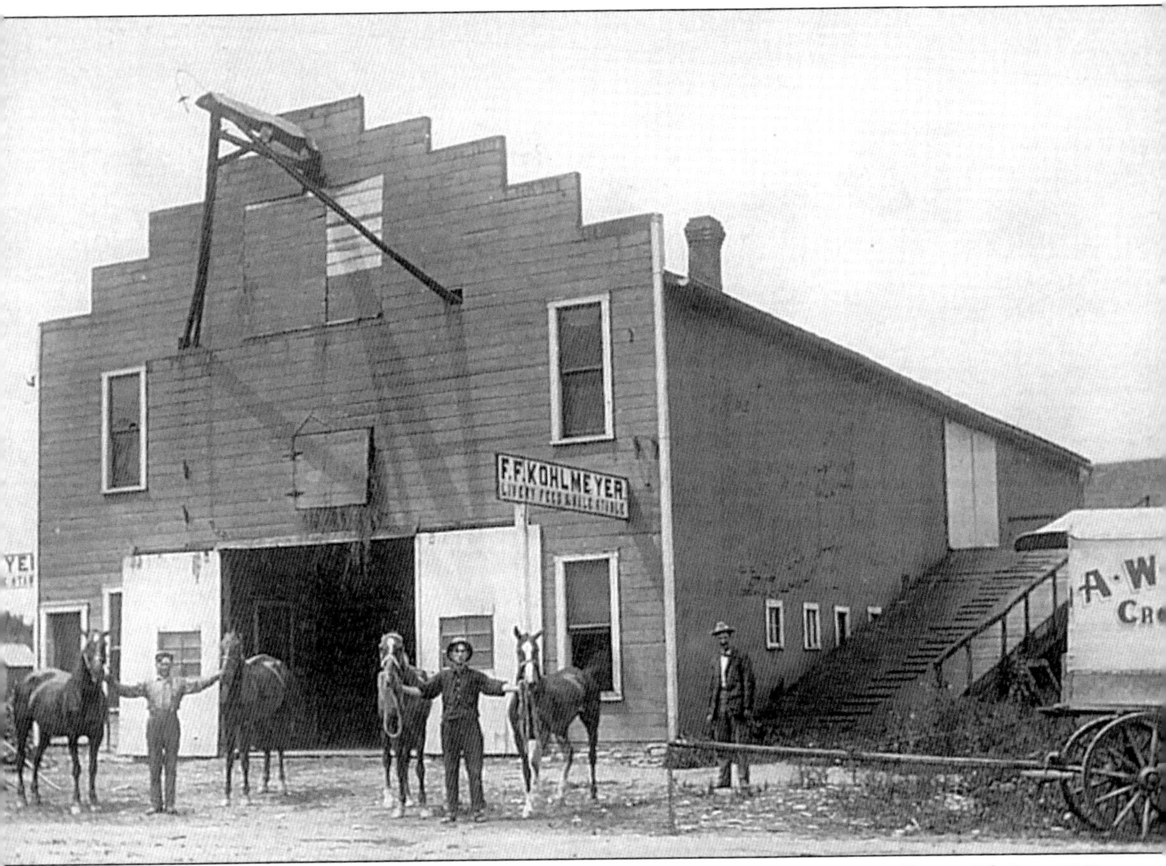

Kohlmeyer's Livery Stable. On the east side of Highway 129 in Cross Plains, F.F. Kohlmeyer operated his large livery stable. In front and at the top of the livery one could see a large pulley affair used to pull heavy objects up to the second floor. A ramp on the right side of the building allowed horses access to the upstairs. A.W. Lomatch's wagon is shown, and two men with teams stand proudly at the stable. (Photograph by unknown photographer.)

CROSS PLAINS

The father of this village was David Taylor, who platted 26 lots in 1826. Lot #16 was set aside for the site of a house of worship. In 1833, a Methodist church was built on this site. In 1876, the population of Cross Plains was 150 souls. At that time the village had a saloon, a church, a mill, several stores, a physician, a blacksmith, and a shingle factory. The town has lost most of these enterprises, but now has a restaurant, bank, store, post office, and many homes.

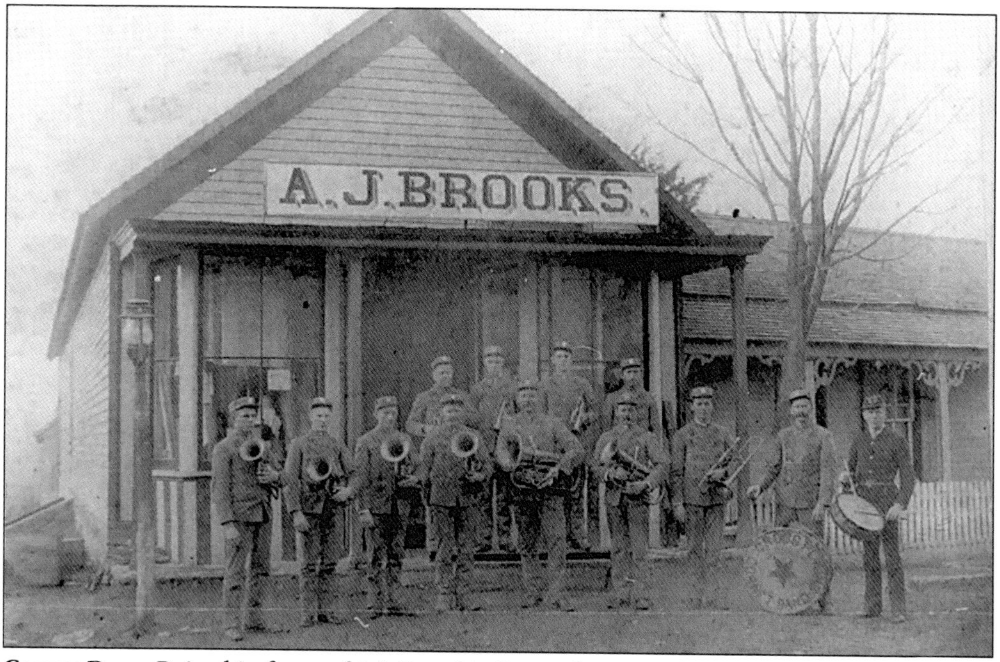

Cornet Band. Poised in front of A.J. Brook's General Store, which stood on the northwest corner of the intersection of road #129 and the Cross Plains–Dewberry Roads, is the Cornet Band. Painted on the bass drum is a star and the words "Cross Plains Cornet Band." The band was made up of nearly all horns, with the exception of a snare drum and a bass drum. Notice the lamp on the side. (Photograph by unknown photographer.)

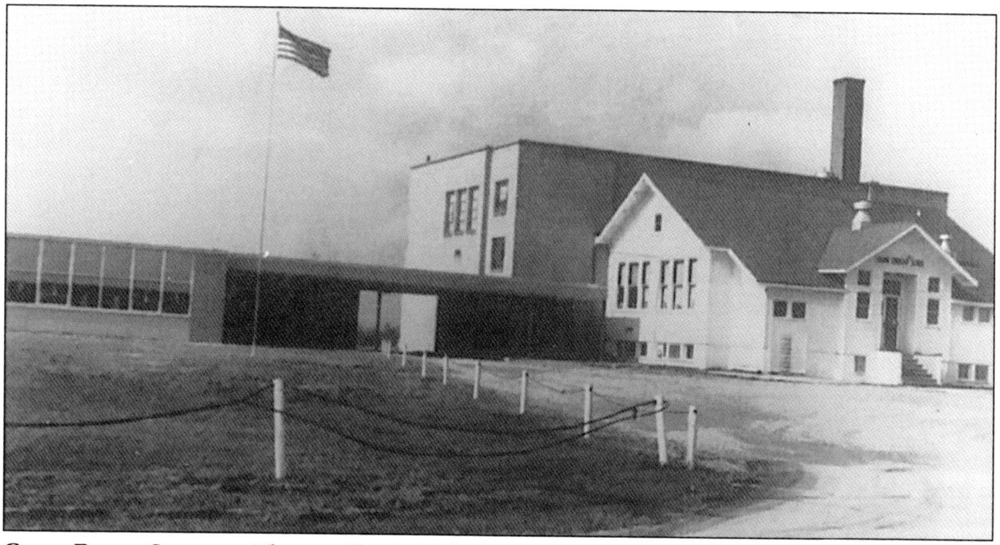

Cross Plains Schools. The small, white-frame school was the same design as the schools in both Friendship and Benham and was used until 1937, when a new brick addition was added to the two-year school. Classrooms, a study hall, and a gymnasium now allowed the school to be a four-year high school. In 1963, the school consolidated with Versailles, New Marion, and Holton to form South Ripley High School. (Photograph by unknown photographer.)

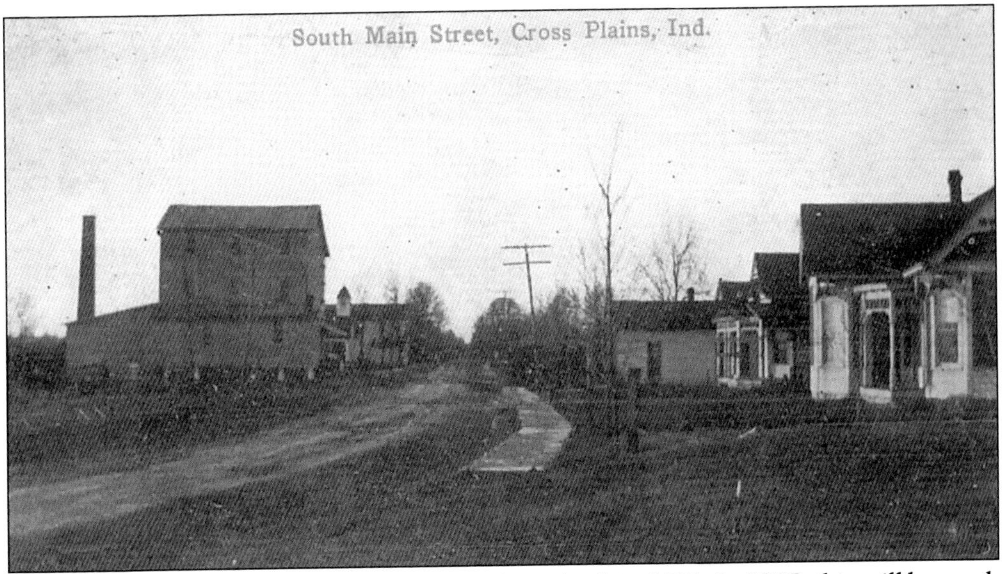

CROSS PLAINS MILL. A new steam-powered mill was built in 1891. In 1905, this mill burned, and William Donselman rebuilt it in 1908. Mills were often victims of fire because of the large amount of combustible dust. The Uhlman family operated the mill, then sold it to the Ripley County Farm Bureau. (Card by Art Mfg. Co., Amelia, Ohio.)

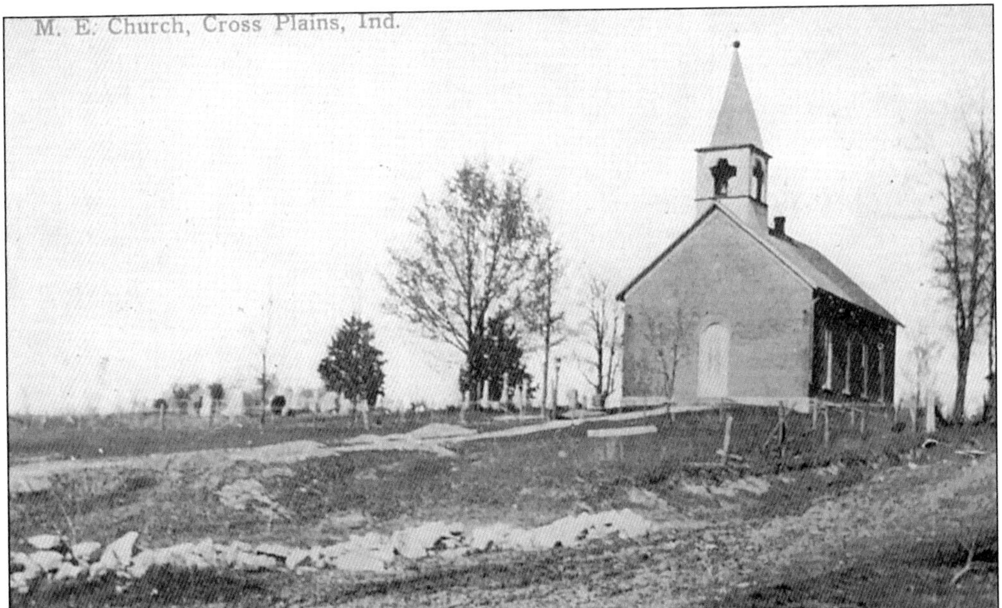

M.E. CHURCH AT CROSS PLAINS. In 1826, lot #16 was platted for a house of worship. Later, in 1833, an acre was added to the original land, and a small log church was built. In 1876, a 32-foot by 48-foot by 17-foot brick M.E. Church was built, at a cost of $2,100. This card served H.J. Miller as an advertising card in 1919. (Card #22990, by unknown company.)

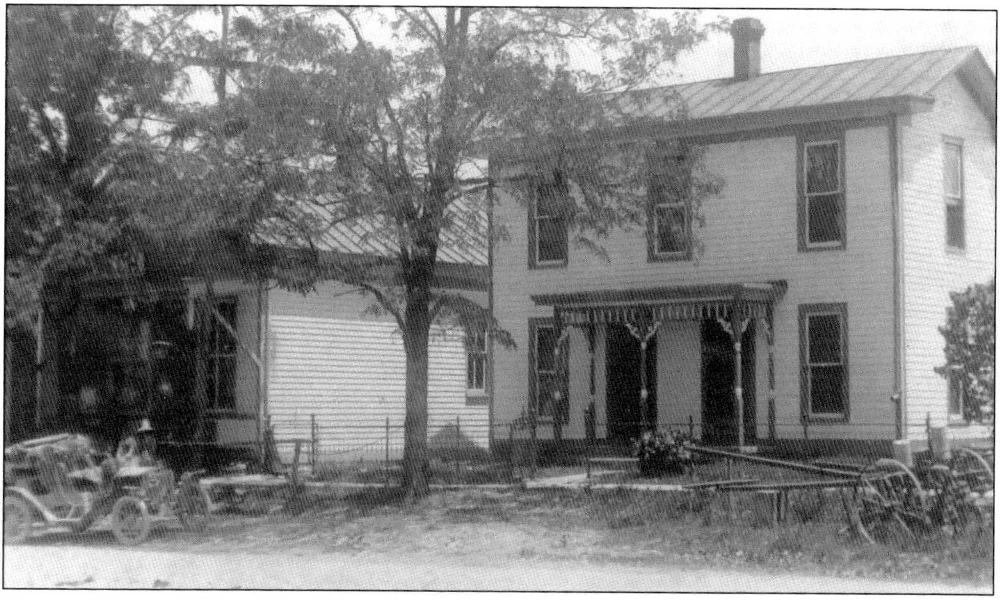

General Store. This white frame home and store was owned by the Lomatch family. The Lomatches operated a large store here for many years. Later, the home and store were taken over by the Morton family, who after years in business closed out in the 1970s. Today the building is used by the 7-Up Bottling Company. (Photograph by unknown photographer.)

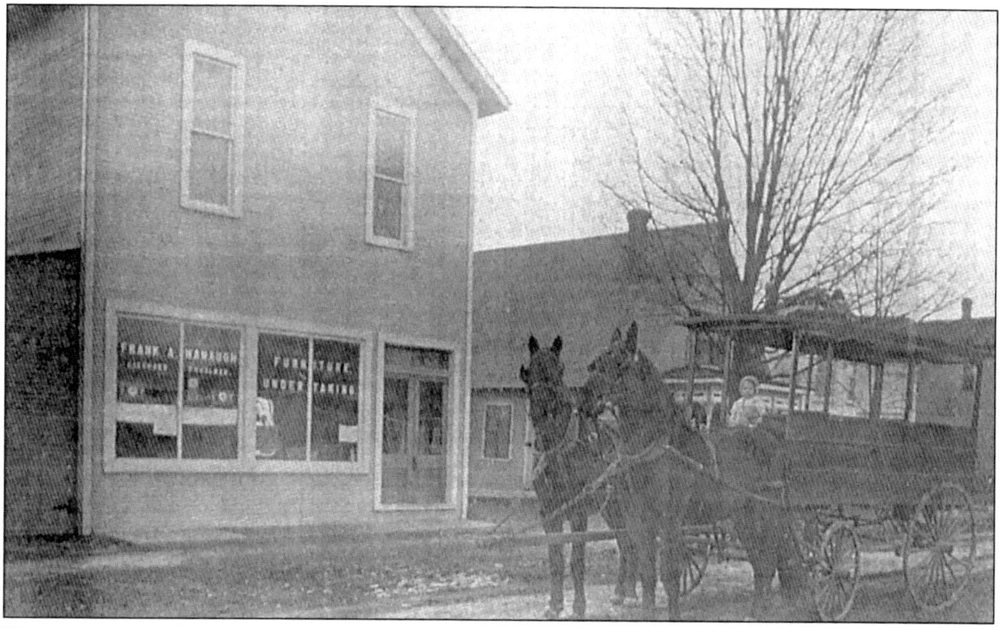

Undertaker and Furniture Store. Frank Manaugh served as a funeral director and furniture store operator in Cross Plains. This combination was not unusual in the smaller communities. Livery stables and furniture dealers often added the business of undertaking to supplement their incomes. Notice the large, open-air hack with the little girl at the controls. This was probably the bus to Versailles. (Photograph by unknown photographer.)

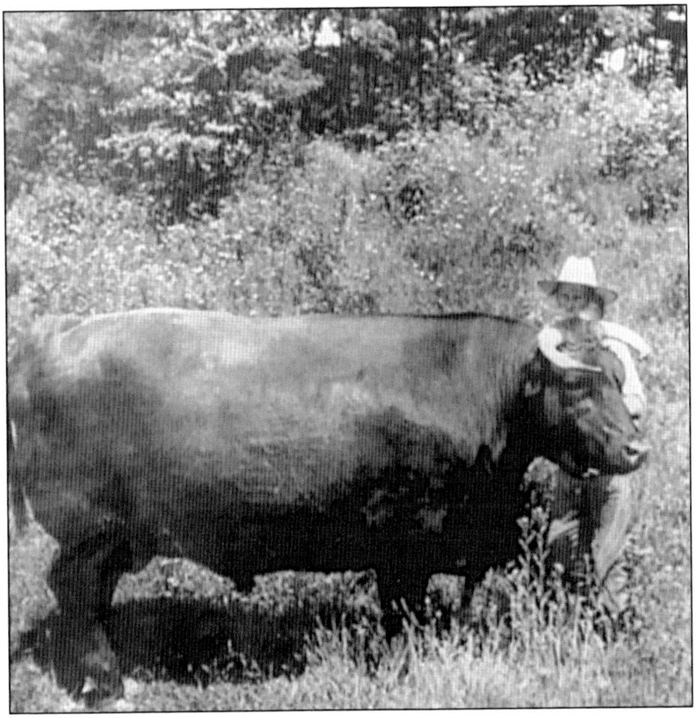

Wooley's Big Cattle. Alonzo Wooley, thought by many to be somewhat eccentric, raised a few very large cattle. Wooley lived the life of a hermit, went barefoot, was bearded (and a little different), and fed the cattle his own secret diet. He showed the big ones in several states, at fairs and other venues. Here is Alonzo and one of the steers. (Photograph by unknown photographer.)

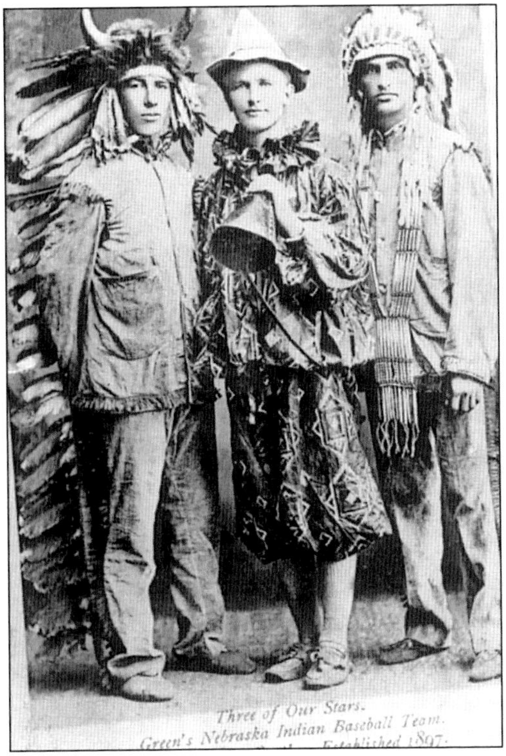

Baseball. Cross Plains and Friendship, like all small towns, each had a men's baseball team that would challenge all comers. Guy Green's "Nebraska Indians" traveled the country, and guaranteed a crowd-pleasing ball game. The Brown Township boys gave the Indians a good, hard-fought game before a capacity crowd. (Green's Advertising Card.)

Five

Washington and Johnson Townships

Washington Township. In May 1922, this small township was formed. It contained 25 full and 7 fractional sections (each comprised of 640 acres) of land on the Greenville Treaty Line. Of course, it was named after George Washington. The township had only two post offices, Elrod and Springdale, and both closed long ago. At one time there were eight schools in the township: Elrod, Caesar Creek, Conn, Stringtown, Smith, Ent, Craven, and Hogan. Today not one of these schools remains.

Johnson Township. One of eight newly formed townships in 1818, Johnson Township is located in Section 12, Township 7, Range 11E. John DePauw, W.H. Eads, and Chas. Beggs selected a 100-acre tract in this township for the new Ripley County seat. John Paul donated 100 acres of his land holdings for this purpose. First listed as "Ripley Court House," the county seat later became Versailles, in honor of DePauw's ancestral home in France. Only one town remains in this township.

Elrod. Washington Township's only village is located on Highway 50, east of Versailles. The village was named after George Washington Elrod, an early storekeeper and postmaster. Elrod once sported two doctors, a blacksmith, a restaurant, garages, a school, a church, and two stores, but no saloon. A. Rezin Johnson owned 1,100 acres surrounding Elrod. Harley May ran the garage at the intersection of Highways 101 and 50. Today, one business remains—Eaglin's Elrod Grain.

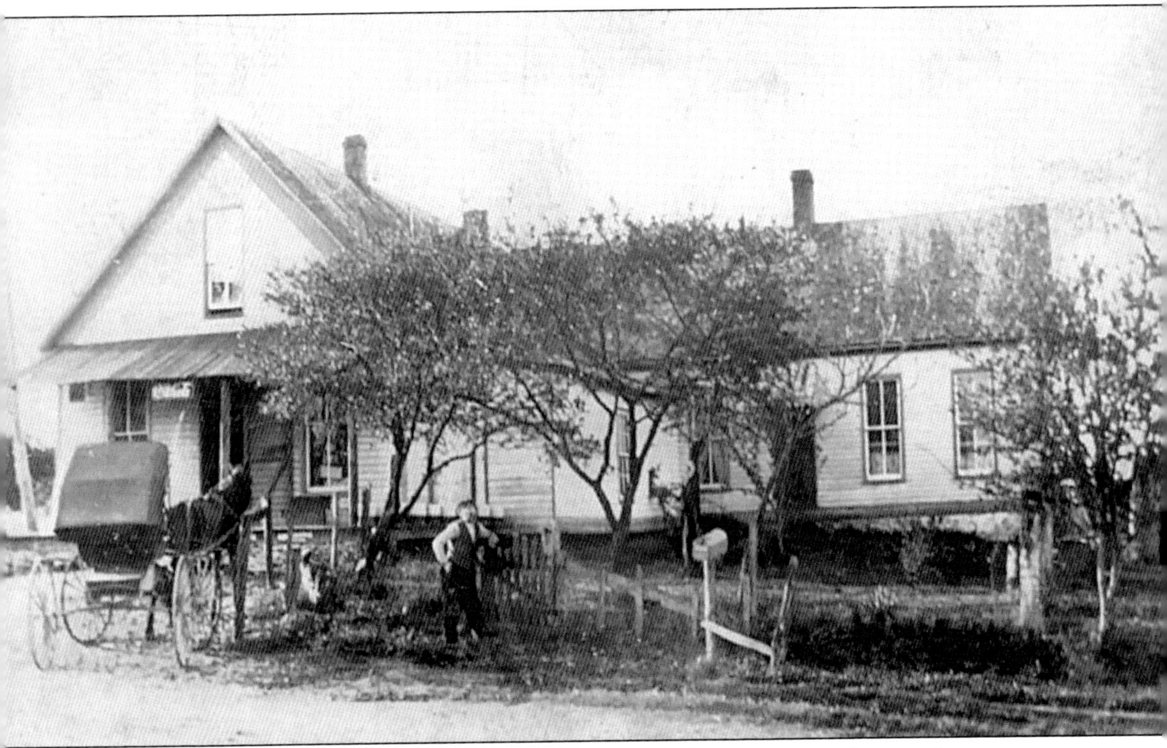

S.F. Franklin's Store. Franklin's Store was Elrod's largest general store for many years. This sepia card from 1900 provides a glimpse of Franklin's home and store in Elrod. Part of this building remains today on the south side of Highway 50. For many years the business was owned by the Baker family. Mrs. Baker sold groceries and gasoline, and her store was then what today is called a "convenience store." Many people remember this old store. (Card by unknown printer.)

VERSAILLES. In 1818, 166 lots were auctioned off for a total of $10,289.75 in the new county seat. Lot # 1 was at the southeast corner of Main and Main Cross Streets, and a public square was placed in the middle of 16 lots. The first post office was erected in 1819, and in 1821 a contract was given for the first court house. The first log jail was on lot #19, at the corner of Washington & Water Streets.

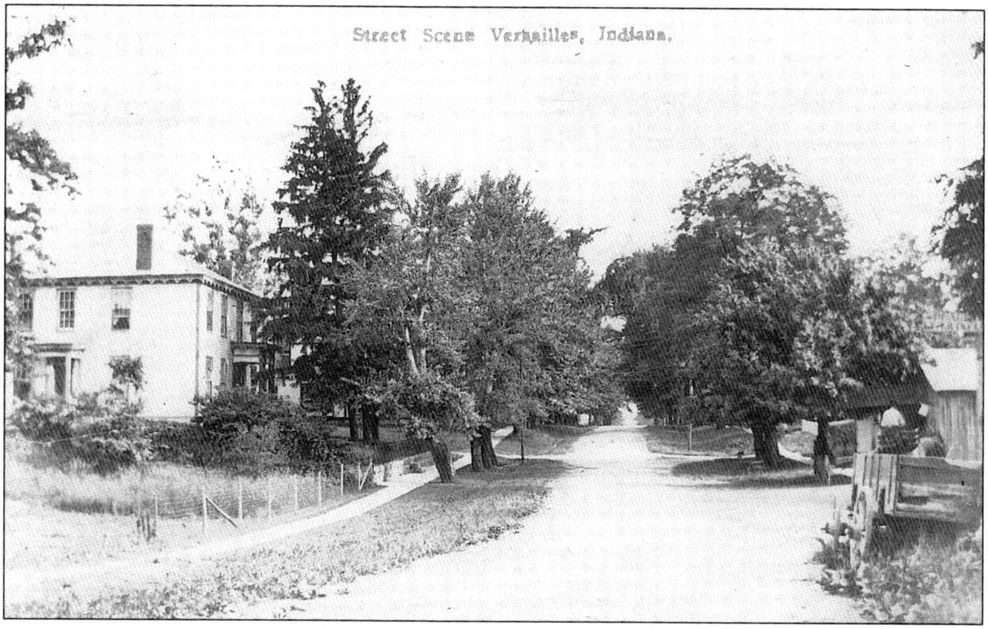

VERSAILLES' MAIN STREET. On Main Street looking south is the home of Carl Smith. This home has been moved to the corner of Tyson and Main Streets, on lot #1, and is now the office for the Schuerman Law Firm. The Colonial Manor Senior Citizens Home occupies the site on the left of this card. The trees are gone and the road paved, but never is a wagon seen on Main Street today. (Photograph by unknown photographer.)

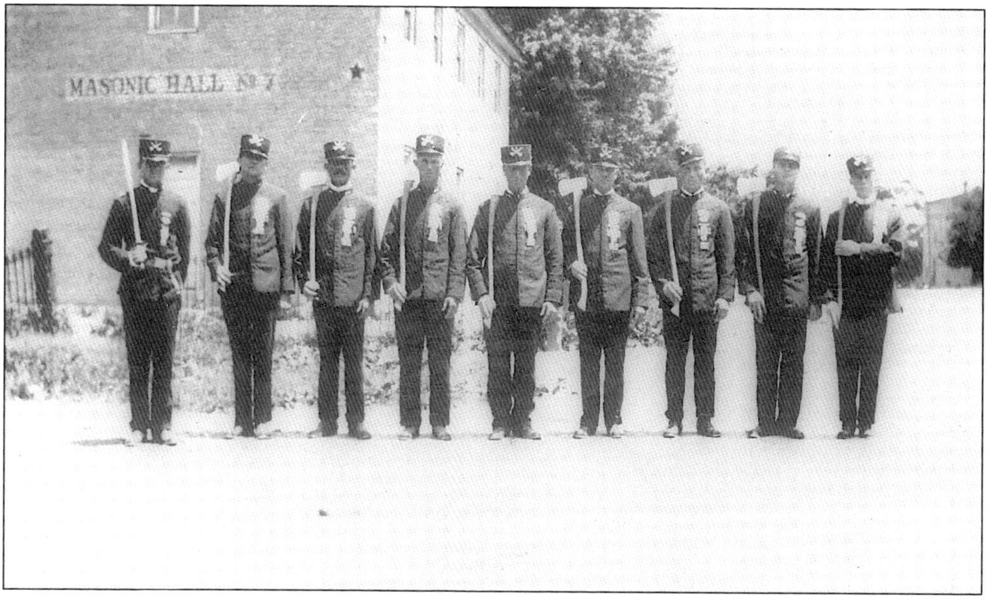

WOODMEN LODGE. Members of the Woodmen Lodge in Versailles are standing at attention, with axes in hand. Masonic Hall F&AM #7 makes the background for the photo. The old hall was located in the courtyard, in the southwest corner, where the canon is located today. The Woodmen Lodge was a large organization during the teens. (Photograph by unknown photographer.)

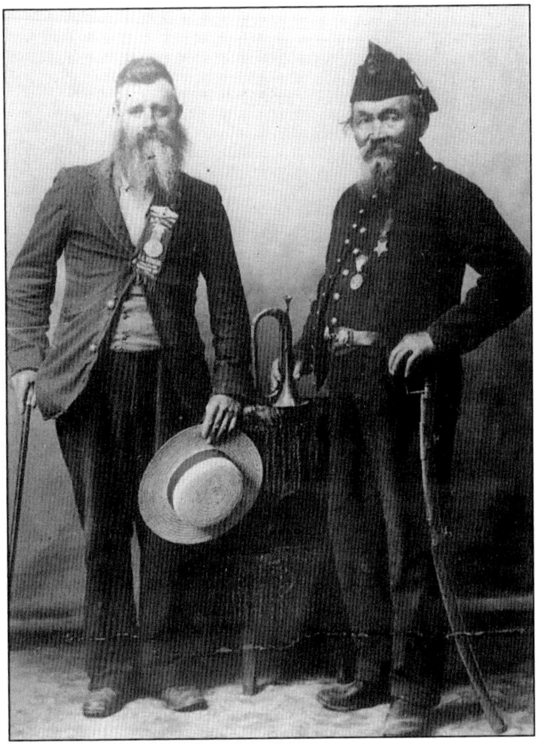

The Odd Couple. At left, with cane in hand, is Robert Hoover, a Civil War veteran and longtime Versailles resident. Hoover helped Dr. Olmstead cut down, wash, and prepare the bodies of the five hanging victims in 1897. At right is Billy Loesnitz, also a Civil War vet. Billy was lamp lighter for Versailles. Loesnitz committed suicide on the grave of his wife, and was buried in his uniform with his bugle and sword. (Photograph by unknown photographer.)

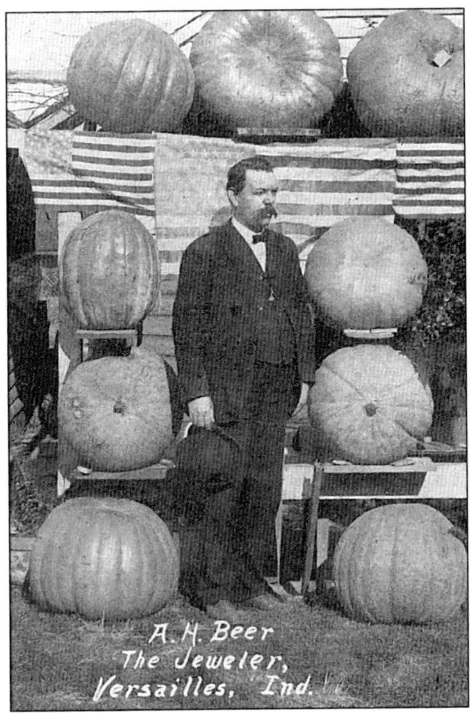

Beer's Pumpkin Show. Alf. H. Beer, a jeweler in Versailles, used many schemes to promote his jewelry shop, but the one that survived through the years was his big pumpkin show. This 1906 card shows "Alf" and the winning pumpkins for the year. Today they weight over 400 pounds, and the weekend show draws quite a crowd. (Card by unknown printer.)

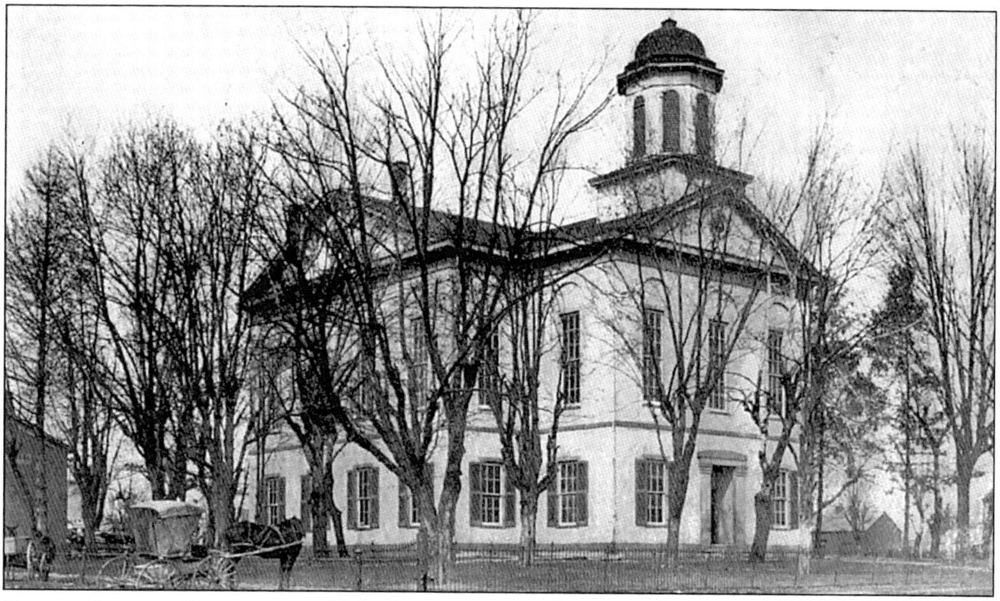

Ripley County Courthouse. This is a very good view of the courthouse, which was built during the Civil War. Looking west on the left corner is the first courthouse. The treasury office in this brick structure was raided by General J.H. Morgan during his 1862 "Morgan's Raid." Notice the old cupola, now replaced with a clock tower, an iron fence, and horse and buggy. (Photograph by unknown photographer.)

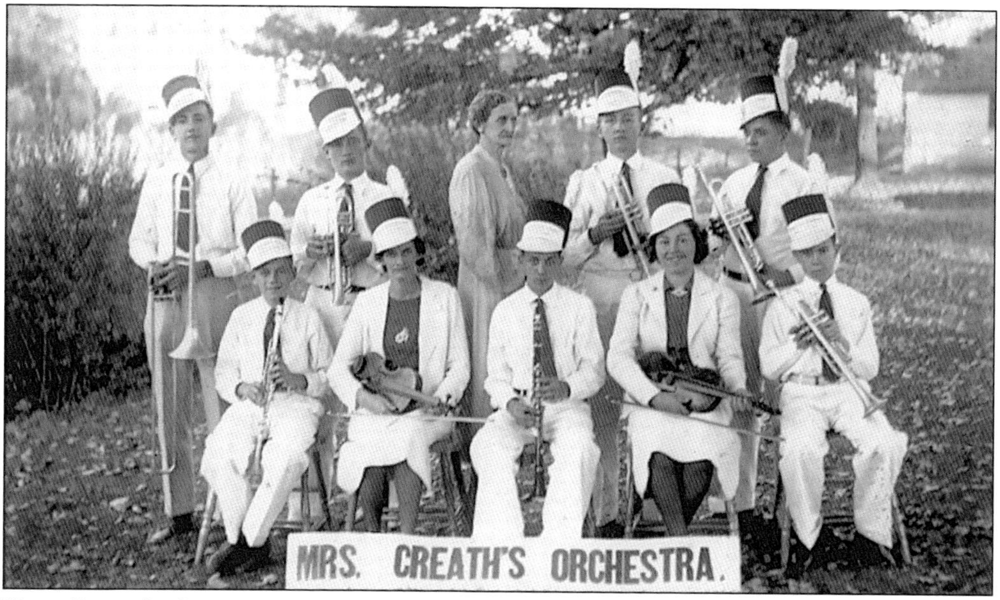

Mrs. Creath's Orchestra. Emma Creath, widow of a Versailles lawyer, made a living for herself and her son Horace by giving private music lessons and teaching music in the schools. "Em" had many different musical groups. Horace possessed perfect pitch and was an excellent pianist. Emma played many instruments. (Photograph by unknown photographer.)

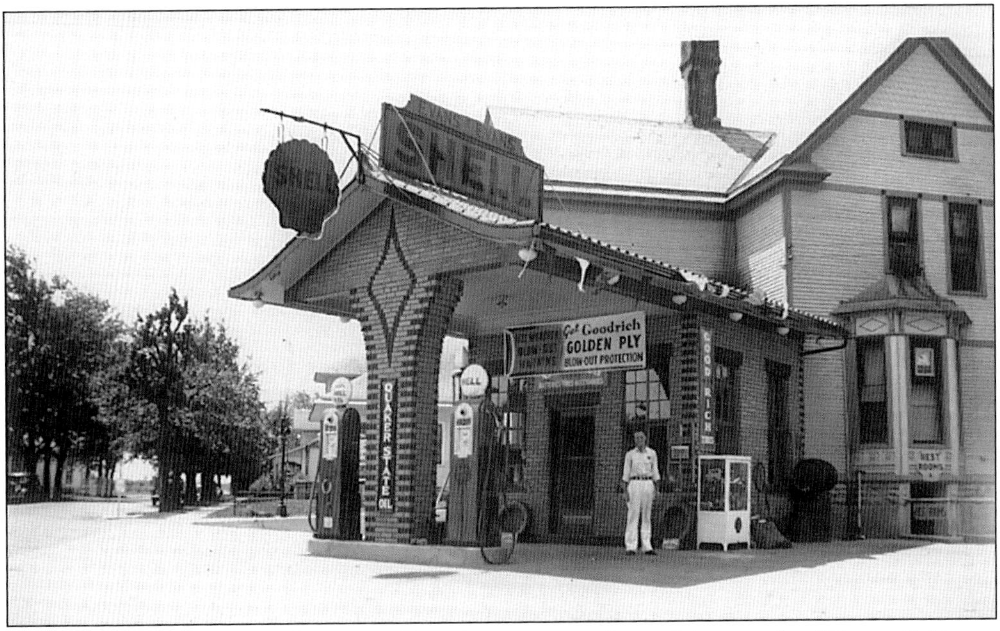

Aker's Shell Station. At the time this picture was taken, this was the "Evans & Evans Shell Station." Locally known as the "Fill-Up," the station and adjoining restaurant were open 24 hours a day, year-round. Elvan Akers is the attendant standing at the window. Elvan operated the popular spot for many years. The corner is now the home of the new McDonald's drive-in. (Photo by unknown photographer.)

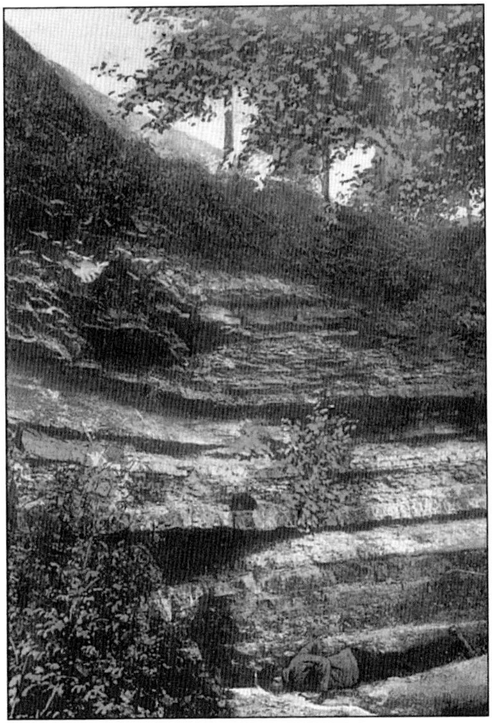

Bluff Spring Near Gordon's Leap. North of town and west of the cemetery was a high cliff with a big spring, known as "Bluff Springs." This spring and the small cave nearby was a favorite spot for the boys of Versailles. In the 1850s, three medical students attempted to rob the grave of a recently buried and interesting cadaver. They were frightened by local citizens, and one named Glass ran the wrong direction and fell over the precipice. Another student named Gordon was credited with the leap, and to this day the cliff is called "Gordon's Leap." (Card by Kraemer Art Co., Cincinnati & Berlin.)

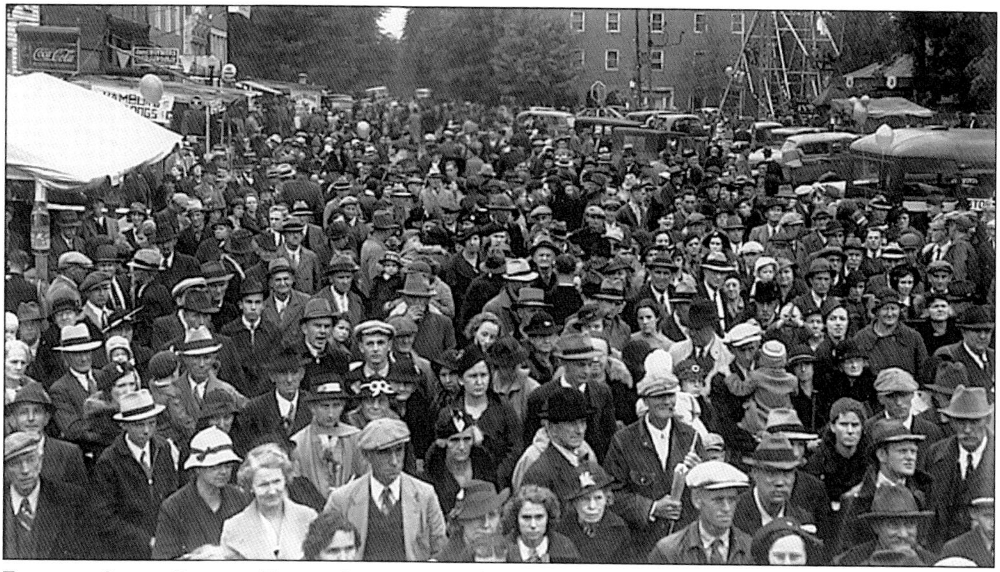

Pumpkin Show Crowd. Tyson Street is packed with a rather somber-looking crowd at a 1939 Pumpkin Show. Jane Withers and Monty Wooley are playing at the Austin Theatre, and the Ferris wheel is at full capacity. This was October, which is the reason for the coats and hats. A sign says "Hamburgers 10, and Hot Dogs 5¢." The crowd should be smiling! (Photograph by unknown photographer.)

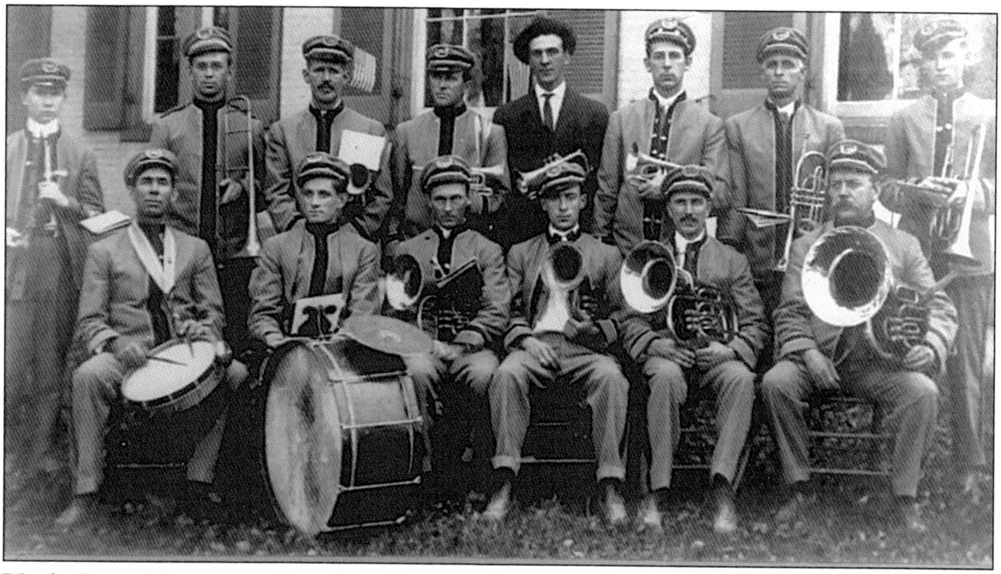

Men's Band, Versailles. Posed by the courthouse is the Band of Versailles. In the early 1900s, men's bands were very popular. Every town, large and small, had a uniformed band. Larger towns paid band directors, and vied for the best band titles. The members pictured in this photograph are, from left to right, as follows: (front row) Clarence Hunter, Otto Busching, Luther Ent, Roy Hunter, Harry Ricketts, and Alf Beer; (back row) Manford Livingston, Walter Beer, Emory Copeland, unidentified, Tony Hunter, George Busching, and Roy May. (Photograph by unknown photographer.)

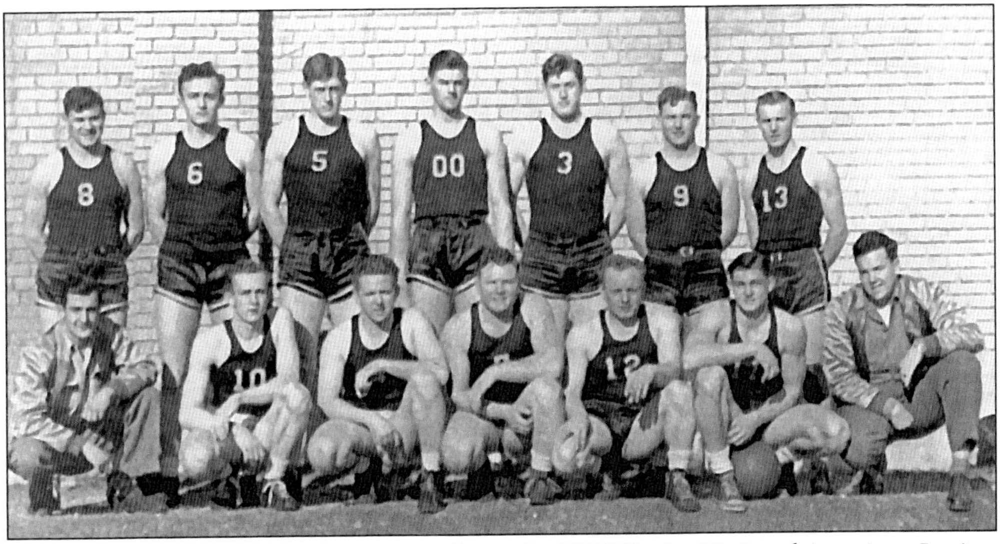

Leora Weare Post 173 Legion Team. At the end of WW II, the National American Legion started a National Legion Basketball Tournament. This was something for the millions of returning young veterans. Each state ran their own state tournament, and the winners went to a National Tournament. Indiana had over three hundred post teams, more than any state in the nation. Post 173, Versailles, won the state of Indiana competition three times: 1947, 1948, and 1950. In 1947, Post 173 lost the National Final game to Midland, Michigan, by three points. The schedule was grueling: at 9 a.m. they defeated North Dakota; at 3 p.m. they triumphed over Reno, Nevada; and at 8 p.m. they lost to Michigan. Michigan drew a bye and played only two games that day. Pictured in the front row, from left to right, are: Bill Hill, Norm Dresselhouse, Rus Martin, Ray Shadday, Les Kelch, James Lemon, and Jim Hall. In the back row, from left to right, are: Jesse Westmeyer, Leland Chandler, Alan Smith, Ken Shaw, Robert Smith, Alf Adkins, and Ray Strimple. (Photograph by unknown photographer.)

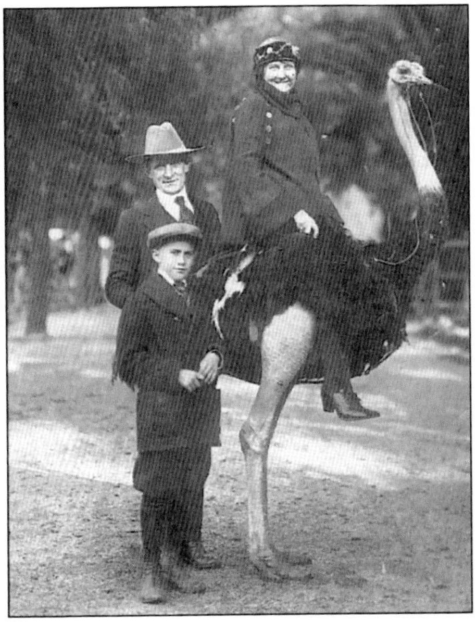

Flo Skeen. This well-known lady of Versailles—pictured here riding an ostrich—is Florence Skeen Pegee, also known as "Flo." This picture, taken about 1920, shows Flo riding while her husband Otto and son Walter Pegee look on. Flo, whose father ran the Court House Inn, was a talented seamstress. She managed a millinery shop and a beer garden, where it was said that no customer was turned down, regardless of the law. A stylish dresser, Flo cut quite a figure in town. A parrot who swore like a teamster was a conversation piece in the beer parlor and home. (Photograph by the Skeen family.)

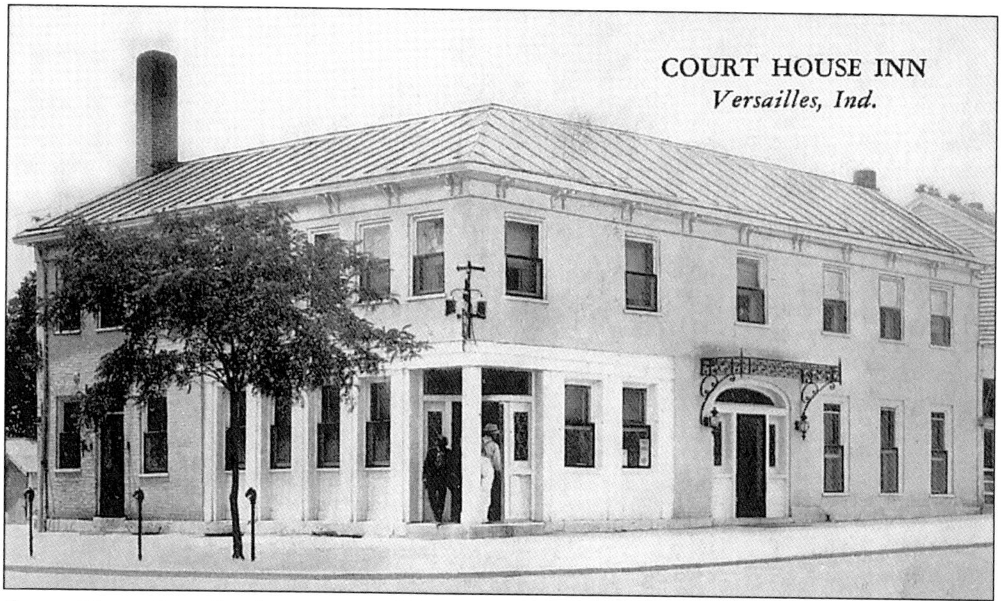

Court House Inn. On the corner of Tyson and Main Streets, on lot 16, is a tavern with a long history. Mr. Skeen owned it in the 1820s, and it continues as a saloon to this date. In the 1930s, a Mr. Thomson of Hamilton, Ohio (and "Old Timbers" fame) purchased the old Hassmer Hotel, and completely refurbished it as a convenient place to stay for those who visited his camp in Jefferson Proving Ground. (1936 card by unknown printer.)

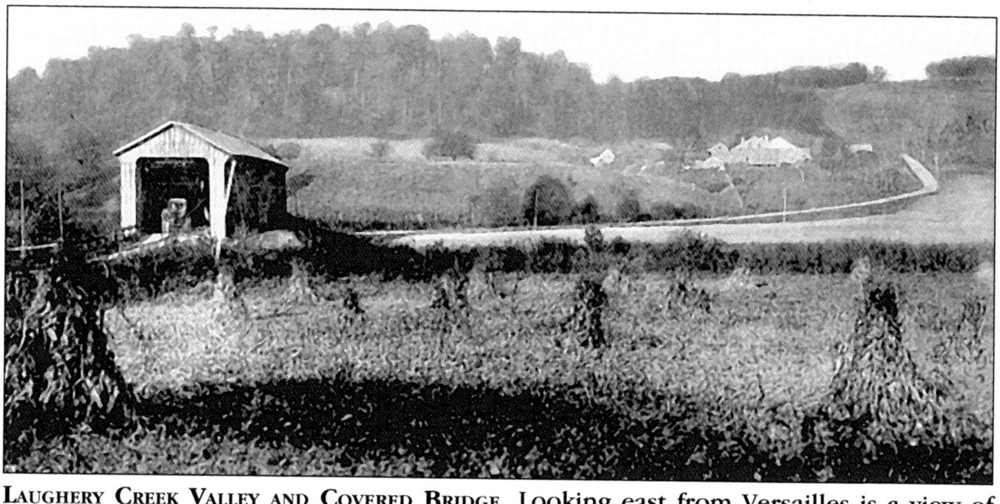

Laughery Creek Valley and Covered Bridge. Looking east from Versailles is a view of the old road to Dillsboro. The Busching Covered Bridge over Laughery Creek is in the distance. The Busching family lived in the old stone home between the barns, thus the name for the bridge. This was the toll gate house back when the road was a pay toll road. Until 1930, this was the highway to the east. Known as road #4 until 1926, the name was then changed to #50. (Photograph by unknown photographer.)

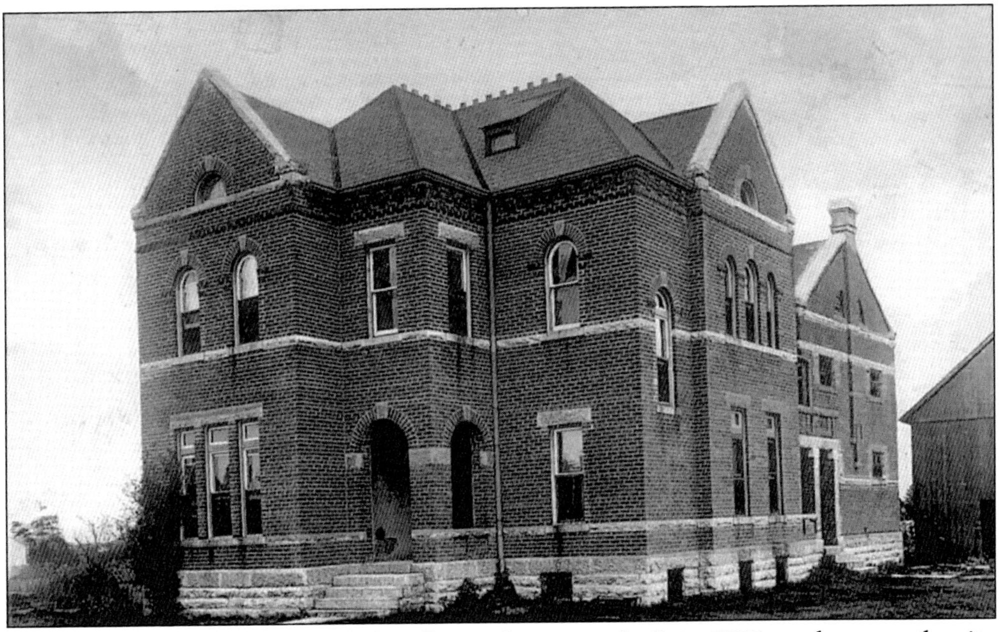

Ripley County Jail. This jail and sheriff's residence was built in 1891, and was on the site of the present jail. In 1897, this jail was featured in the famous "1897 Hanging." The sheriff was conveniently out when the mob entered the jail. They beat and dragged (by the neck) five inmates from the jail, and hanged them from an elm tree nearby. (Card #2662, Kraemer Art Co., Cincinnati & Berlin.)

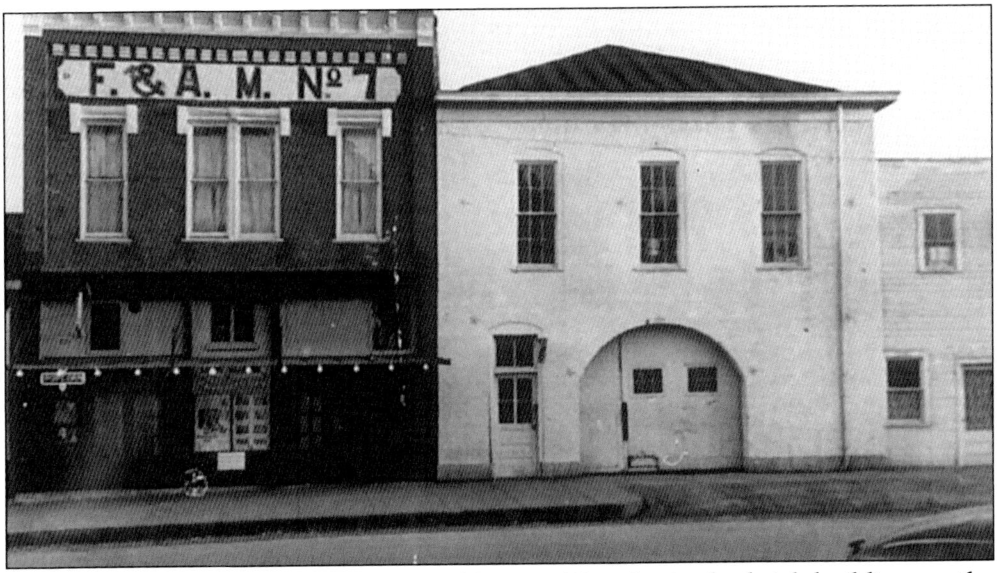

Masonic Lodge Hall, Livery Stable, and Theatre. Upstairs in the brick building on the left was the Masonic Lodge Hall #7. Below, on the ground floor, was the old Austin Theatre. The Austin ran movies from 1925 well into the 1960s. To the right is the old Livery Stable building, whose upstairs served as the school gym for some time. The hall was a skating rink, gym, play house, and office for the *Republican Paper*. (Photograph by unknown photographer.)

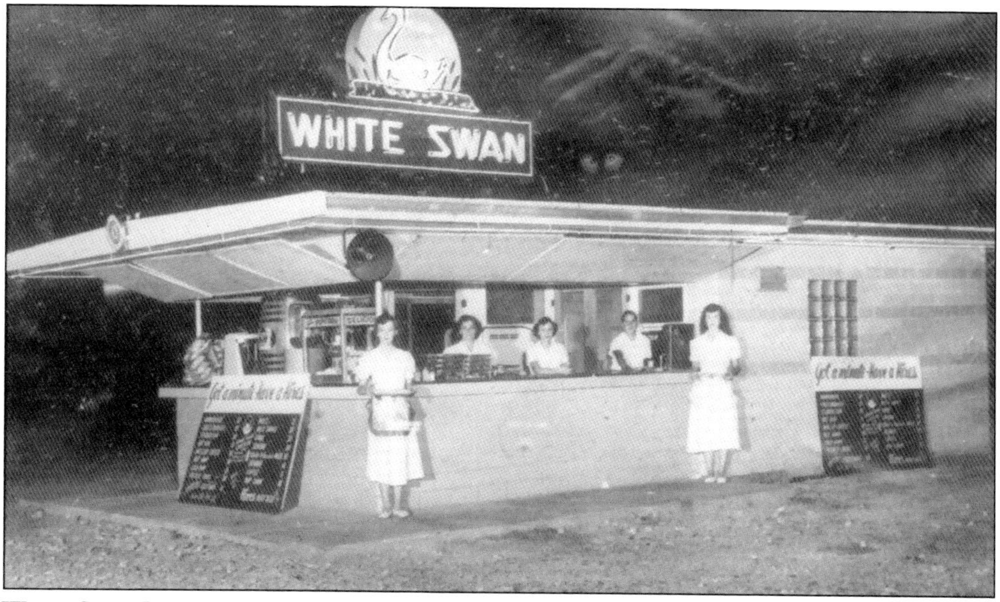

White Swan Drive Inn. An early drive-in in Versailles was the White Swan, called by local boys "The Ruptured Duck." It was located on the north side of roads #421 and #50, across from the Southeastern Indiana Vocational School. A popular hangout for the youths who had wheels, the "Duck" was destroyed by fire (probably too much grease). (Photograph by unknown photographer.)

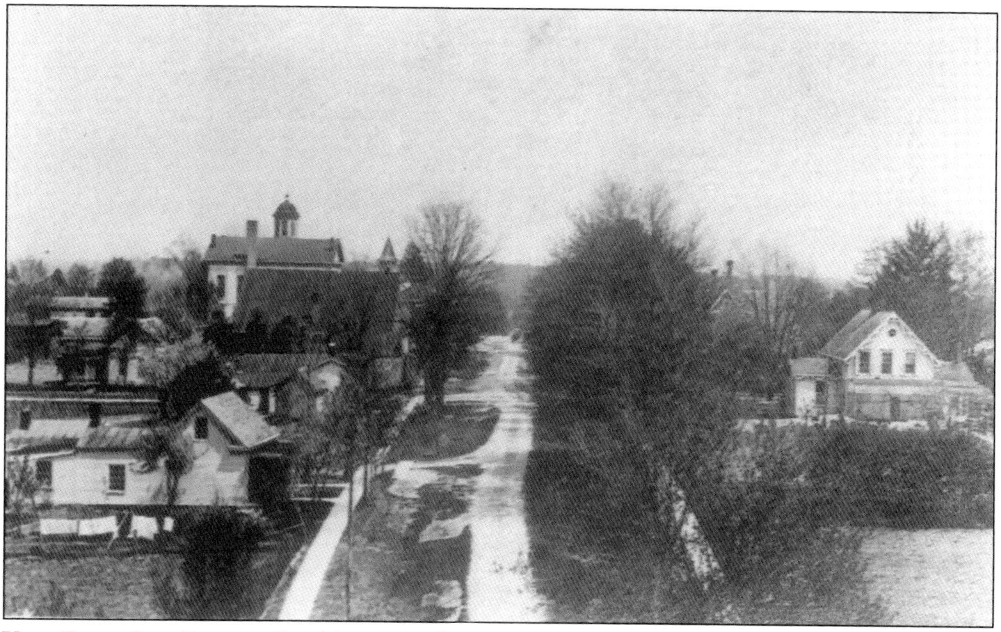

View From Old School. Looking east down Main Cross (Tyson) Street from the roof of the old school, this 1900 photograph reveals a large part of town. On the right is the back of Austin's home on Adams Street. To the left are several small homes, followed by the old Methodist church. In the distance, the roof and cupola of the courthouse can be seen. (Photograph by unknown photographer.)

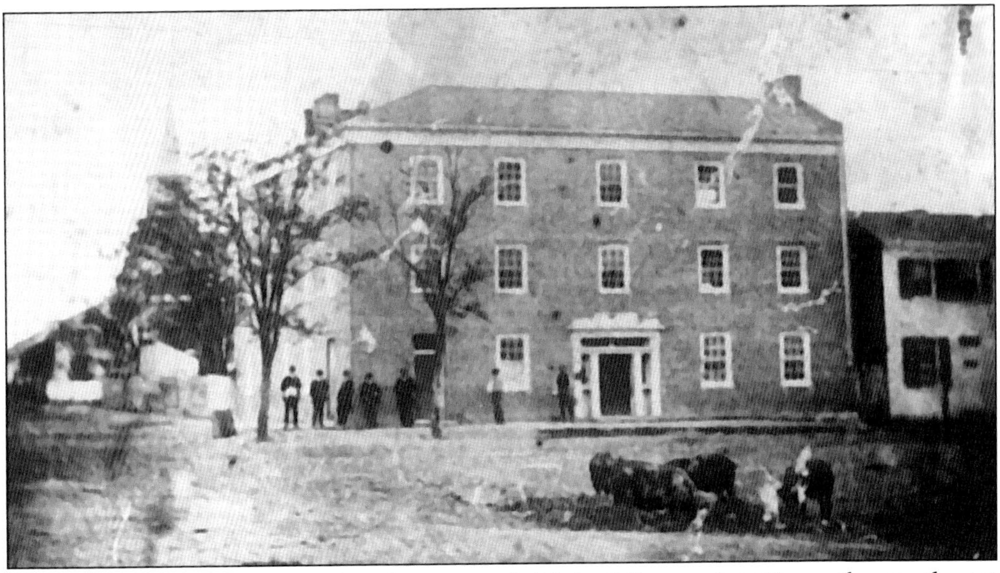

Anderson Medical Building. This three-story brick building on lot 12, on the southwest corner of Washington and Tyson Streets, was the site of an aspiring medical college. Dr. Anderson trained a few young students here before the Civil War. At one point, J.F.D. Lanier purchased this lot for $200, and later sold it for $100. J.F. was not usually known for this type of transaction. Notice the hogs in the mud-hole, and the lodge members, whose hall was on the third floor. (Photograph by unknown photographer.)

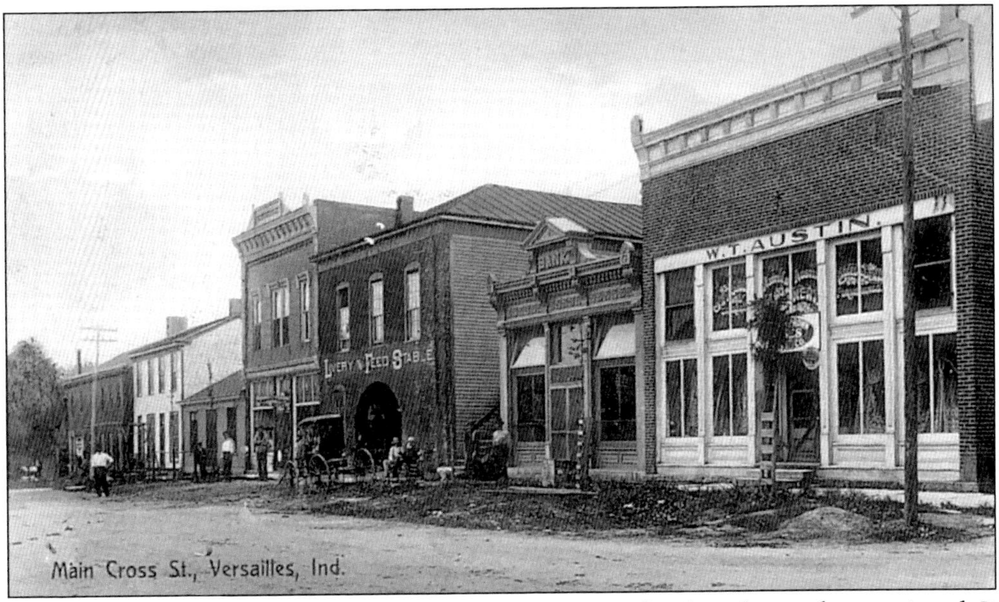

South Side of the Square. This was Main Cross Street at the time the card was printed. It is now known as Tyson Street, named in honor of James Tyson, who was the benefactor of Versailles. W.T. Austin's Store is on the corner of lot 13, and the second building is the Old State Bank. Next in line is the livery stable, and the last building is the Hassmer Hotel. Much later this was the Court House Inn. (Card #2668, by Kraemer Art Co., Cincinnati & Berlin.)

Six

Delaware Township

Delaware Township. In May 1825, Delaware Township was formed and named after the Delaware Indians who were once in the area. In March 1841, a part of the northern section was given to Laughery Township. There are 25 full sections, and Laughery and Ripley Creeks can be found in Delaware Township. At one time the township had Mud Pike, Kelley, Lookout, Stewart, and Baylor Schools. Now all of these are closed.

Rei/Delaware. Delaware Township's main town was originally named Rei, and the post office remained under that name until 1885. However, because the Delaware Indians had once inhabited the area, Delaware became the town's new name. In 1866, a normal college called Delaware Academy was built. The Academy trained young teachers and served as a high school. A large brick building that once served as a dormitory for the Academy remains in town today. Delaware once had a drug store, a depot, a church, a mill, a blacksmith, a saloon, general stores, a grain elevator, a hardware store, physicians, a cigar maker, and an Odd Fellows and Woodman Lodge. All that remains today is a British Petroleum Mini-Mart.

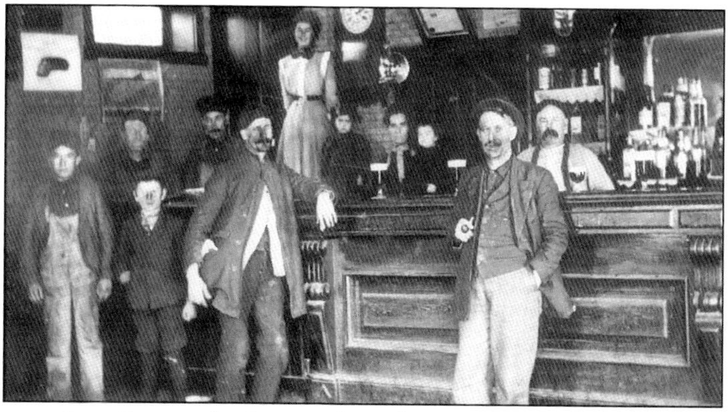

Delaware Saloon. Standing at the bar in the saloon are several men with black on their faces. This was first thought to be coal, but it turned out to be charcoal instead. A few enterprising farmers burned wood for charcoal, and these men worked at that trade. I think the attractive barmaid, not the taste of the beer, drew this crowd to the saloon. Pictured in the front, from left to right, are: Henry Schmaltz, Frank Schmaltz, Henry Starkey, and Henry Broerman. In the back row, from left to right, are: unidentified, unidentified, Carrie Schmaltz Crum, Daisy Schmaltz Asche, and Mrs. Martha Schmaltz holding Georgia and Steve Schmaltz. (Photograph by unknown photographer.)

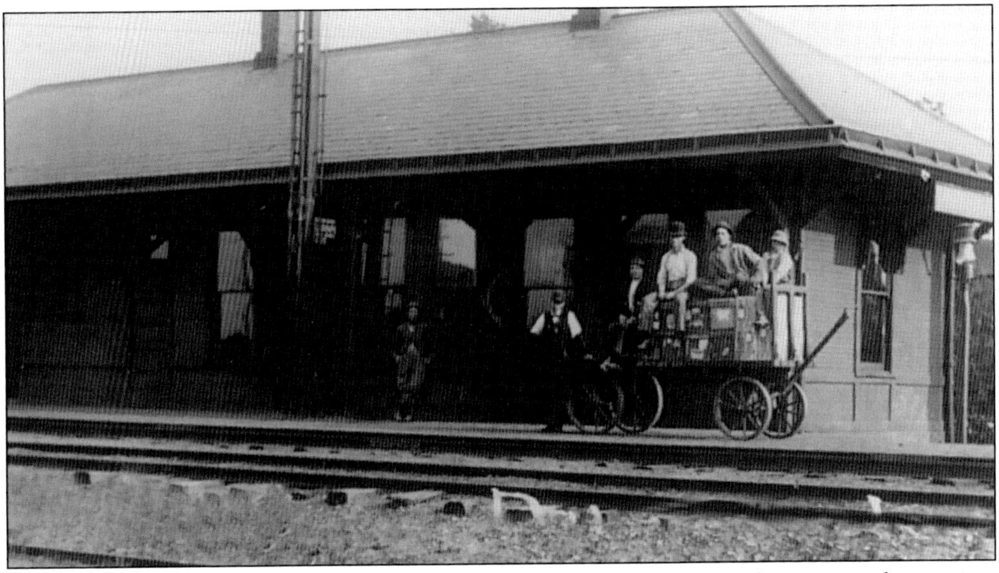

Delaware Depot. In 1854, the first O&M train passed through Delaware, and a station was established at Rei. The station was called Delaware Station. Later, the Baltimore & Ohio bought the O&M, and moved the rails 1.5 miles south. In 1900, this new station was called the new Delaware Station. It looks like the boys are awaiting the next train. (Photograph by unknown photographer.)

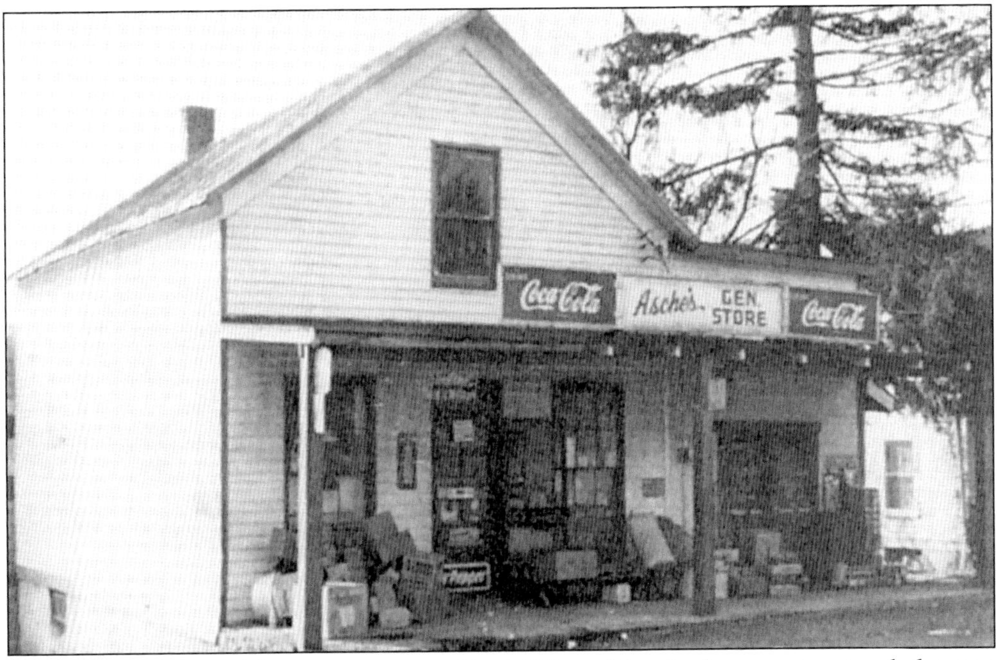

Asche's Store. This old store was started in 1889, and has had many structural changes through these many years. In 1951, Gerald Asche purchased the business from Russell Kelley and operated the store for years. In the late 1950s, Highway 350 was widened and the old store building razed. Later, a small store occupied the spot. (Photograph by unknown photographer.)

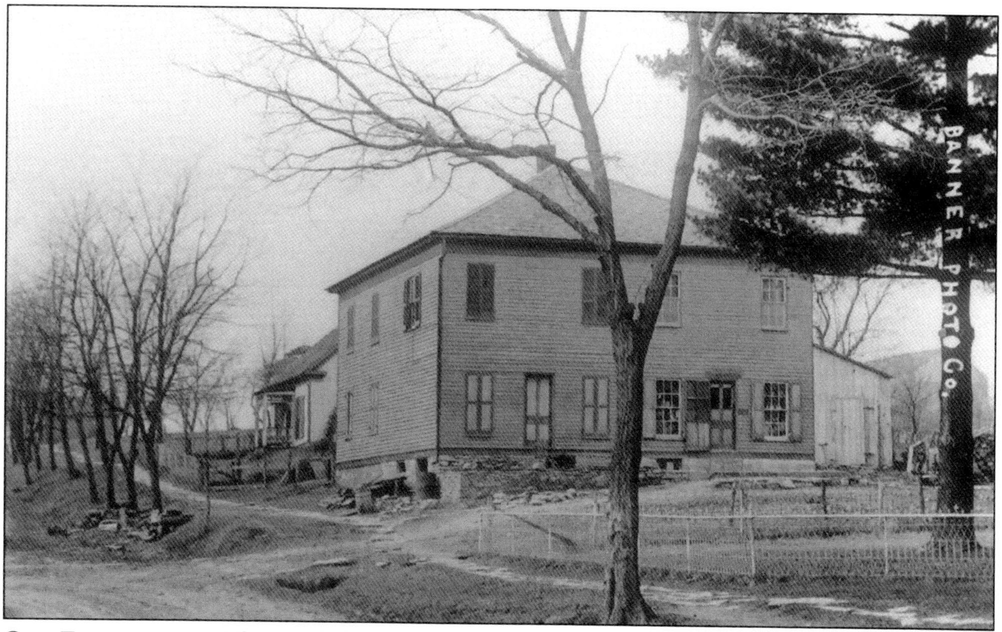

ODD FELLOWS HALL. The I.0.0.F. lodge hall was a large-frame, two-story building on the northwest corner of College and First Streets. The far right door was the entrance to Raney's Store. The lodge was a Chapter #172 Order of Odd Fellows, a popular lodge in the early 1900s. The Modern Woodman's Lodge Hall was farther down this same street. (Photograph by unknown photographer.)

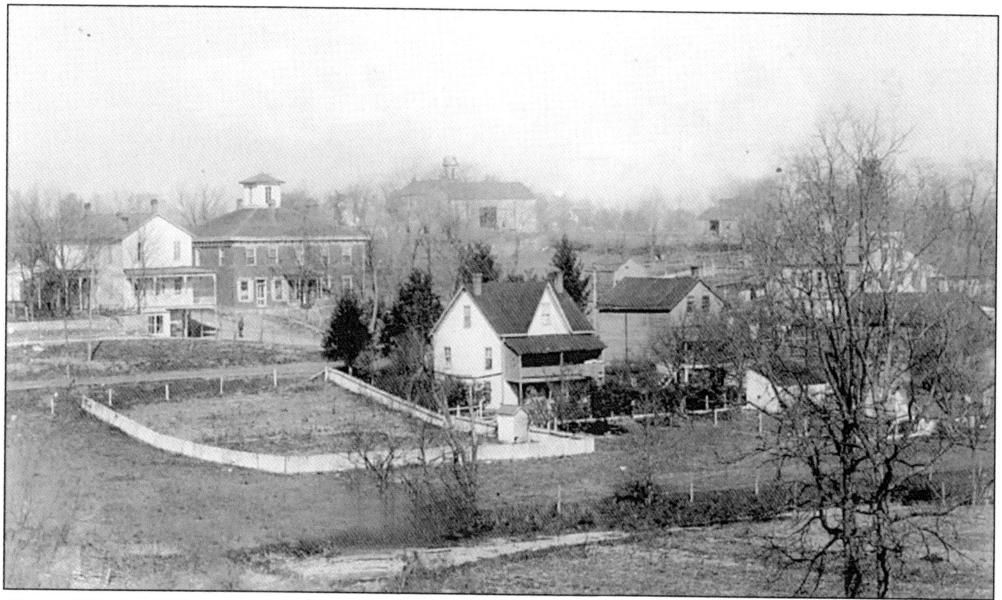

GREAT VIEW OF DELAWARE. This sepia picture encompasses most of Delaware. The large, square, brick building with the white cupola was the Delaware Academy, built in 1866, on what was called College Hill. The Academy was a normal school used to train young teachers. At center is the all-important little building in the back. A stock pen and unpaved streets are also visible. (Photograph by unknown photographer.)

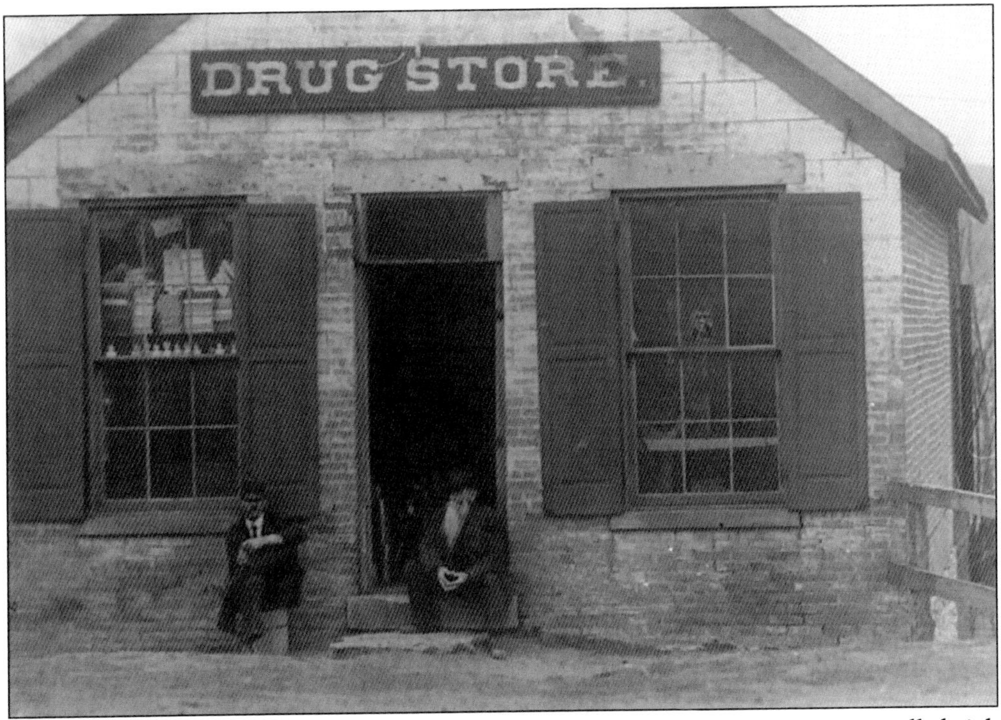

Delaware Drug Store. Elias Davis Mullins built this drug store. It was a small, brick building just east of the general store. Elias operated the store until 1880, when he sold it to Clint Carnine. Elias sent his two sons, Geo. and Holman, as well as Clint Carnine, to pharmacy school, then retired. Two elderly loafers hold up the store in this photo. (Photograph by unknown photographer.)

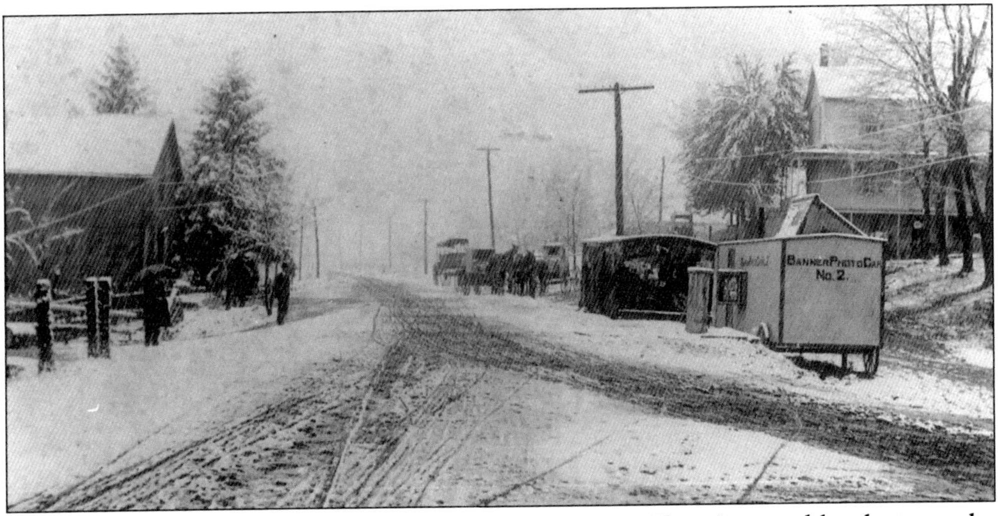

1908 Snow Scene. In the right of this picture is Banner Photo's portable photography laboratory. This lab was on wheels and could be moved very easily. A Mr. Roberts was the photographer, and he captured many valuable street scene pictures in the area. A box car warehouse is next in the scene, then a milk, or mail wagon. Pharmacists Clint Carnine and Elias Mullins walk in the snow. (Photograph by Banner Photo.)

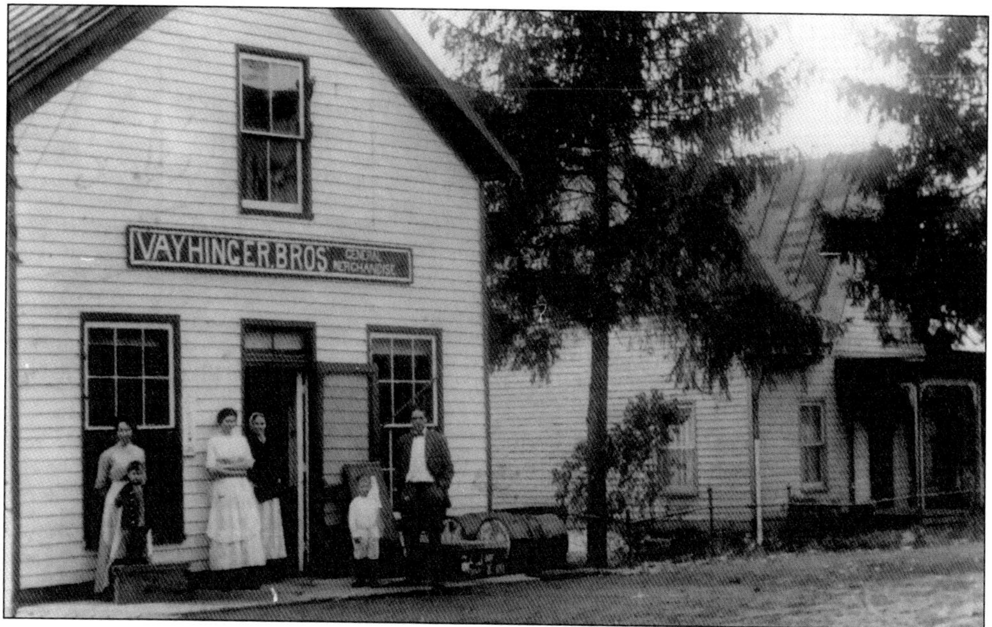

VAYHINGER BROS. Vayinger's General Merchandise Store is pictured here in 1912. The two barrels on the right are sure to be cheap and better kerosene (coal oil), sold at most general stores. One brother lived in the home at right. Pictured, from left to right, are: Fannie and Clyde Vayhinger, Eva Koechlin, Lettie Johnson, and young Gilbert and Bert Vayhinger. (Photograph by unknown photographer.)

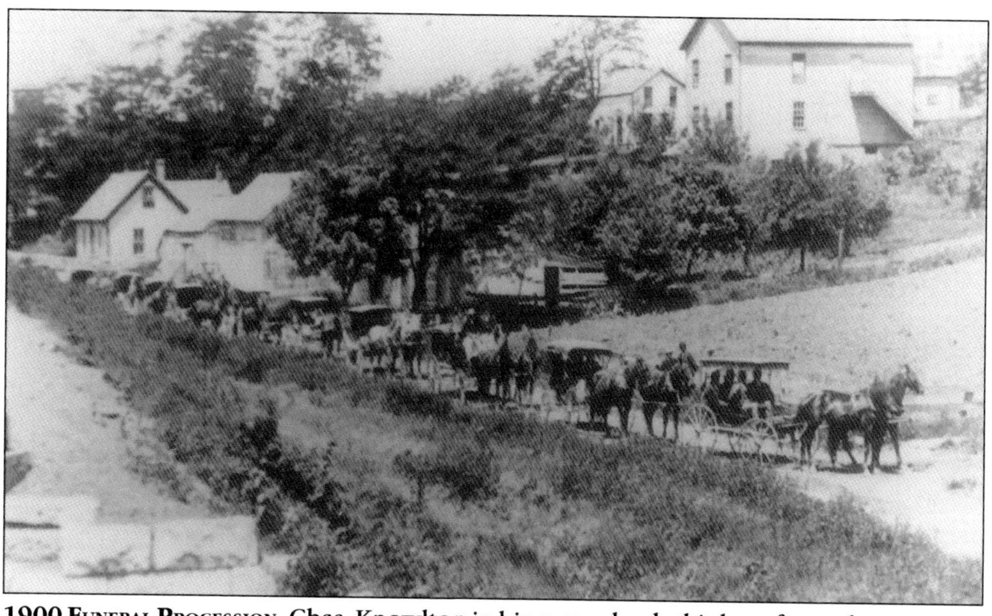

1900 FUNERAL PROCESSION. Chas. Knowlton in his surrey leads this long funeral procession for a Mr. Edwards, who lived in the large brick house across from the store. Wm. Dunbar, Knowlton, Harvey Monroe, and Clint Carnine were pallbearers at this funeral. At this time the railroad still went through Delaware. The third vehicle is the horse-drawn hearse. (Photograph by unknown photographer.)

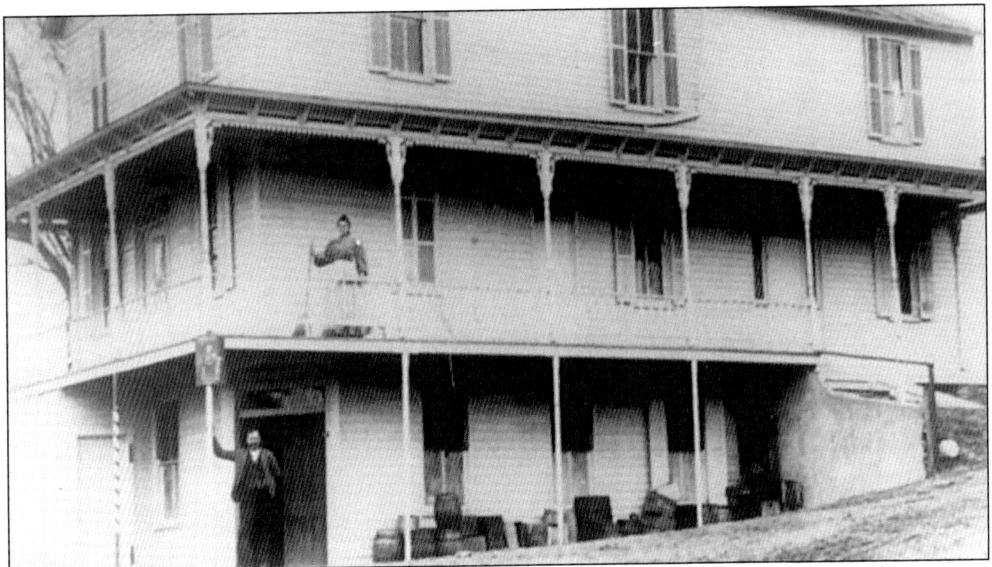

Delaware's Saloon. Ready to serve the thirsty was this large saloon run by Edward and Mary Koechlin. In 1900, the bar room was on the ground floor, while the Koechlins lived upstairs. Later, the saloon was owned by Steve Schmaltz, then George Tholke. In earlier days the saloon also served as a hotel, common in those days. (Photograph by unknown photographer.)

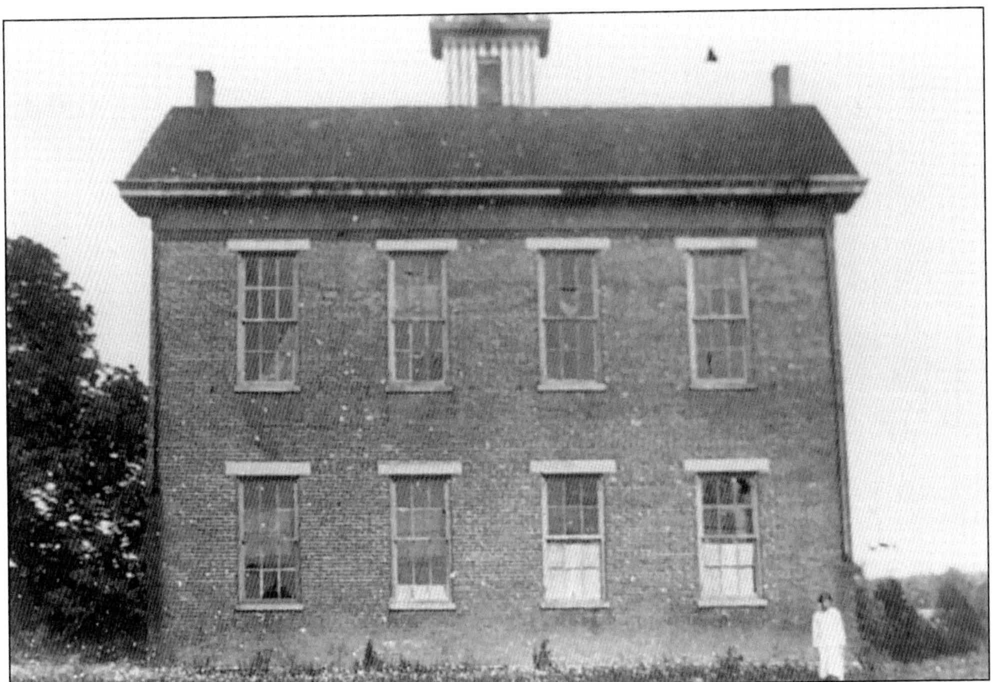

Delaware School. This red brick building had two classrooms downstairs, a hall, and two upstairs classrooms. First, a two-year high school was taught for many years. Then, a three-year course was given. A four-year school only operated for two years. In 1923, it became an elementary school only. (Photograph by unknown photographer.)

Seven

Shelby Townships

This area was settled early in 1814. In 1818, Mr. Beggs, Mr. DePauw, and Mr. Eades were appointed to select the site of the new Ripley County seat. They met at Mr. Brown's home in New Marion, and soon chose Versailles as the new site. Shelby Township consisted of Haney's Corner, New Marion, St. Magdalene, Marble Corner, Rexville, and Titusville. Michigan Road was also within its borders. In the late 1930s, the government practiced Eminent Domain and acquired a large portion of Shelby Township to be used for the Jefferson Proving Ground. As a result, Shelby Township suffered from the loss of many taxpayers.

NEW MARION. New Marion was Shelby Township's largest town. It was laid out in 1832, but the neighborhood was much older than that. The intersection of Old Vernon and Michigan Roads was at the center of New Marion. In its early years, New Marion was home to a saloon, a general store, a school, a bank, a physician, a dentist, a mill, and an undertaker. Like many small towns, it lost its industries. It was the town's death toll when the Jefferson Proving Ground purchased everything to the town's west.

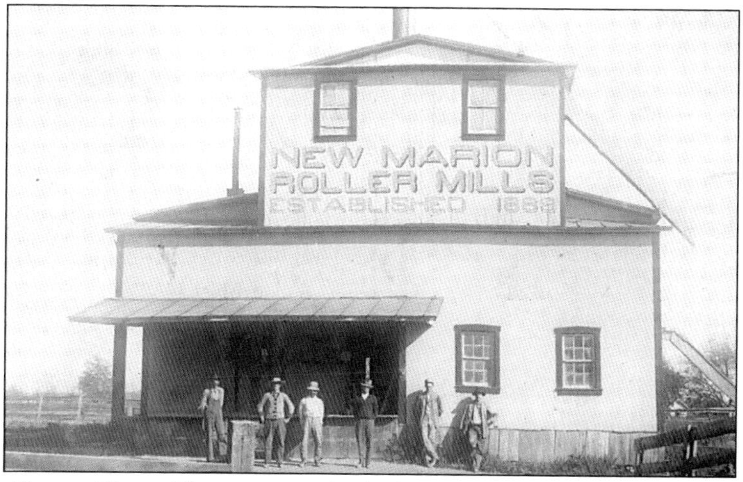

New Marion Roller Mills. Three stories high, featuring a porch halfway across the front with a floor the height of a wagon bed, this 1869 mill was one of New Marion's busiest spots. A steam boiler furnished the power for grinding flour and mixing feeds. The men pictured in front are, from left to right, as follows: Unknown, Clarence Kieffer, Bert Ebel, Holman Burton, Alex Miller, and Jack Titus. (Photograph by Carl Ebel.)

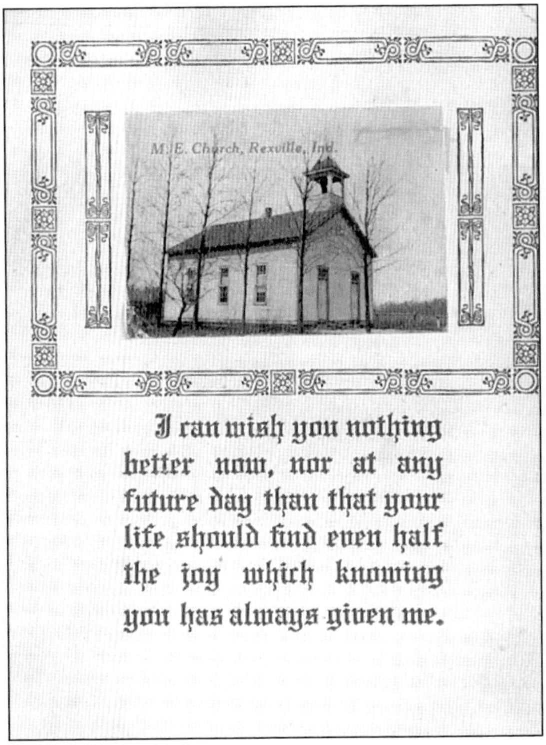

REXVILLE M.E. CHURCH. Rexville Church was on the west side of Highway 421, on the north end of Rexville, and once had a membership of 130. Rexville, at the time this picture was taken, had a post office, stores, an I.O.O.F. Lodge, a school, and two doctors. This church was the only church in Rexville. (Card by Auburn Post Card Co., Auburn, Indiana.)

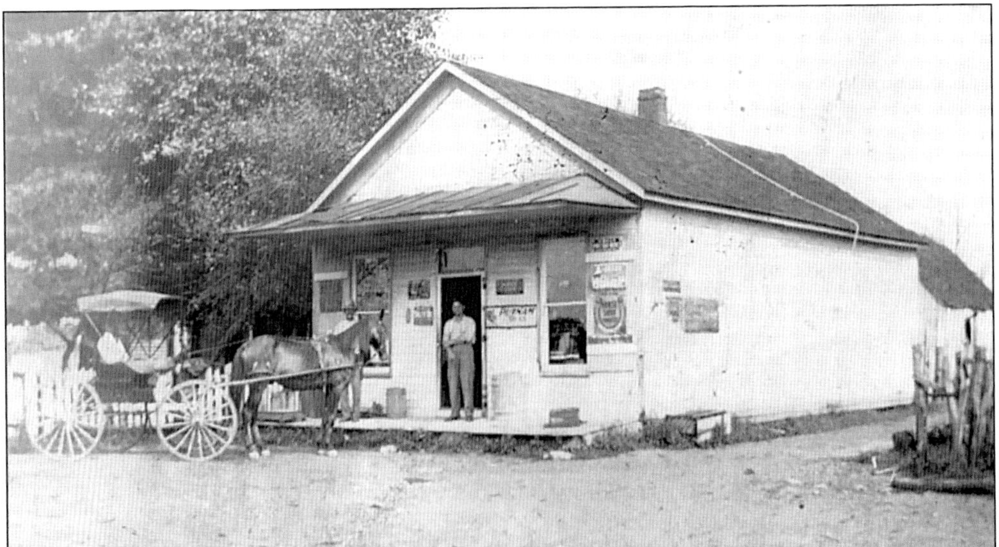

REXVILLE GENERAL STORE. One can see signs on the front of this store advertising Horse Shoe Tobacco, Putman's Dye, soft drinks, and several other products. Horses with buggies are hitched to the rack, and two men are talking to the driver. Virgil Orem was proprietor of the store. This was a typical rural store. (Photograph by unknown photographer.)

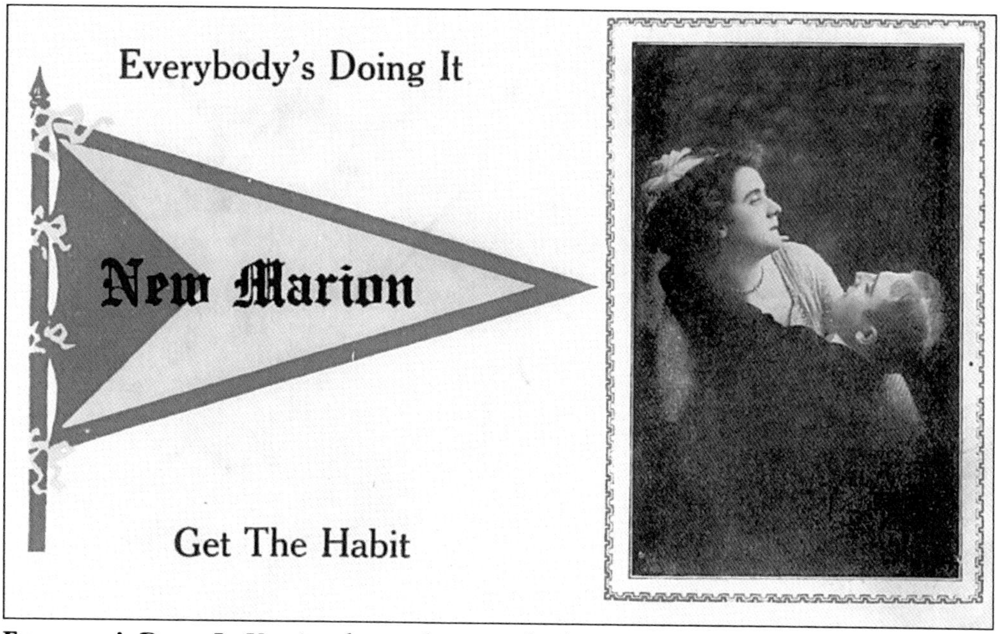

Everybody's Doing It. You just know that everybody is going to New Marion, so get in the habit! Nearly every village and town had these cards printed to boost their hometowns, usually with pretty girls on the front or some eye-catching logo. These cards were sent with short messages. They served two purposes—to convey friendly messages and to promote hometowns. (1913 Romantic photograph by unknown photographer.)

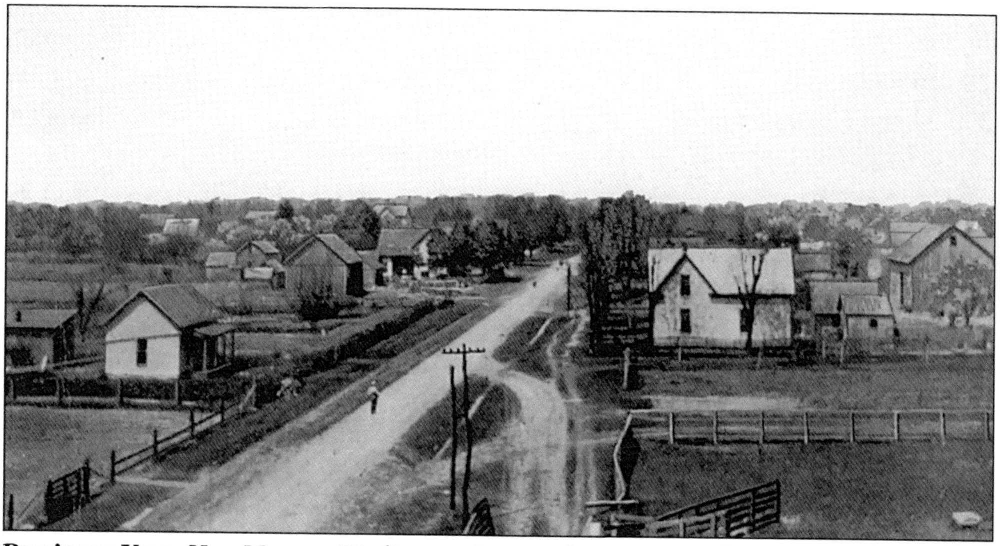

Bird's-eye View, New Marion. Bird's-eye view cards were popular with all the towns. A photographer would find a high spot, make several shots, and publish the cards. This card shows Meisberger's Stock Yard Pen, the dirt road through town, one buggy, and a lone pedestrian walking up the main drag. This is a typical bird's-eye view. (Card #19526, by unknown photographer.)

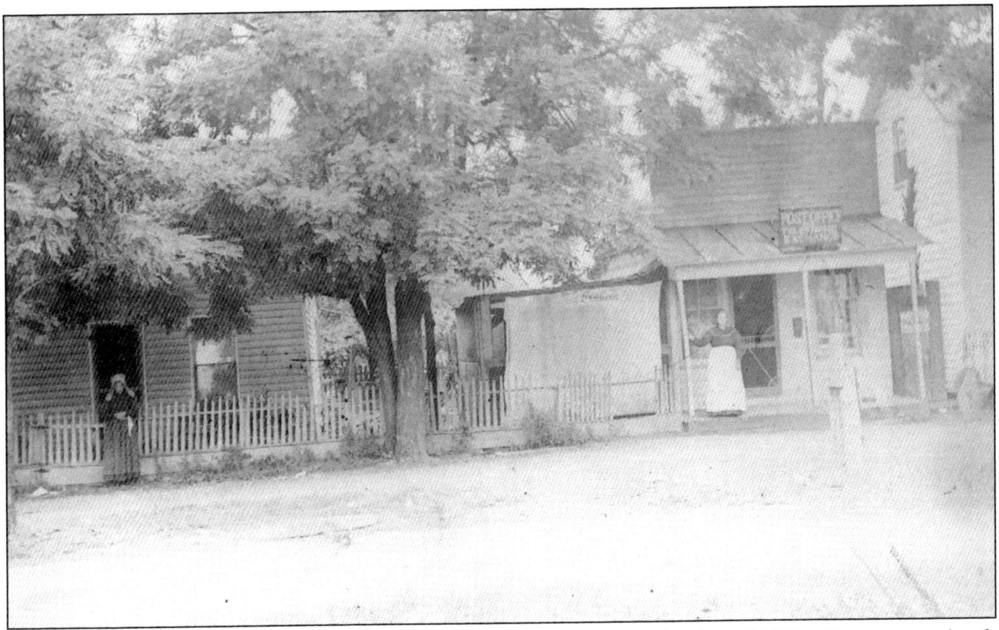

OLD NEW MARION POST OFFICE. This photograph, taken just before 1900, gives one a look at the very small post office and Telephone Exchange. The barely legible sign on the small building to the right tells this tale. The woman in a long dress and bonnet in front of a picket fence dates this photograph. (Photograph by Wilbur Meyer.)

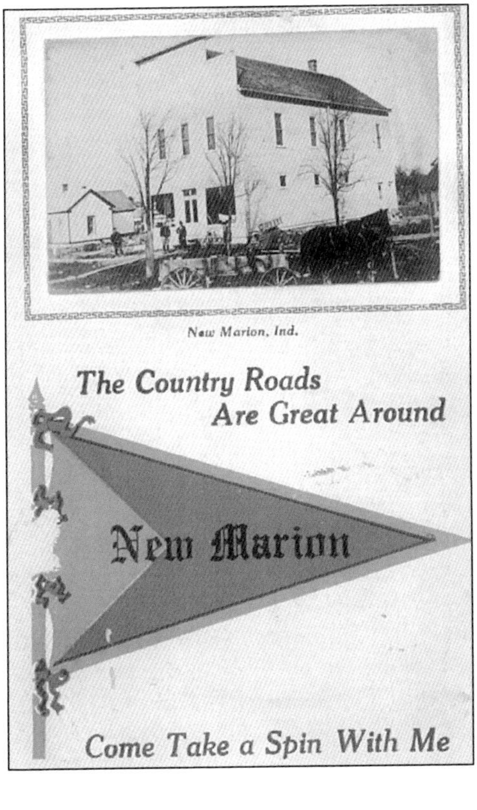

COUNTRY STORE. "The Country Roads Are Great around New Marion." Don't believe it, although they can be great in dry weather. At the top is the large store belonging to John Holzer. This card was mailed in 1920 to Ike Harrell from his cousin Millie. Holzer later moved to Versailles and continued in business. (Unnumbered card by unknown publisher).

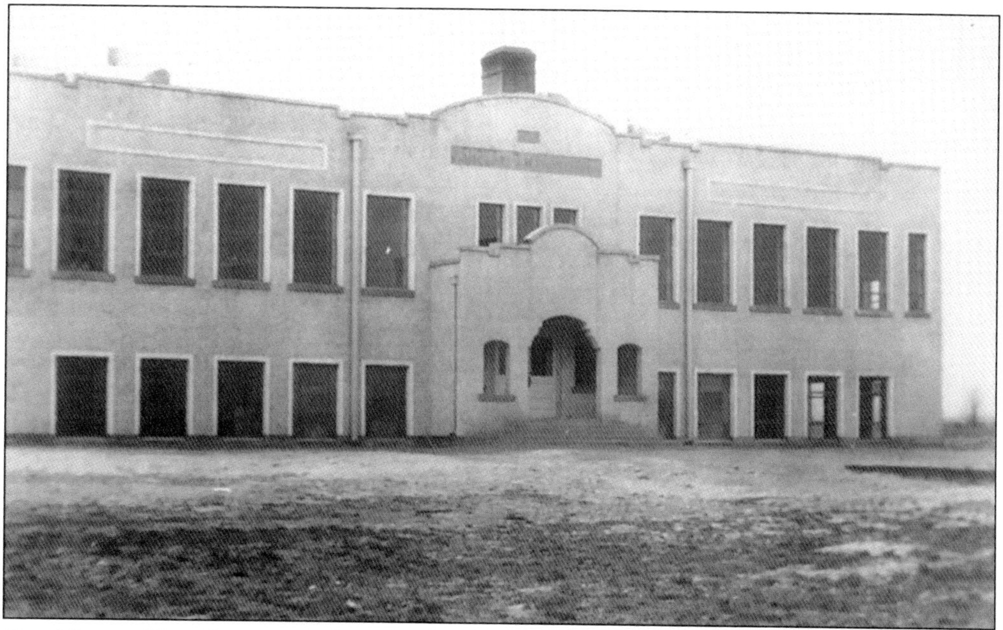

New Marion High School. Before this building served as the high school, several smaller structures were used. In 1936, a new gymnasium was added, as well as six classrooms, making the school appear like this photograph. The school has an almost "Alamo" look to it. In the 1960s, New Marion was absorbed into the South Ripley school system. (Photograph by unknown photographer.)

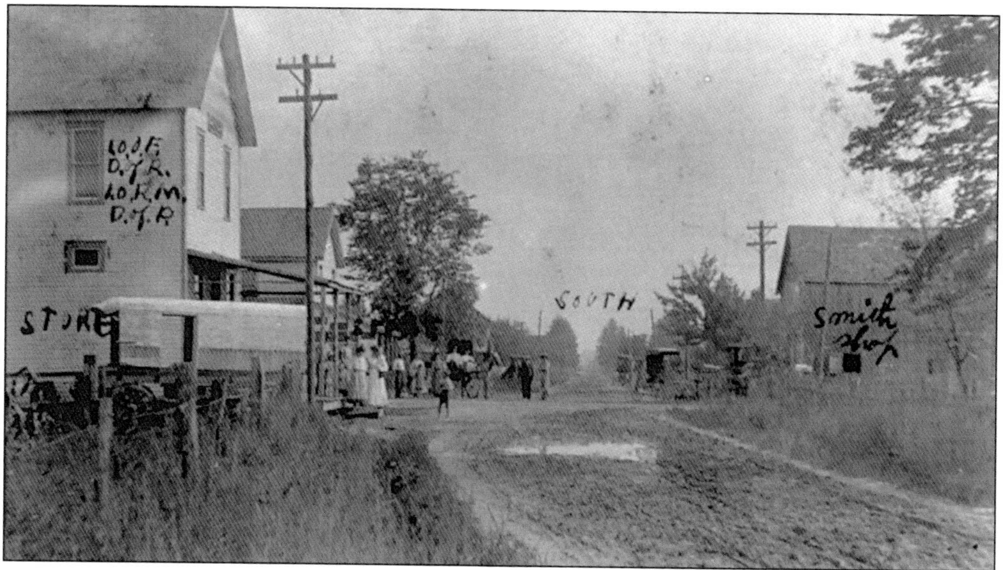

Marble Corner Street Scene. This postcard shows how Marble Corner looked in 1908. The upper story of the building on the left is the Big Creek Lodge #461 I.O.O.F. Hall. In the downstairs of this building was the general store run by Colonel Wildman. Frank Reed was the huckster and postmaster in the next store. On the right was the blacksmith shop of Mike Kramer. Marble Corner received its name because of its location near Marble Creek and the corner of the township. (Photograph by unknown photographer.)

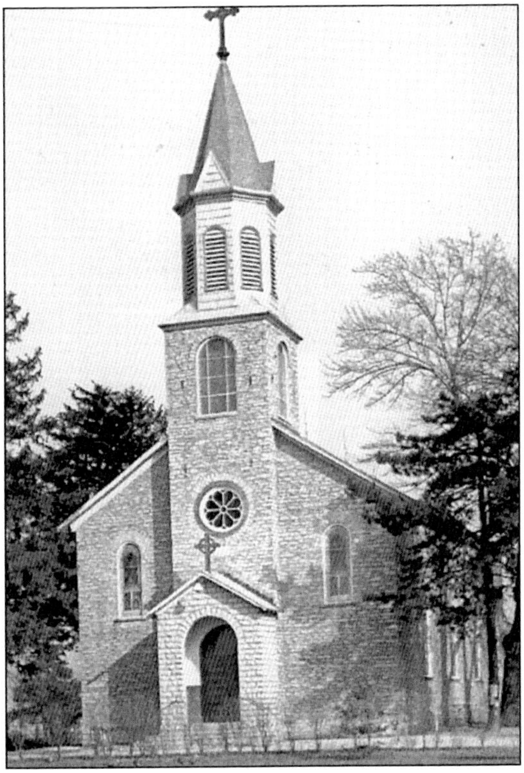

St. Magdalene Church. This Catholic church 4 miles south of New Marion was organized in 1834, and was called "The Dutch Settlement" because its members were all German. Finley Meisberger was the village's postmaster, saloonist, storekeeper, and farmer. The stone church was built in 1861, and held its last service February 16, 1941. Jefferson Proving Ground destroyed the church and moved its cemetery. Services are now held in the Old Bank Building in New Marion. (Photograph by unknown photographer.)

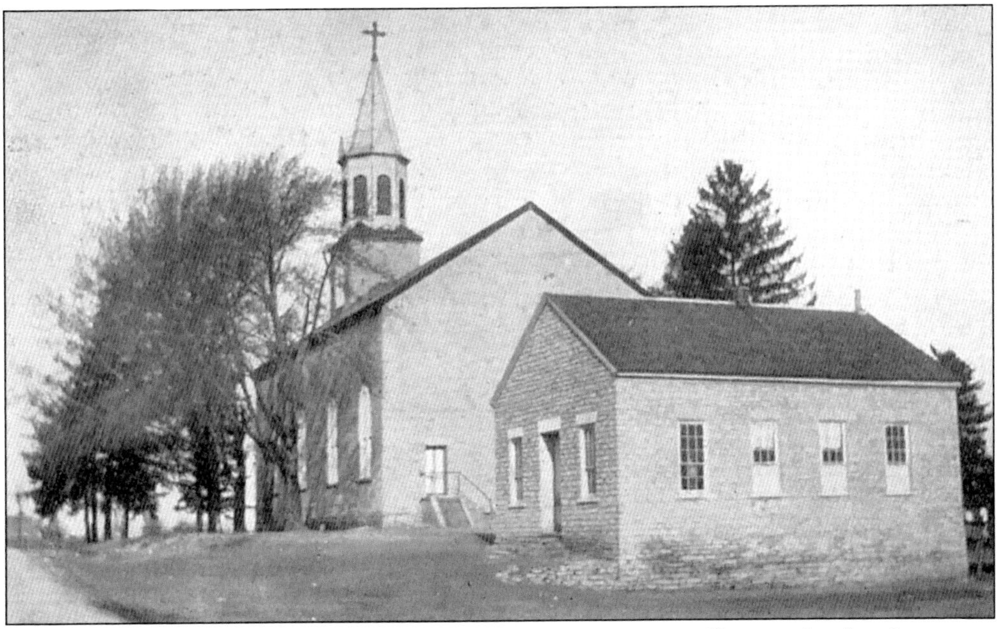

St. Magdalene Church and School. The school was a one-room affair, made of native stone, and sat behind the church. This parochial school served the area well for many years, but like all small schools it finally closed, and the students were sent to New Marion. The local priest was usually the teacher. (Card by E.C. Kropp Co., Milwaukee, Wisconsin.)

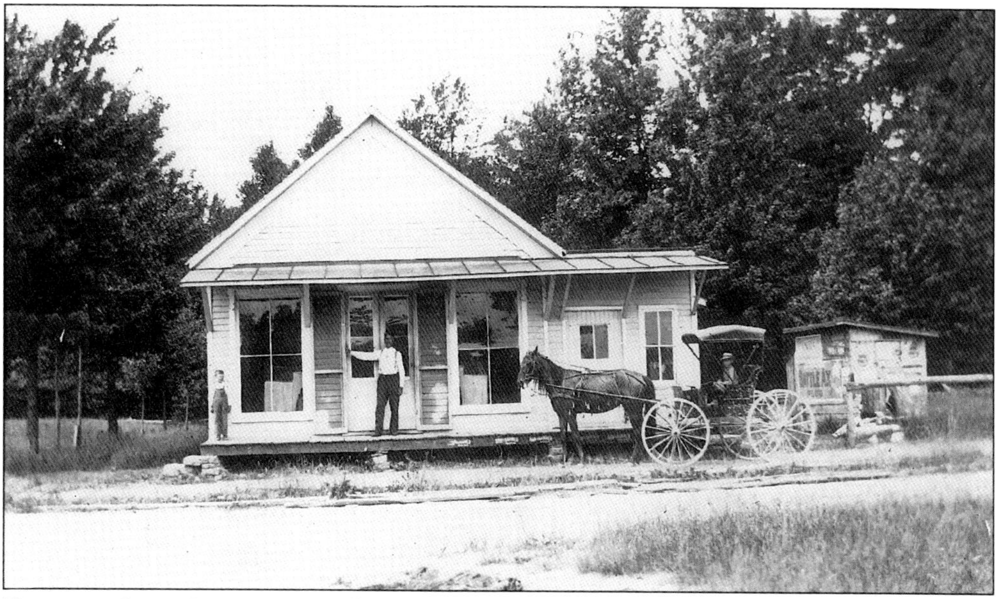

Titusville Post Office. Titusville was located on the west side of Highway 421, north of Rexville. A general store and post office were practically all there was to the town, although once there was a Titusville Schoolhouse. A buggy with a young driver is parked in front of the store. On the side of the shed at right, a sign advertising "Battle Axe Plug Tobacco" is easily seen. On the porch is Thomas Rayburn with a small boy. Titusville simply forgot to grow. (Photograph by Alan Smith.)

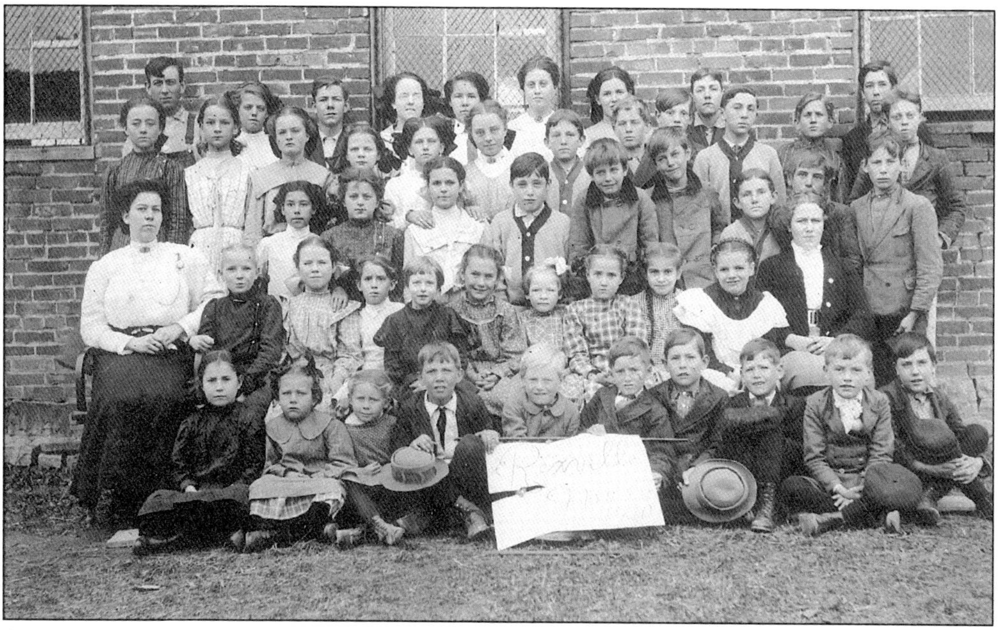

Rexville M.E. Church. T.S. Vawter, Z.T. Hytt, James Rea, John Paugh, Peter Sales, and T.N. Russell were early citizens of Rexville. The M.E. Church once had a membership of 130 souls. Thomas Flint was an early superintendent. (Auburn Post Card Manufacturing Co., Auburn, Indiana.)

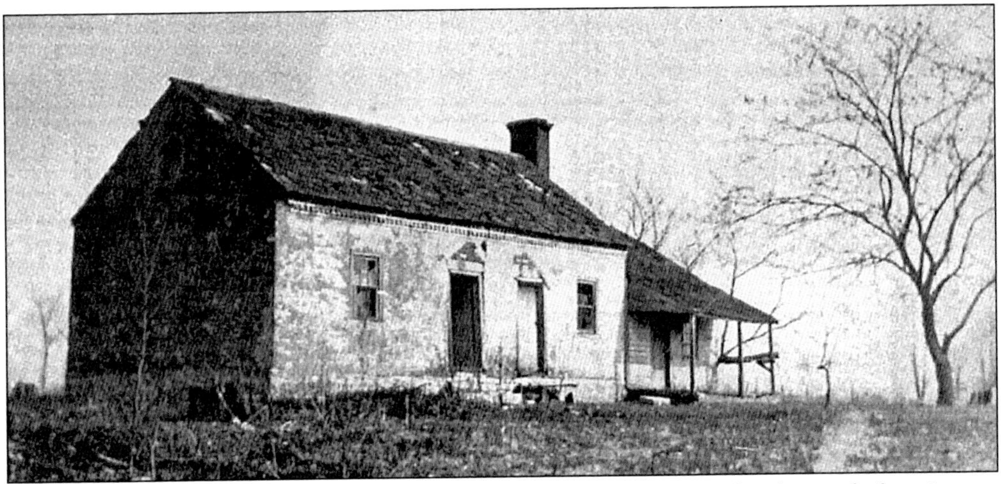

Benjamin Brown House. The first Ripley County Court met in this home belonging to Benjamin Brown on July 23, 1818, just two years after Indiana became a state. Judge John Test presided as president and judge of the Circuit Court. Governor Jonathan Jennings appointed the first county officers. Brown's home was at the present site of New Marion in Shelby Township. The court immediately moved to Versailles after this first meeting.

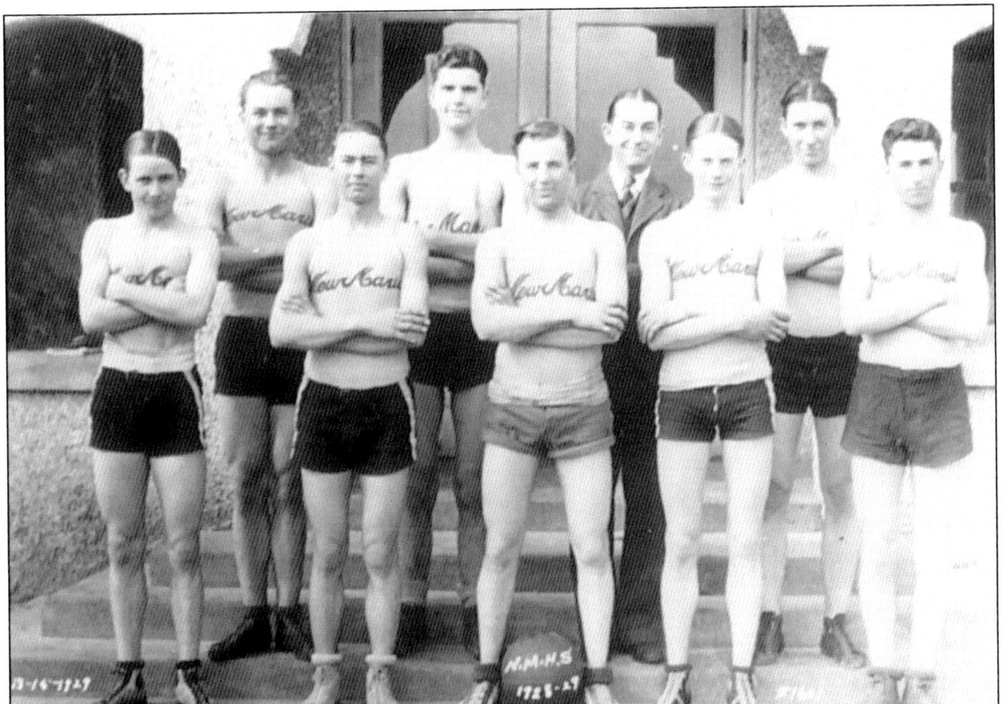

1928–1929 Basketball Team. The Panthers are, from left to right, as follows: (front row) Bill Strubbe, Edgar Nauret, Bud Thomas, Irvin Fruedenstein, and Ray Pavey; (back row) Lawrence Giegrich, George Leineweber, Dave Fruedenstein, and Albert Miller. The Panthers were one of New Marion's better teams. (Photograph by unknown photographer.)

Eight

Otter Creek Township

In November 1827, Shelby Township was divided in half, and the northern half became Otter Creek Township. In 1841, Laughery Township was created from the northern portion of this new township. Later, in 1858, the boundary was shifted southward. Because otters were very plentiful in the area, the area was named Otter Creek. Also contributing to its name, the township featured three creeks: Brushy, Otter, and Sugar. Poston (now called Dabney) and Holton are the only towns that remain in Otter Creek. The Michigan Road, Highway 50, and the B&O Railroad transverse the township.

HOLTON. Albion Redlon surveyed this town in June 1854, and 131 lots were sold. Jesse Holman ran a store here, as well as a post office, a saloon, and a mill. The first train ran through town on July 4, 1854. In 1860, vast numbers of pigeons roosted near town, blocking out the sunlight. They were killed, and local residents shipped wagon loads of the pigeons for 25¢ per dozen. The town suffered through several fires, but always bounced back. At present, Holton has a saloon/restaurant, a bank, several churches, a liquor store, a grocery store, and many homes.

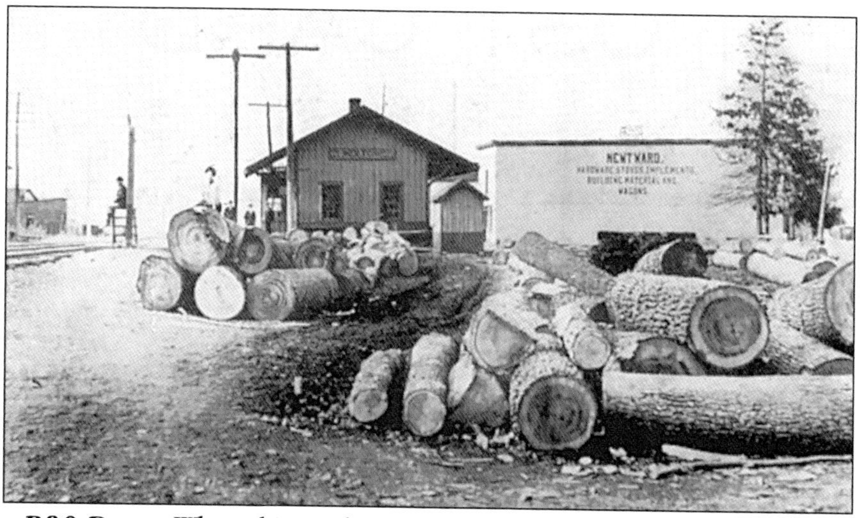

Holton B&O Depot. When this card was made, Holton's Depot was the busy spot in town. Some very large walnut logs are piled on the right of the picture, and a lone man can be seen sitting atop of the mail catcher. A train is approaching. Newt Ward's large store looms up in this black and white picture. (Card by unknown publisher.)

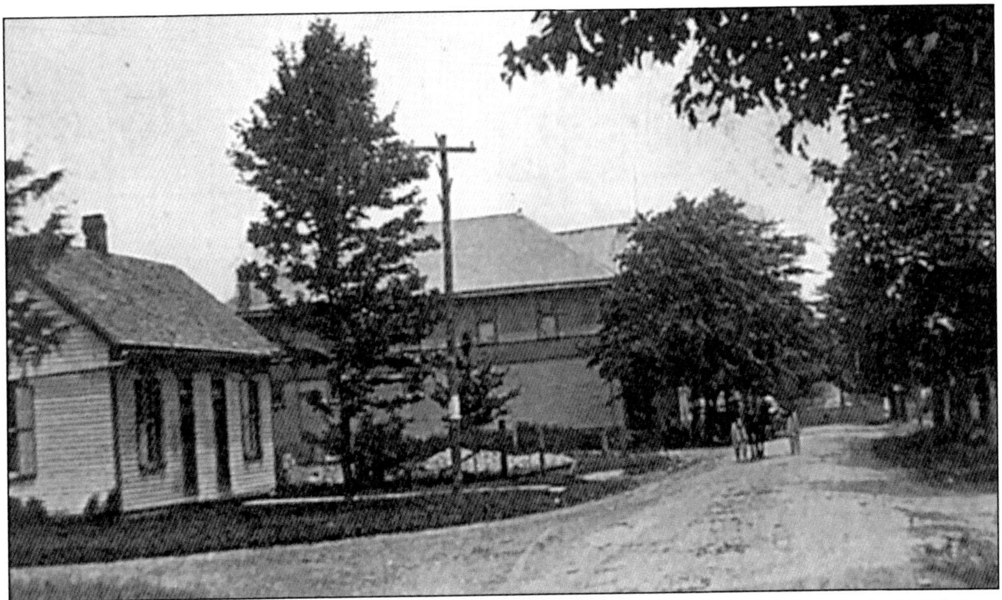

Twin Views of Holton. In the top view, a gravel street named New Marion Street has a fine residence on the left. Beyond this is a large store. A single horse and buggy plod along this main street. Below is the large frame home of O.P. Shook, located on the outskirts of town. (Card #23830, by unknown photographer.)

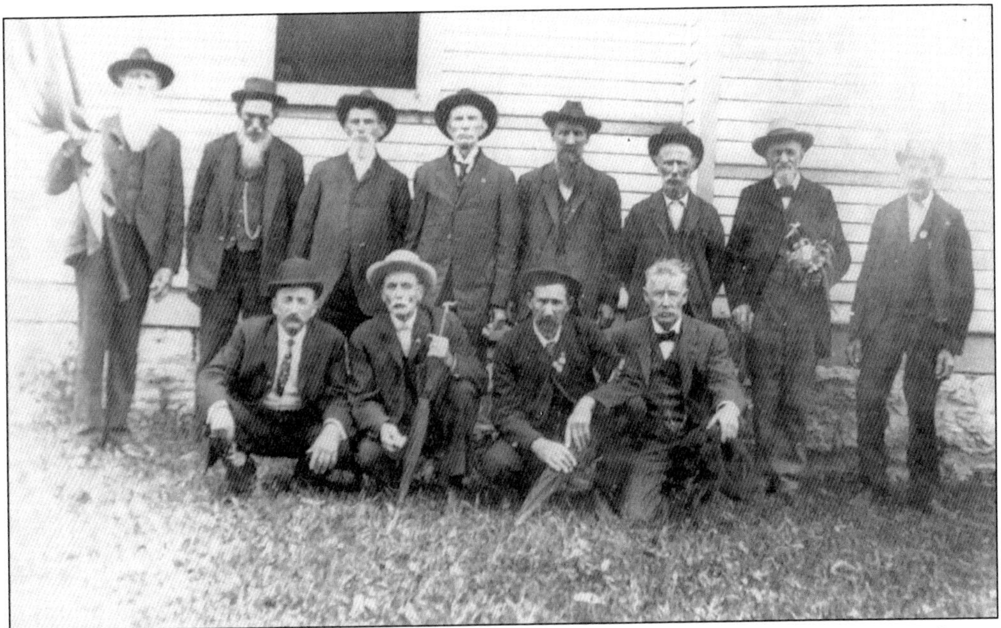

Holton G.A.R. Post. Holton's Grand Army of the Republic was Post 495, and was named for J.B. Holman Post. First Lt. Jesse B. Holman, Co. D. 37th Indiana Infantry, was killed in the Battle of Stone River on December 31, 1862. In 1905, the post had 22 members, but later joined posts with Versailles. Smith Harrel is pictured in the front row, fourth from the left. The other men are unidentified. (Photograph by unknown photographer.)

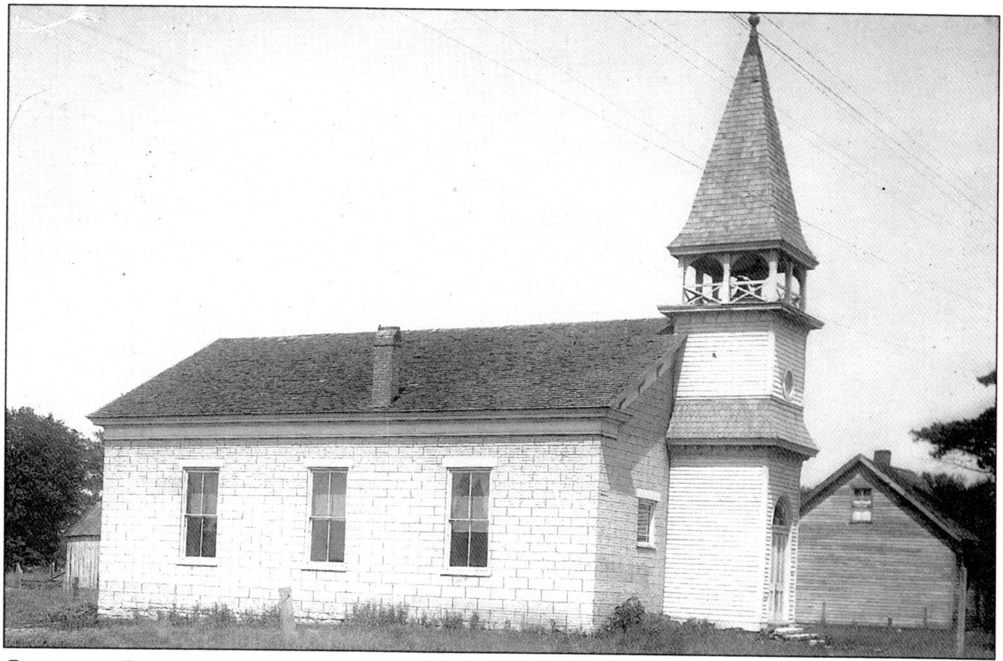

Christian Church. In 1855, one year after Holton was formed, a few families met to organize a Christian church. Long after the first log church was constructed, lot 56 and half of lot 55 were purchased, and a new brick church was built. In 1916, two rooms were added to this church, and over the years many improvements have been made by the congregation. (Glossy card by unknown photographer.)

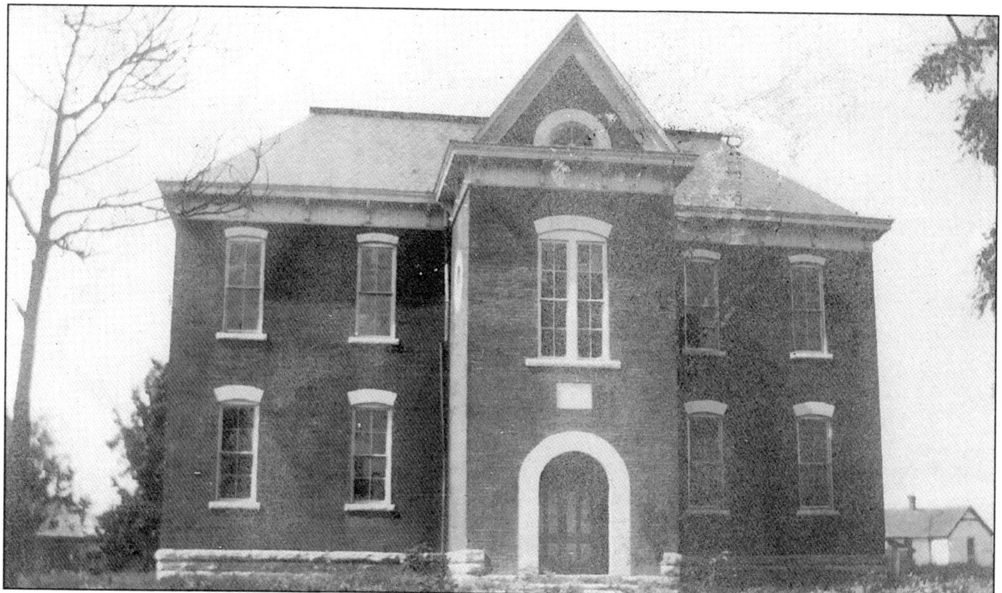

Holton High School. This four-room high school building was the second permanent school in Holton. It was used as the seat of education for Holton for many years, but finally fell victim to progress. Two school buildings have since replaced this structure. (Sepia card by unknown photographer.)

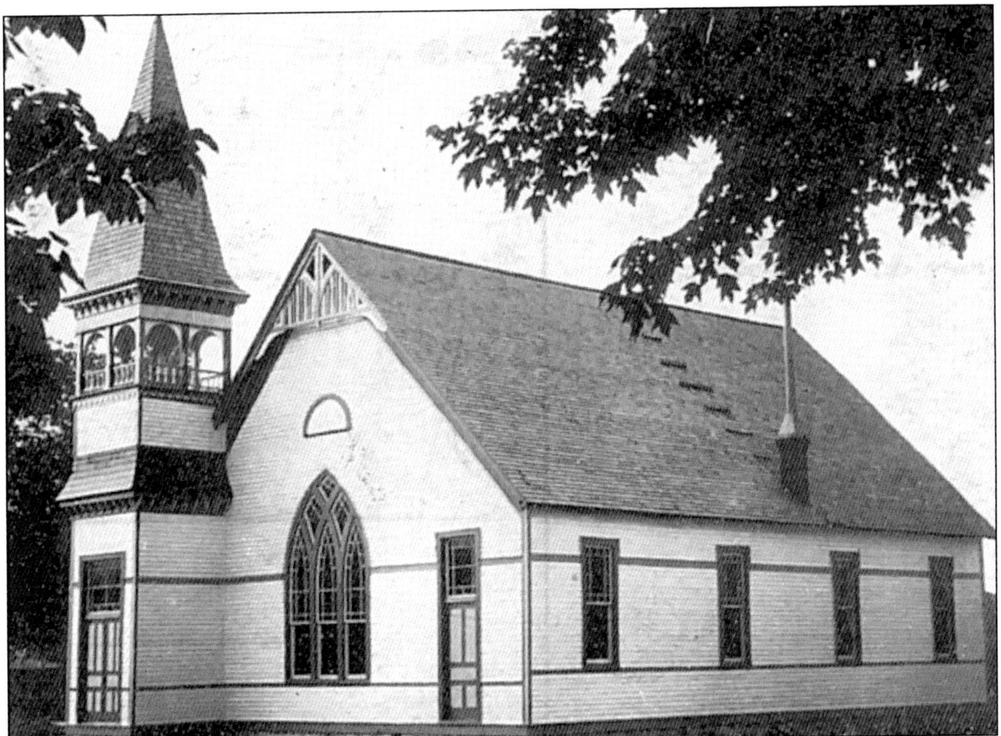

METHODIST CHURCH. On March 29, 1859, several families of Holton met at the home of John Downey to organize a Methodist church. A permanent church was built in 1897, and in 1948, a basement was added to this structure. In the years that followed, many improvements were added to the 1897 church. (Card by unknown printer.)

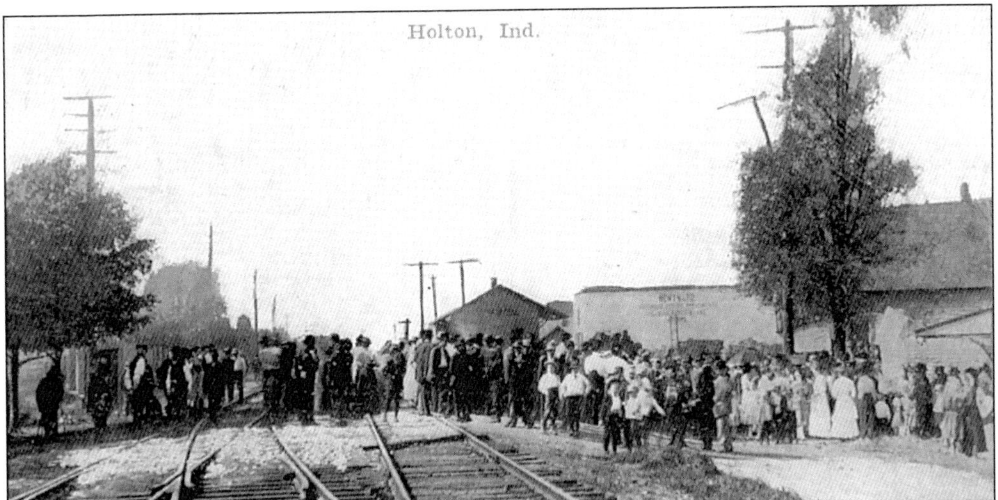

A BIG CROWD IN HOLTON. I hope there wasn't a train due in Holton when this photograph was made. The occasion that drew such a large crowd is unknown, and why the people are assembled on the tracks is open for speculation. The dresses are an early 1900s style. Freight cars are sidetracked on the spur rails at the depot. (Card by unknown photographer.)

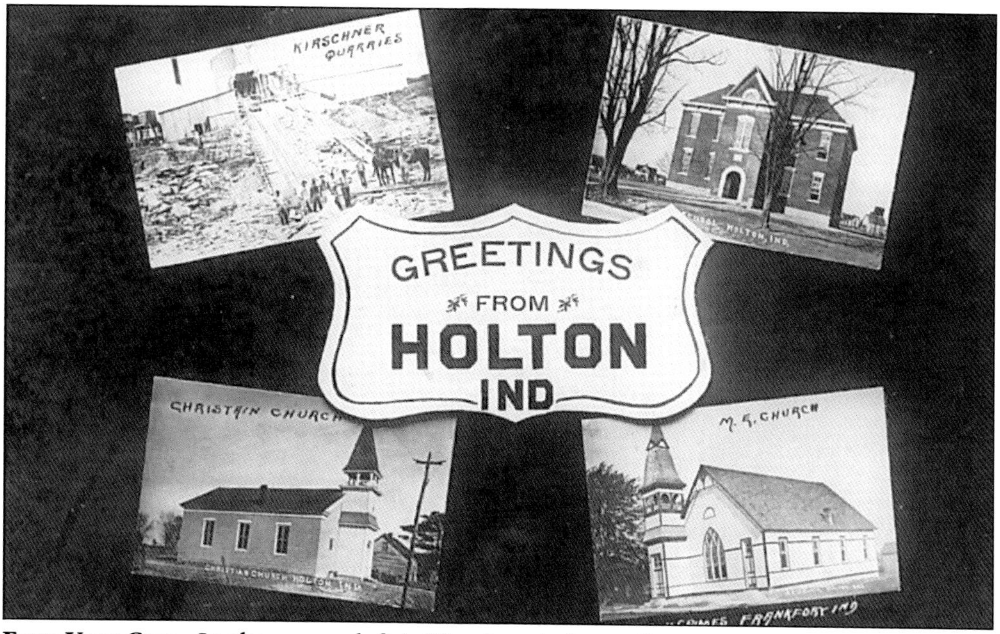

Four-View Card. In the upper left is Kirschner's Large Stone Quarry. The Old Holton Brick School is seen in the upper right, and Holton's Christian Church is shown in the lower left. The Holton M.E. Church occupies the lower right corner of this card. Multi-view cards were a way of showing several local scenes at one price. (Card by unknown photographer.)

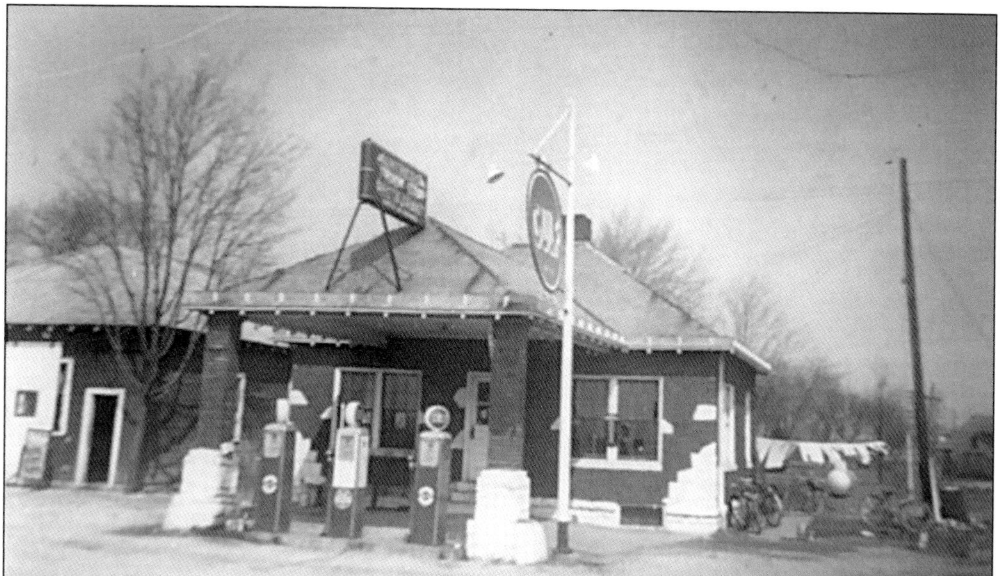

Holton's Gas Station. Located on the north side of Highway 50 in Holton, this station was a favorite congregating place for Holton's loafers. Many towns had few places to gather, and the gas station supplied gas, food, free air, and gossip at a nominal price. (Photograph by unknown photographer.)

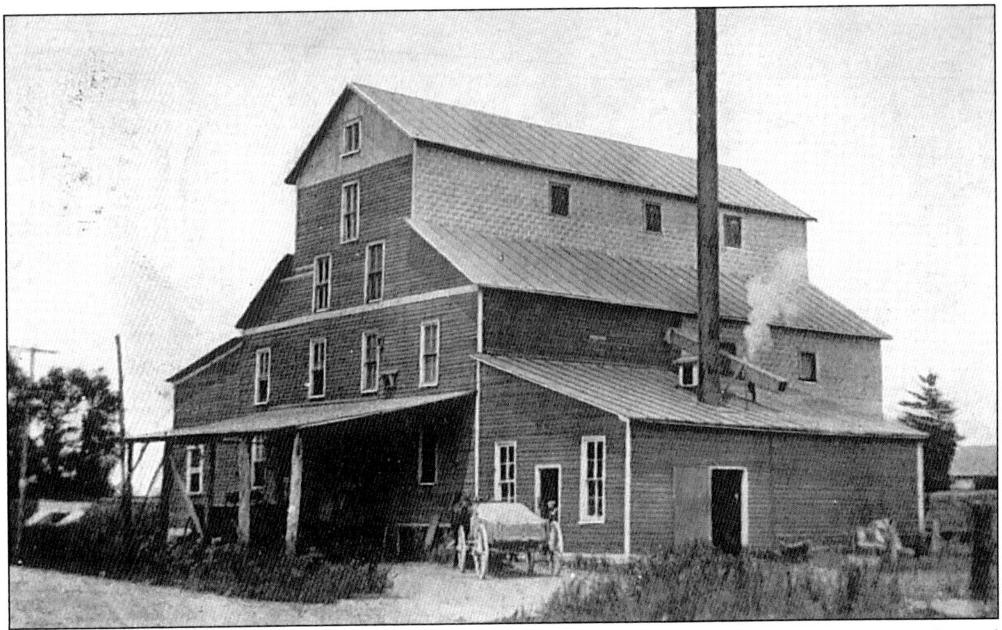

Holton Flour Mill. For years, mills were very important for rural towns. They purchased wheat, corn, rye, and beans from local farmers. They also ground and mixed feed for farmers for a share of the grain. Flour was their most profitable product. Often mills were powered by steam, and they were a natural to supply towns with electricity. (Colored card by E.C. Kropp Co., Milwaukee, Wisconsin.)

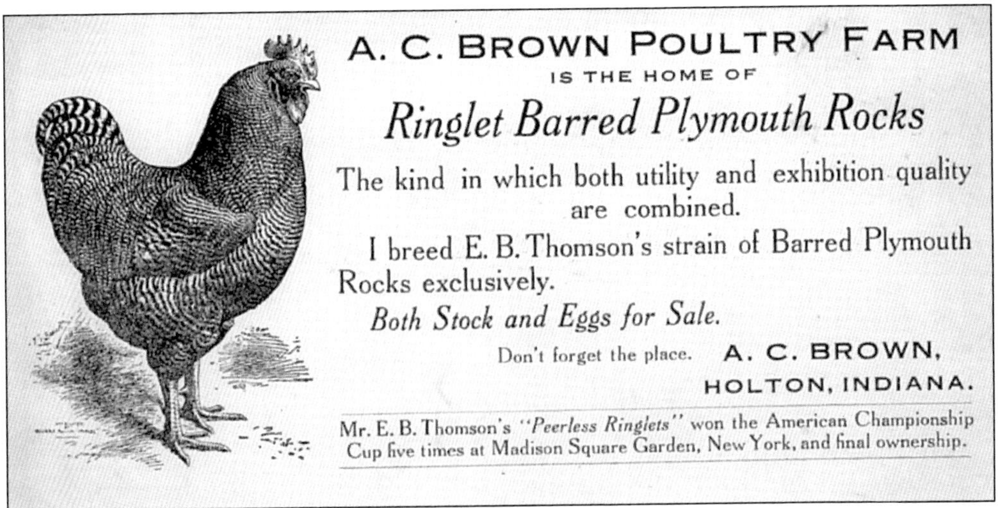

Brown's Poultry Farm. A.C. Brown, a local Holton farmer, was at one time the state of Indiana's Corn King. Brown also raised and sold Plymouth Rock Chickens. A favorite breed of chicken was the Barred Plymouth Rock, and Brown, being a good promoter, used these cards to advertise his special fowl. (Card by unknown printer.)

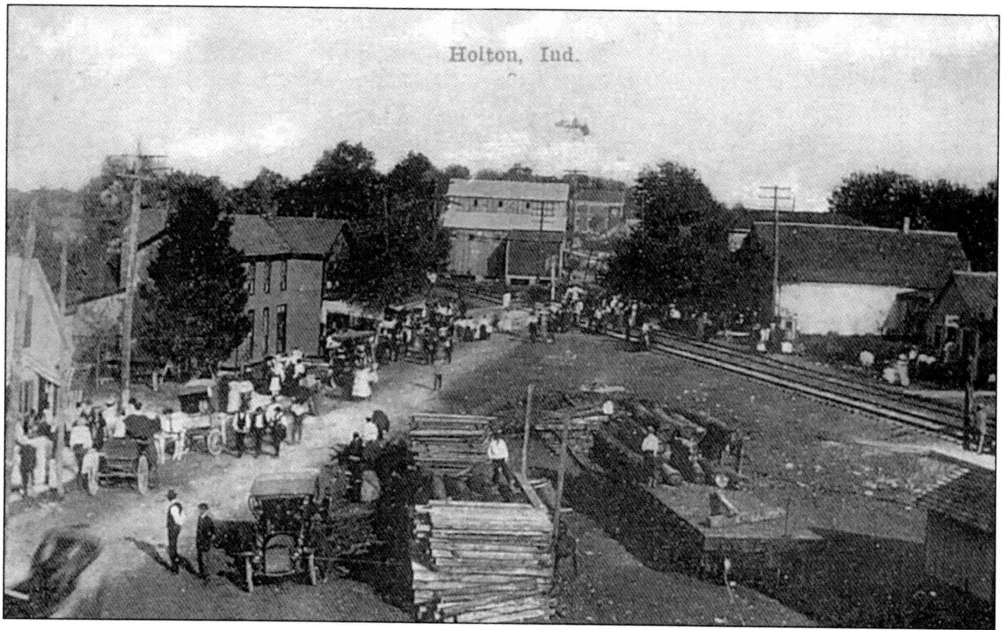

VIEW OF HOLTON. A large pile of logs and railroad ties are stacked near the railroad tracks. Several business buildings are seen to the left on the unpaved street, and the mill is in the distance. A crowd of buggies and wagons has gathered for some special occasion. (Colored card by unknown photographer.)

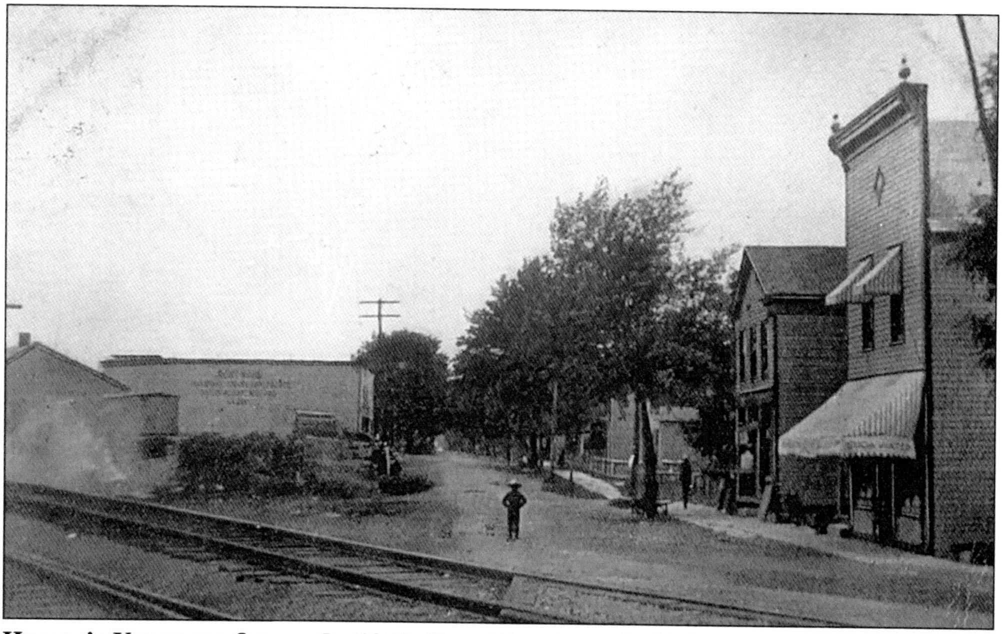

HOLTON'S VERSAILLES STREET. In 1912, Versailles Street in Holton was an unpaved road that crossed the B&O Railroad tracks. In this card, a young boy trudges past a pile of logs awaiting shipment. Further down the street, a store features the once-popular tarpaulin sun awnings, now a thing of the past. (Card by unknown photographer.)

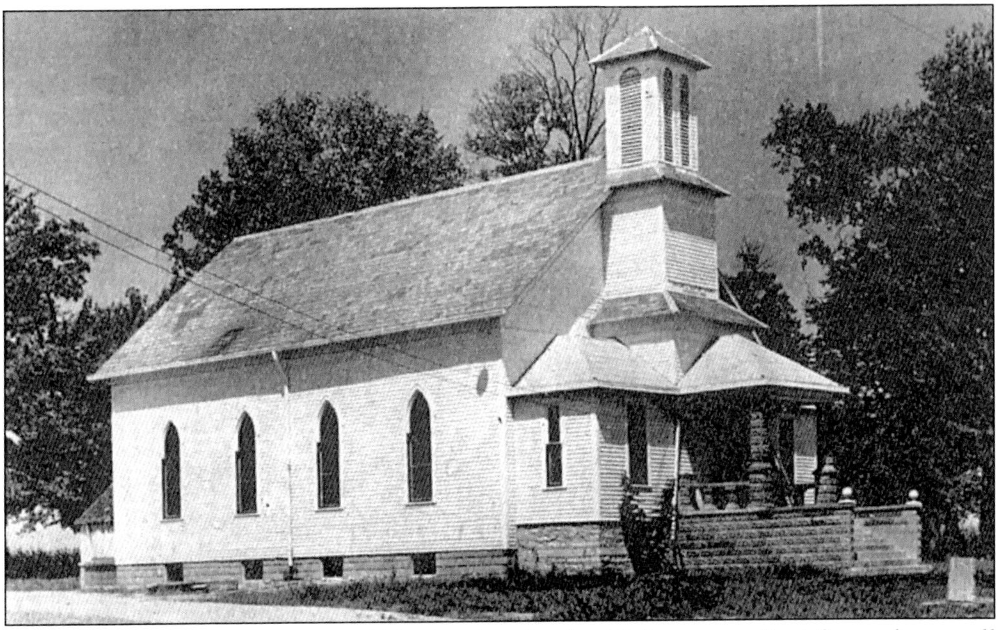

Hopewell Baptist Church. In 1839, Baptists in the Holton area first formed a small church. It wasn't until years later, in 1895, that this church was built. For 95 years the church served the community well, but on June 2, 1990, a tornado completely destroyed the house of worship. On April 26, 1992, a new, large, beautiful church was dedicated. (Card by Whitsett Print Shop, Seymour, Indiana.)

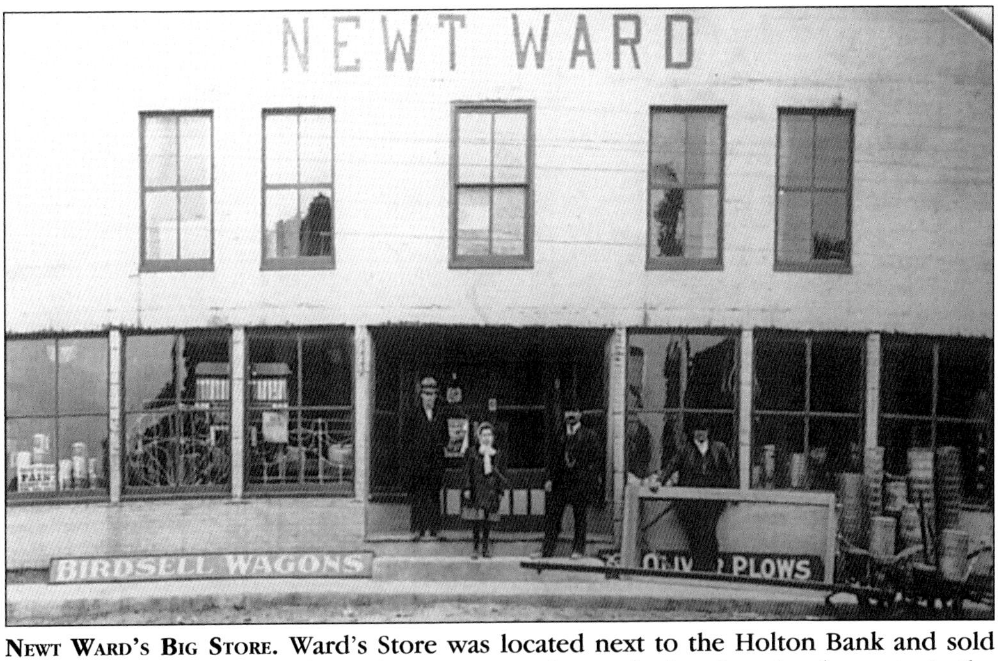

Newt Ward's Big Store. Ward's Store was located next to the Holton Bank and sold Birdsell's Farm Wagons, Oliver Plows, woven wire, and other farm implements. In the window, a billboard advertises a local fair. A few loafers pose in the picture. (Photograph by unknown photographer.)

Nine

FRANKLIN TOWNSHIP

In May 1822, Franklin Township was formed. It was made up of 32 whole and 6 partial sections. Lynville, Stumpkes Corner, South Milan, Milan, and Pierceville post offices were in this township. John Snodgrass first settled here in 1815, and in 1820 the first school house was erected. In 1825, settlers cut a hole in a big poplar tree on the Versailles–Brookville mail route, and called it "Post office Poplar." The first post office (in a building) was in Harding's Store in Old Milan, often called North Milan.

PIERCEVILLE. Three miles west of Milan, on the B&0 Railroad along Highway 350, is the village of Pierceville. At one time, the town had a physician, a blacksmith shop, a church, a depot, stores, a school, and a saw mill. Today, a store is all that remains. Joseph Seagrams Distillery has several very large warehouses in Pierceville today.

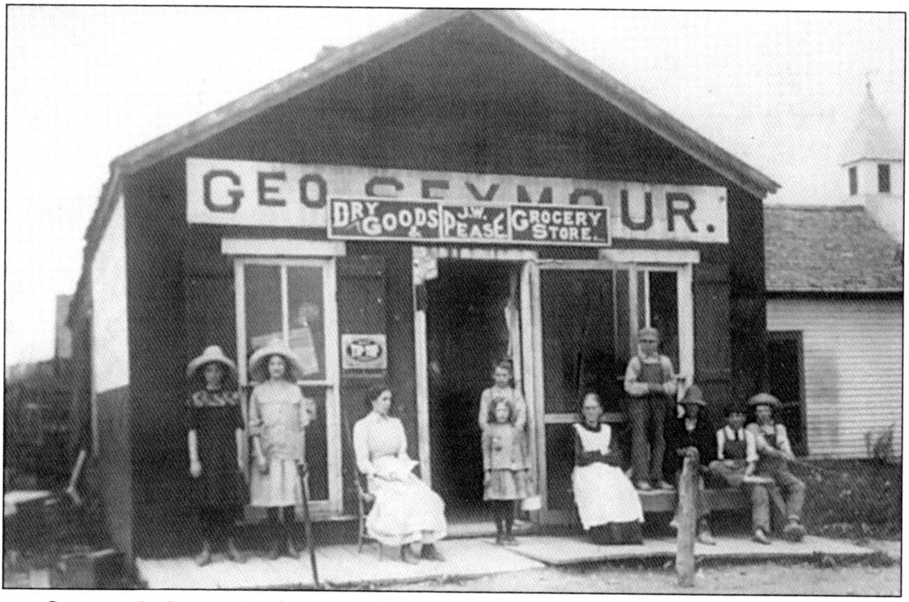

GEORGE SEYMOUR'S STORE. At the time this 1912 card was mailed, J.W. Peace operated this store in Pierceville. Peace's advertising sign lists dry goods and groceries. Two young ladies, two small girls, and four boys are seen taking it easy in front of the store. In the background at right, a church is in view. (Photograph by unknown photographer.)

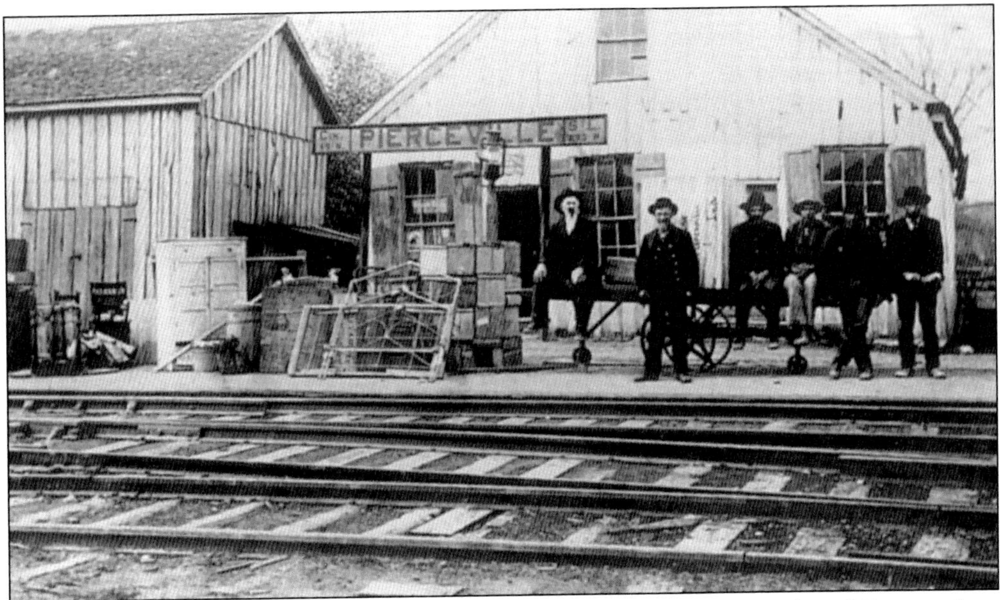

The Pierceville Depot. This very old photograph features the O&M Railroad Depot when it was housed in a small post office and store. A larger depot was later built. The sign in front lists the distance to Cincinnati as 45 miles, and St. Louis as 293 miles by rail. A group of loafers awaits the next train. On the deck is a large stack of freight awaiting shipment. (Photograph by unknown photographer.)

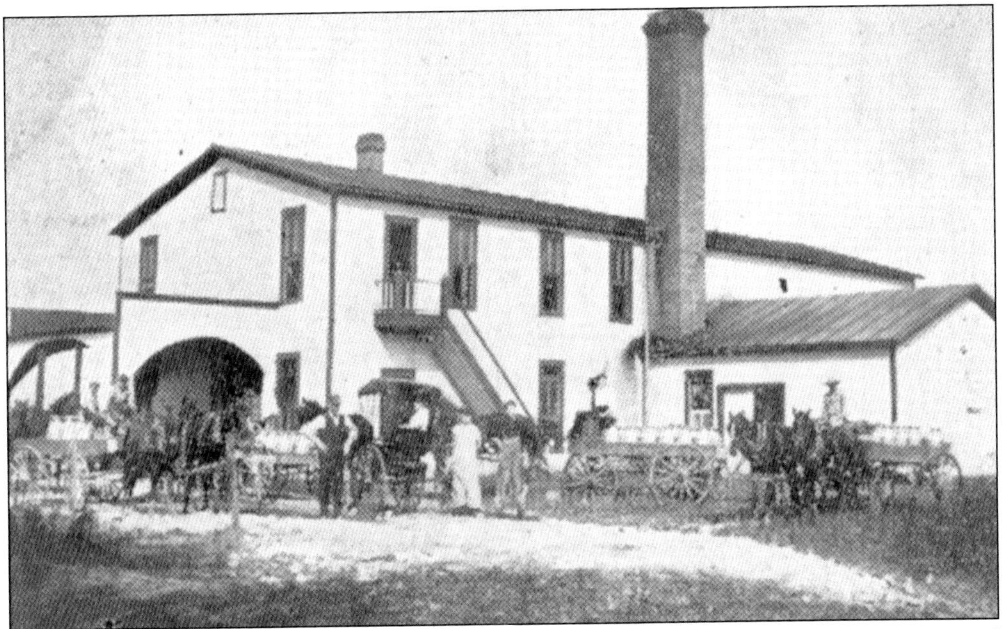

New Pierceville Creamery. This large creamery was built in the 1880s. Milk, cream, and other dairy products were shipped by rail to larger cities, which created a mutually profitable enterprise for both the creamery and local farmers. Adolph Neff operated the creamery, and Charles Tuttle later purchased the business. It must have been a busy day, as five wagons are in the picture. (Photograph by unknown photographer.)

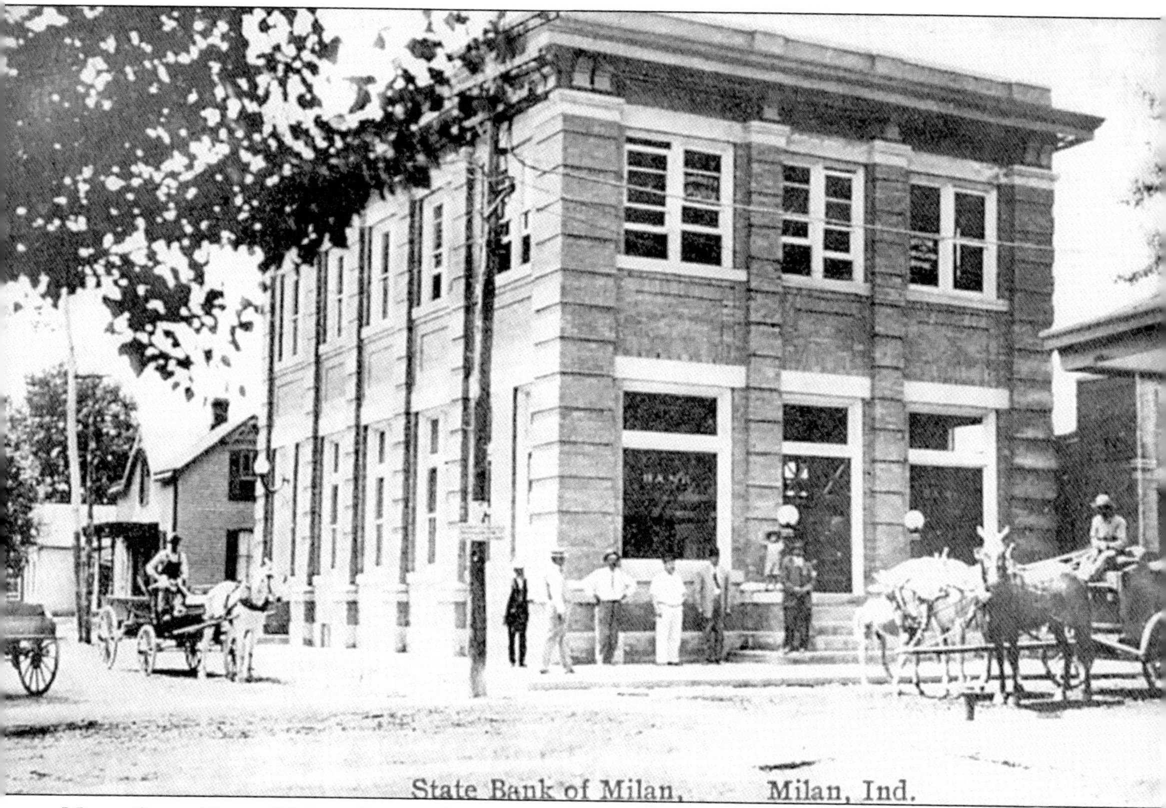

MILAN STATE BANK. This color card was mailed in 1923, and reveals a lot of activity on Milan's Carr Street. Horses, wagons, and a few ever-present loafers are seen on this picture. Behind the bank, a house is in view. Jim Haney later built a movie theatre on this site. (Colored Kraemer Art Co., Cincinnati, Ohio.)

MILAN

Milan was first settled in what is now called "North Milan" at Harding's Store in the early 1830s. The first post office address was Harding's Store, and was named in honor of lawyer Stephen Harding. Harding became the first governor of the State of Utah. In the 1850s, the Ohio Mississippi Railroad laid its tracks 1 mile south of North Milan, causing the town to move south with the railroad. The name of the new post office then became Milan. Milan became a household name in 1954, when its high school basketball team won the state championship title.

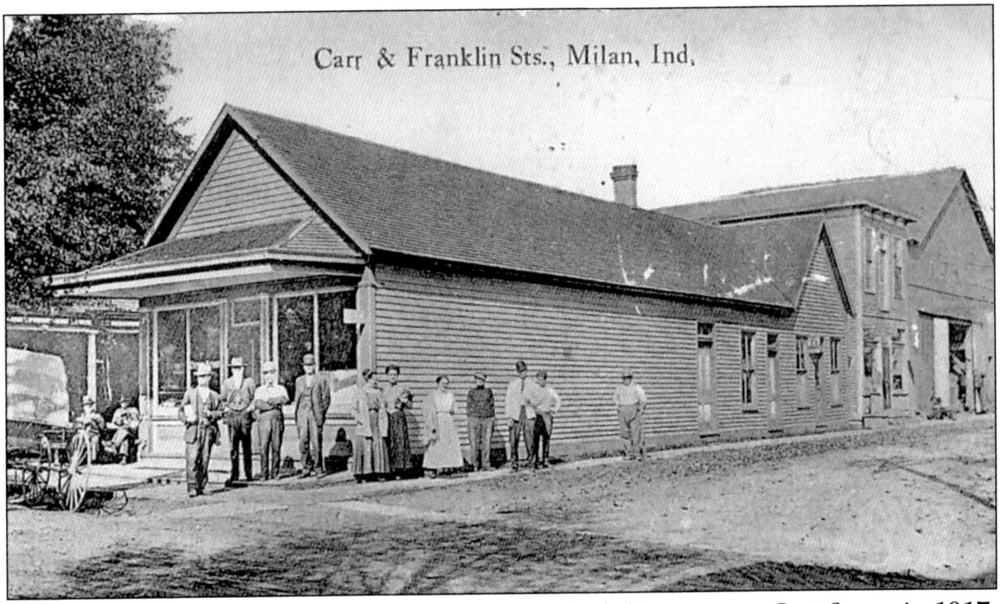

Milan Drug Store. Newt Peters owned and operated this store on Carr Street in 1917. In 1919, Emmett Lawless purchased the store and remained in business until 1963, when Andy Hand took over. A tailor shop and livery stable can be seen behind the old drug store. It seems several locals wished to be in this picture. (Kraemer Art Co., Cincinnati, Ohio.)

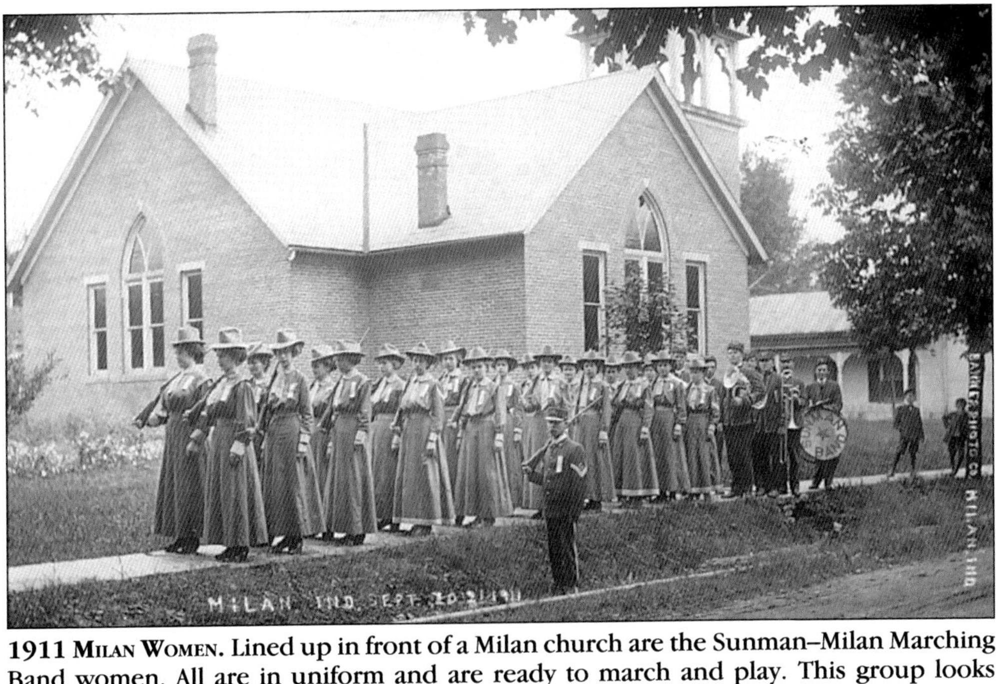

1911 Milan Women. Lined up in front of a Milan church are the Sunman–Milan Marching Band women. All are in uniform and are ready to march and play. This group looks pretty snappy. There were two or three different view cards printed featuring this popular band. (Photograph by Banner Photo, Milan, Indiana.)

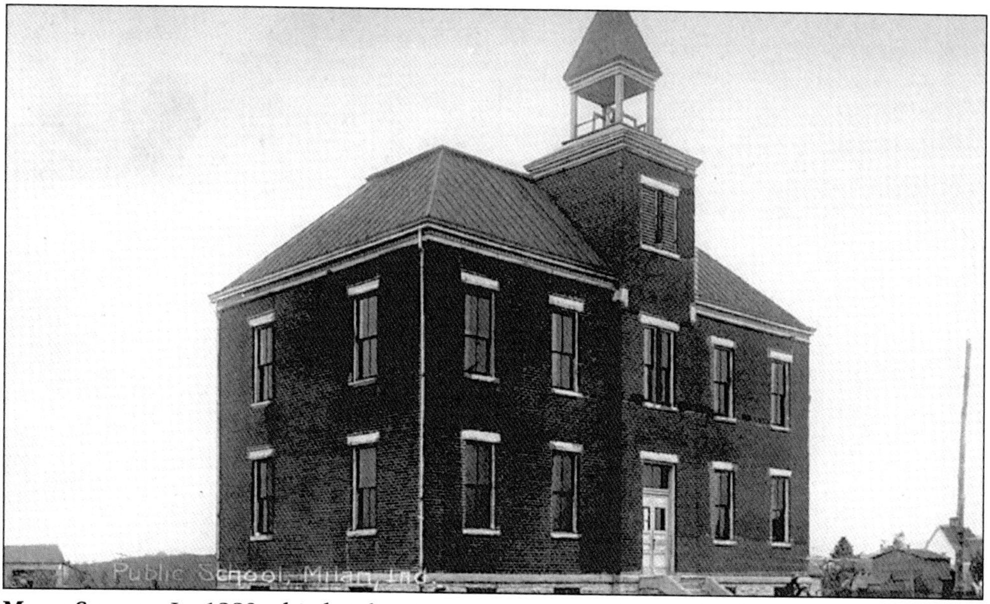

Milan School. In 1889, this brick school house was Milan's third school. Some of the bricks in this four-room school were taken from an older school building. In 1901, a two-year high school was started. This school was on the south side of what is now Morrel Street, and at present the front doors are located on Catherine Street. (Card # 2694 by Kraemer Art Co., Cincinnati & Berlin.)

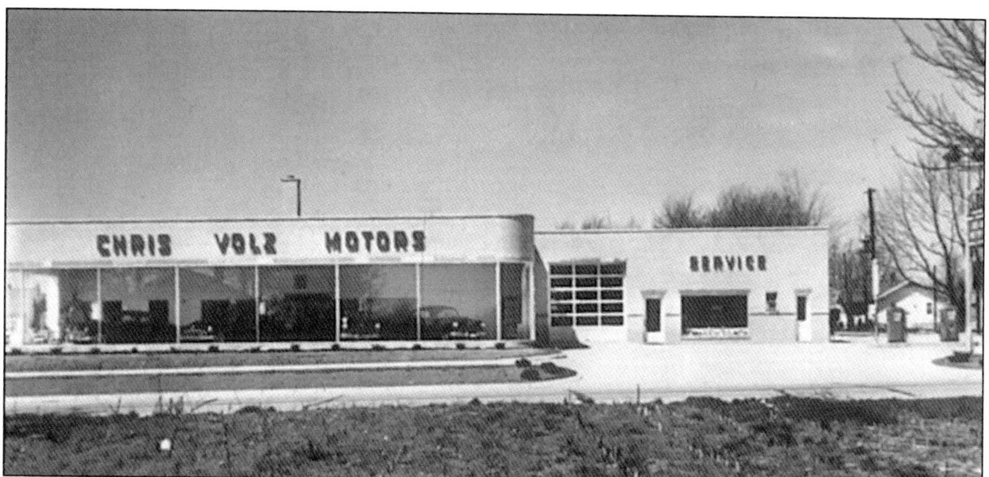

Chris Volz Garage. Volz's Garage and Car Agency was first located on the north side of Carr Street. After outgrowing the Carr Street location, Volz built a large, modern building at the south edge of town in 1950. It is said that ten thousand people attended the grand opening of this new car agency on April 1, 1950. A very successful agent, Chris Volz was the only General Motors dealer to sell all GMC products, trucks, and cars. Many notables purchased cars at Milan. (Photograph by unknown photographer.)

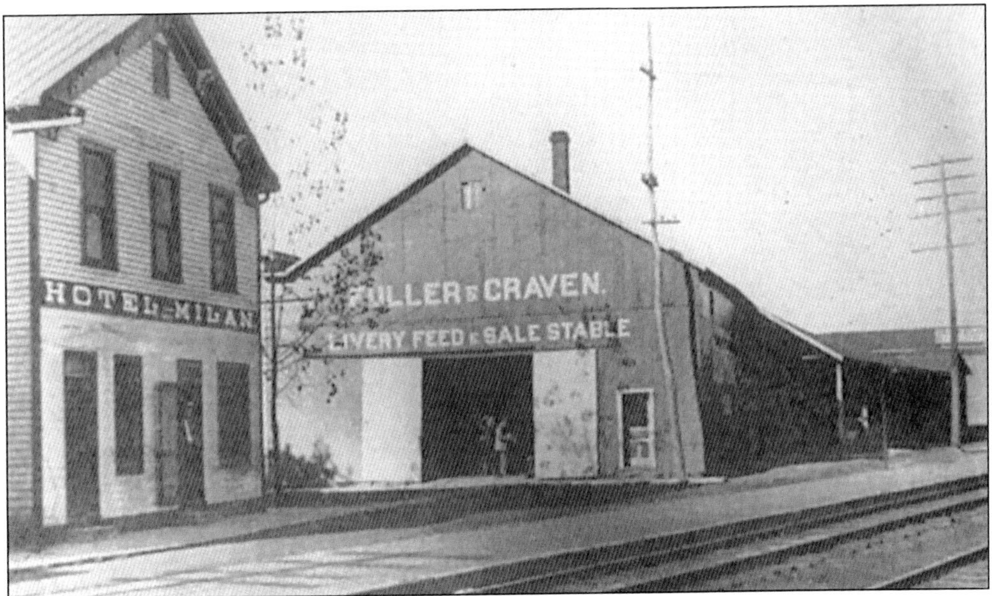

HOTEL AND LIVERY STABLE. The Milan Hotel and the Fuller & Cravens Livery Stable were conveniently located on one side of the B&O Railroad tracks. Businesses such as these were often located near a depot and hoped to serve rail travelers. Hotels rented rooms, and liveries rented out horses and buggies—a great combination. (Photograph by unknown photographer.)

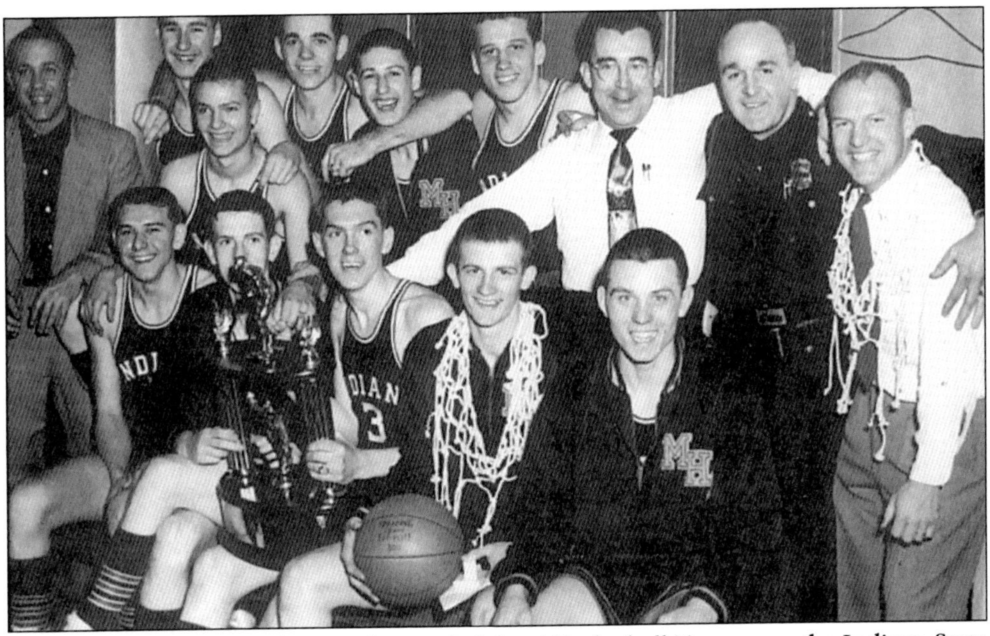

STATE CHAMPIONS. In 1954, the Milan High School Basketball Team won the Indiana State Basketball Championship. This team defeated the "Big Boys" in the state, something that hasn't happened since, and probably never will again. Their record was 28 wins and 2 losses, a great season for any club. The Indians defeated Terre Haute, Indianapolis, and Muncie, quite a feat for a small school. (Photograph by unknown photographer.)

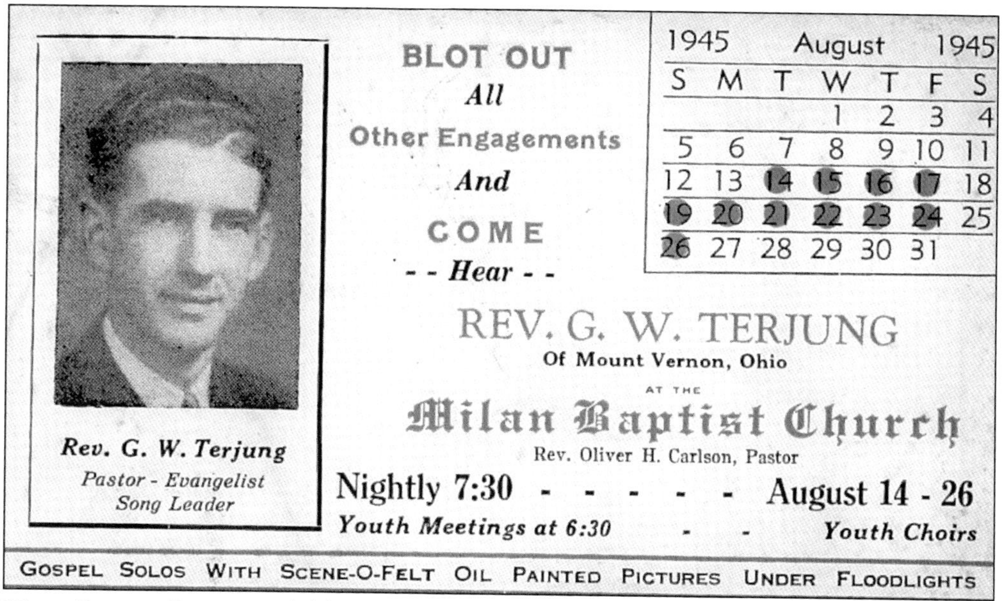

MILAN BAPTIST CHURCH. Ink blotters were once a popular means of advertising, and the Reverend O.H. Carlson of Milan used this method to bring out the crowds at his church's evangelical services. A calendar showed the dates on which one was supposed to attend his church. On this novel blotter, 12 dates were scheduled. (Unknown printer.)

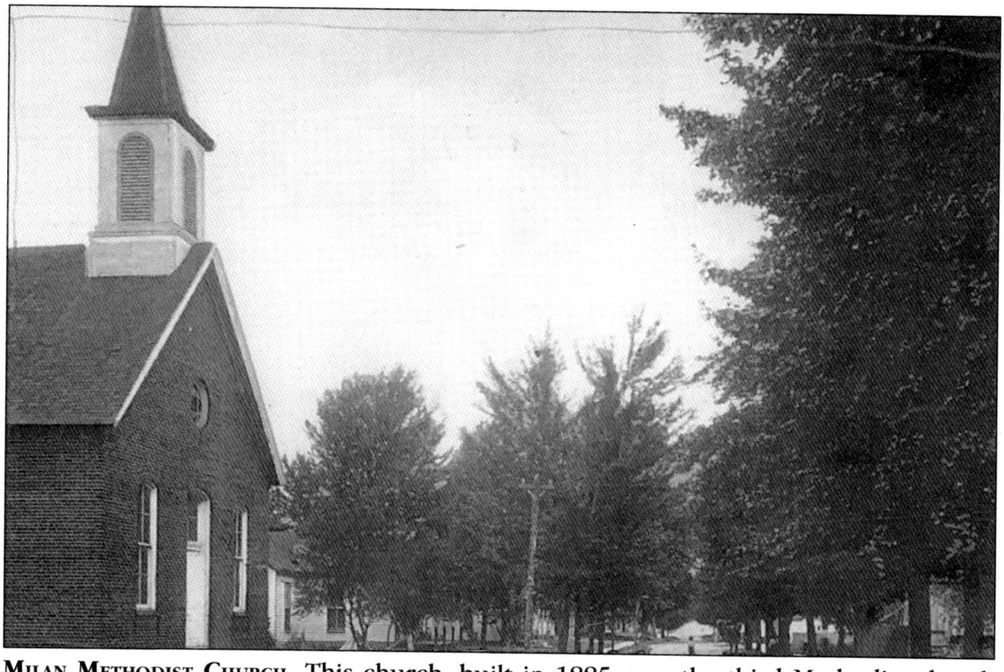

MILAN METHODIST CHURCH. This church, built in 1885, was the third Methodist church building in Milan. In 1920, after outgrowing the church pictured, the congregation erected a new structure on this same site. That fourth church survives today and is active in Milan affairs. (Card #2687 by Kraemer Art Co., Cincinnati & Berlin, for C.N. Peters.)

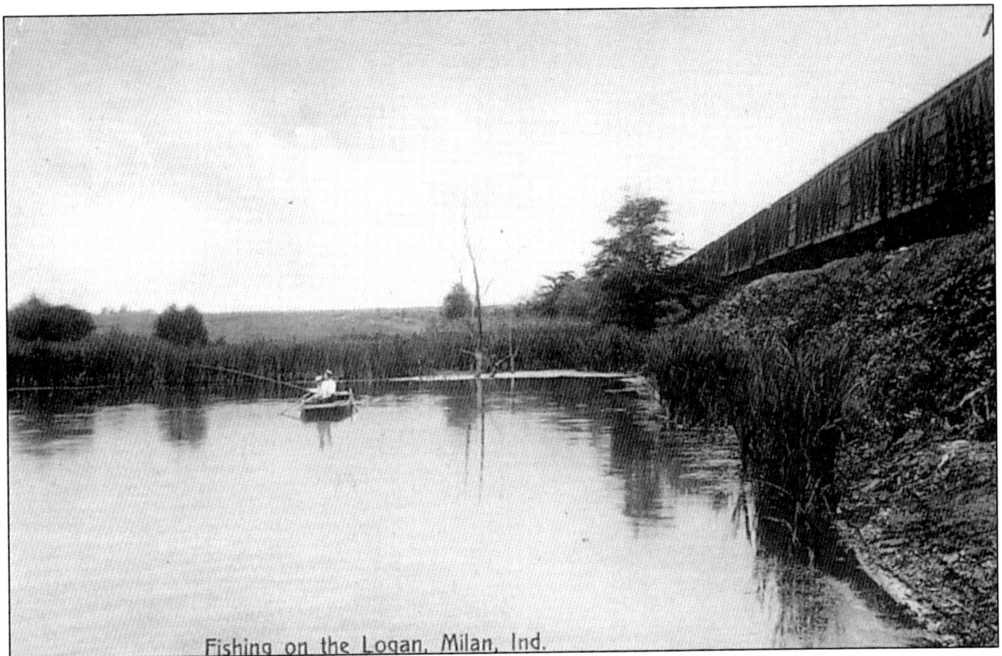

Logan Lake. In this card, two fishermen and a B&O freight car can be seen next to Milan's Logan Lake. Logan Lake was dug by the railroad as a source of water for steam engines. Many Milan fishermen enjoyed the company's lake. (Card #2681 by Kraemer Art Co., Cincinnati & Berlin, for C.N. Peters.)

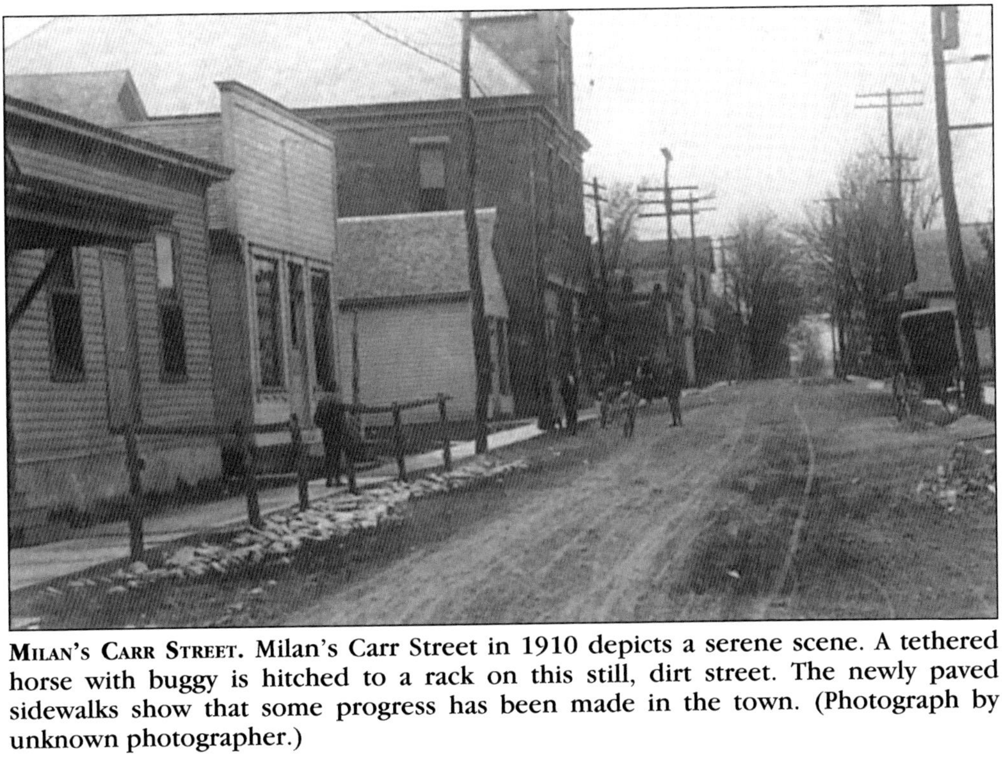

Milan's Carr Street. Milan's Carr Street in 1910 depicts a serene scene. A tethered horse with buggy is hitched to a rack on this still, dirt street. The newly paved sidewalks show that some progress has been made in the town. (Photograph by unknown photographer.)

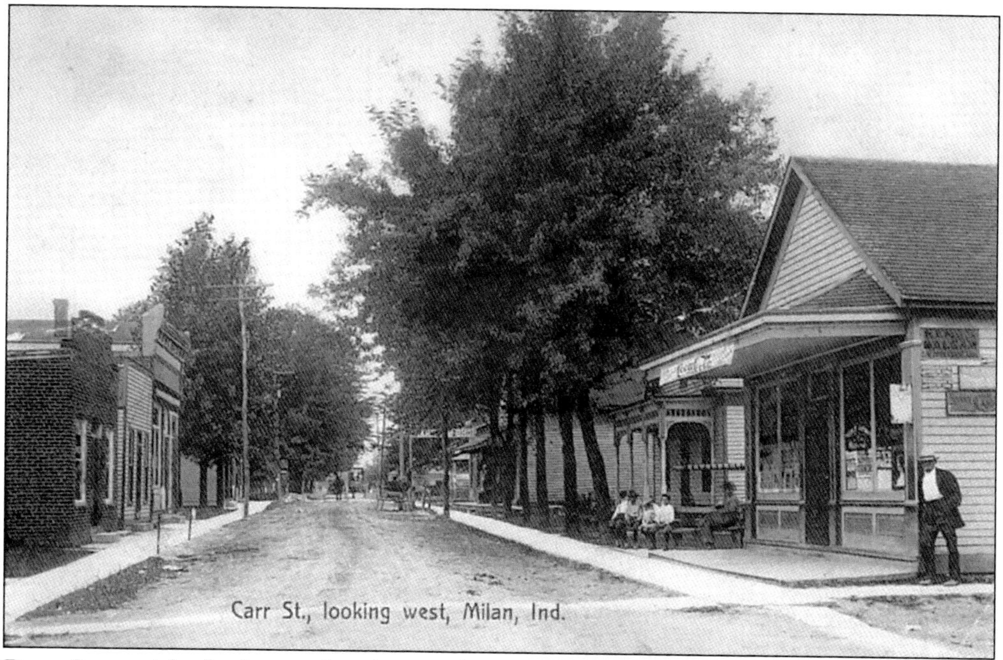

Drug Store. A loafer is seen leaning on the popular drug store on Carr Street. The store was on the corner of Carr and Franklin Streets. The date was 1900, and one can see a telephone pole but no electric lines in this print. (Card #2688 by Kraemer Art Co., Cincinnati & Berlin.)

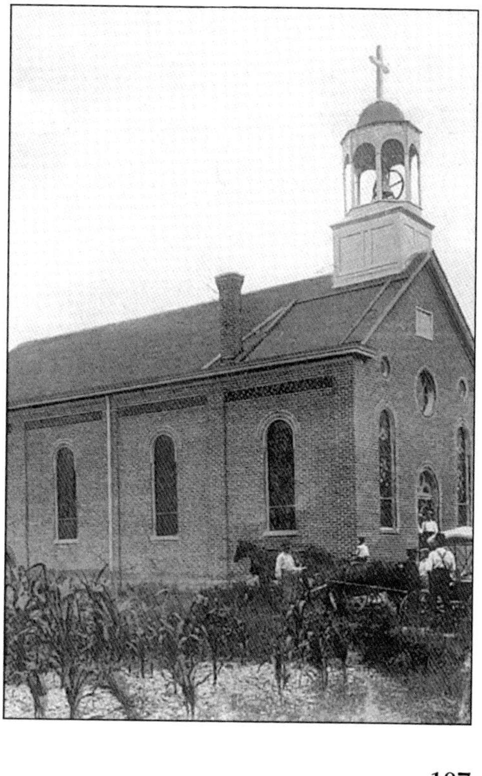

St. Charles Catholic Church. The ground for this church was donated by Mrs. Newt Peters, and the church was dedicated on August 8, 1908. The church was named after St. Charles Borromeo, Bishop of Milan, Italy. A cornfield is on the side of the church at this time, which probably dates the card close to dedication time. (Card #2692 by Kraemer Art Co., Berlin & Cincinnati, for C.N. Peters.)

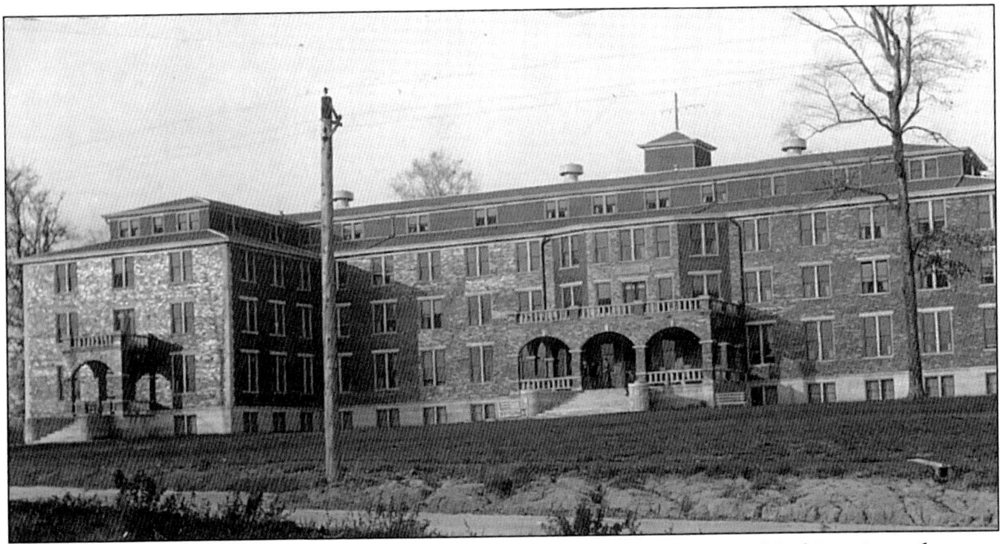

MILAN HEALTH RESORT. Named "The Miwogco Mineral Springs Hotel," this mineral water health resort opened its doors in October 1920. Named after the Milan, Indiana, Water, Oil, and Gas Company, the resort was a carbon copy of the Dillsboro Sanitarium. James Bailey of Dillsboro was the architect for both health resorts. Sunday dinners drew patronage from a large surrounding area. For eight years the springs prospered, but on February 12, 1928 (the first year of the Great Depression), a fire completely destroyed the insured resort. (Card by unknown company.)

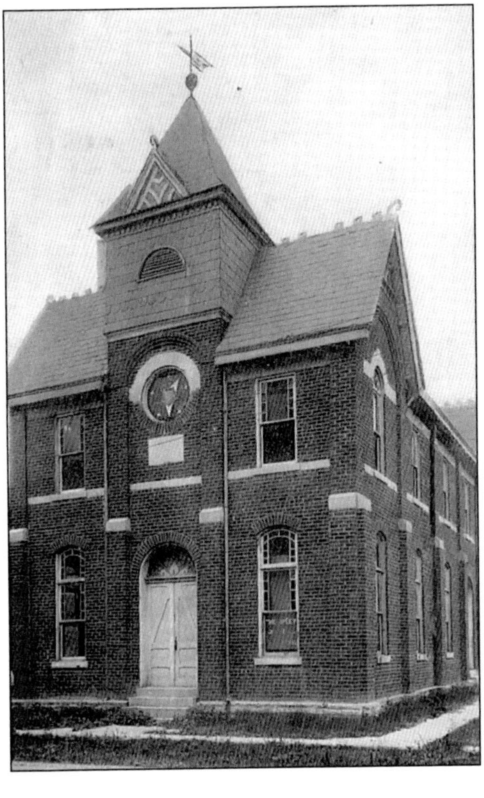

MASONIC TEMPLE. Milan's Masonic Lodge #31 was moved from the city of Moores Hill. The lodge was first located in Old North Milan, then later moved to present Milan. The chapter was chartered May 26, 1846. The lodge celebrated it's 100th natal day on October 22, 1946. (Card # 2685 by Kraemer Art Co., Cincinnati & Berlin, for C.N. Peters.)

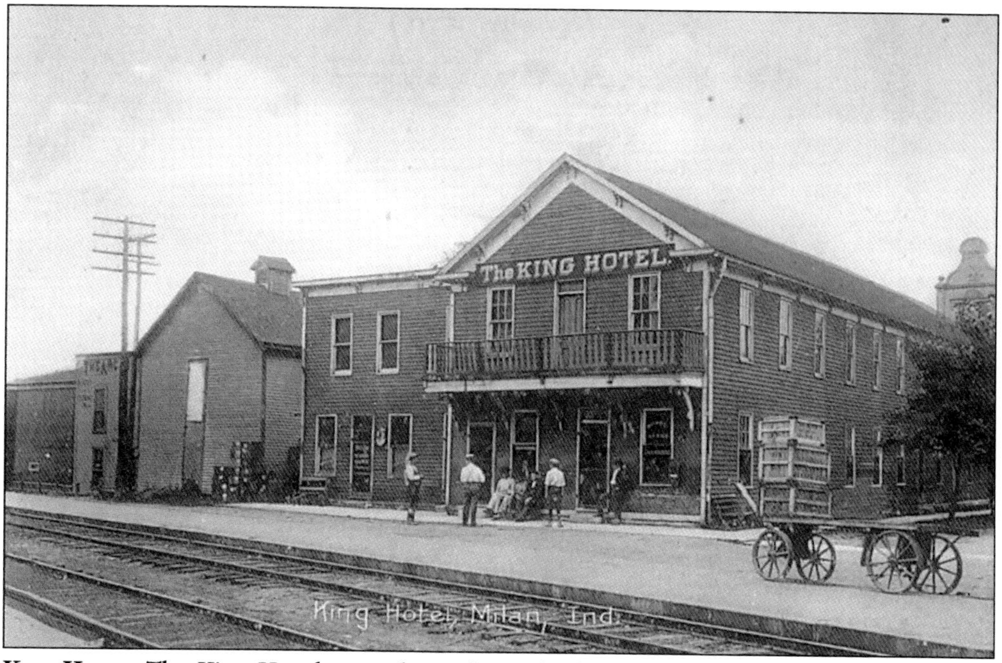

King Hotel. The King Hotel was a large frame building near the B&O Railroad station, and was a convenient hotel and saloon for railroad passengers as well as for Milanites. Near the depot is a freight wagon with several locals awaiting the next train. (Card #2693 by Kraemer Art Co., Cincinnati & Berlin, made in Germany.)

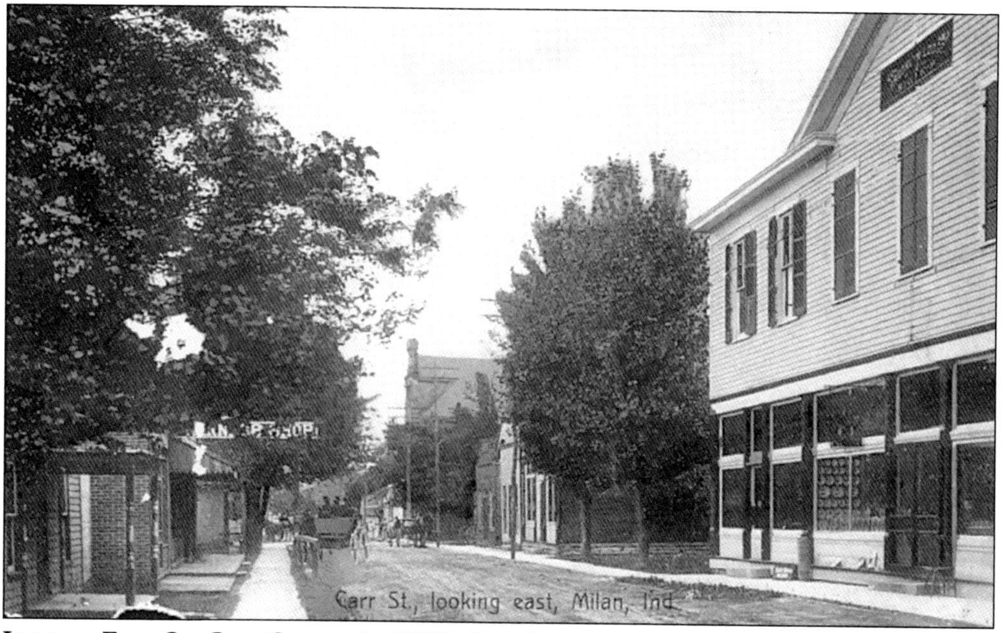

Looking East On Carr Street. In 1900, Carr Street was as yet unpaved, but the tree-lined street was Milan's main thoroughfare. A buggy and wagon slowly wind their way to unknown parts. On the right is one of Milan's large frame stores. (Card #2689 by Kraemer Art Co., Cincinnati & Berlin, for C.N. Peters.)

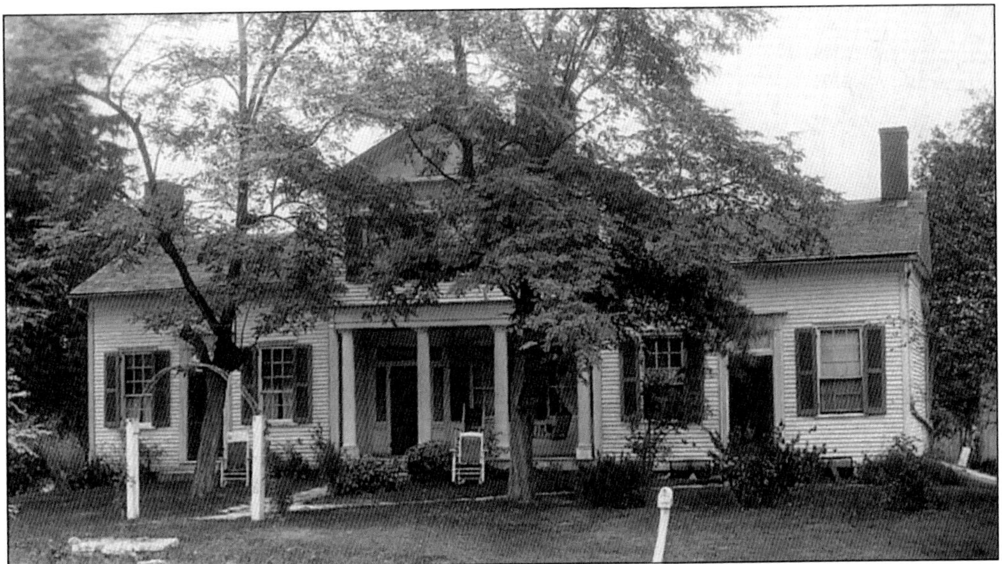

Harding Homestead. The Harding homestead was located in Old, or possibly North Milan. Stephen Harding lived here in his youthful years. The homestead was Station #7 in the Underground Railway system. A red front door designated that it was a stop for runaway slaves. Harding gave an abolition speech at the Ripley County Courthouse, which at the time was so unpopular that a crowd of men intended to hang him. Had it not been for the women of the town, Harding would have met a bad end. Harding later became the first governor of the state of Utah. This home survives to this day. (Photograph by unknown photographer.)

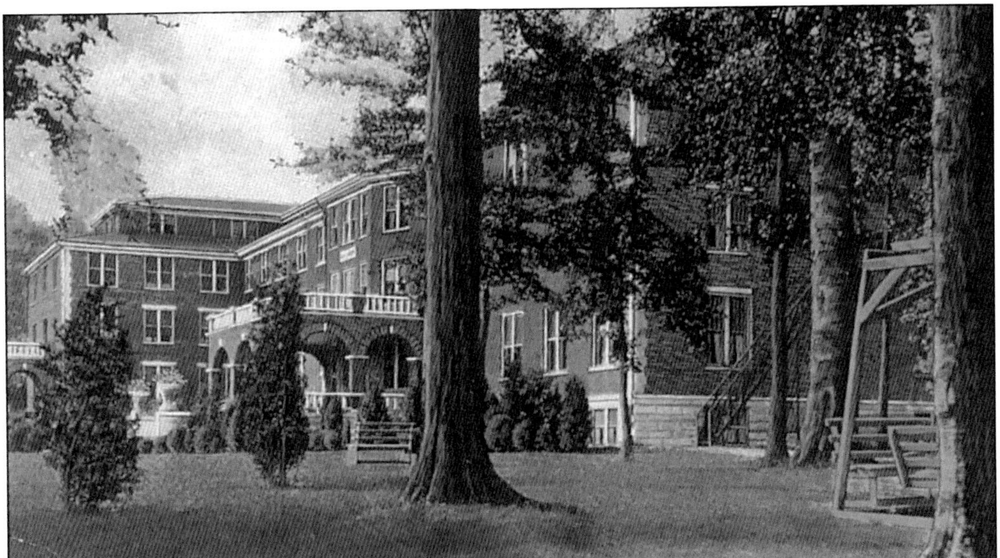

Front View of Miwogco Hotel. The front and one side of this hotel are shown in this 1922 card. The Milan Springs Hotel was a very busy resort for a number of years. The *Versailles Republican* newspaper stated that when the hotel burned, it was the greatest loss ever in Ripley County. The loss was estimated at $400,000, a tidy sum in 1928. (Photograph by unknown photographer.)

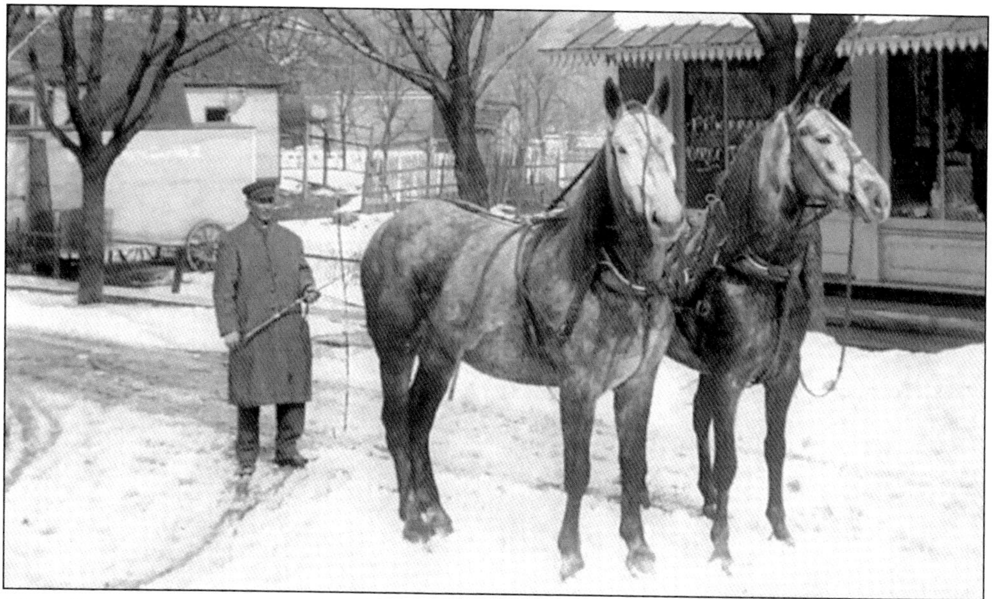

Milan Funeral Home. Edward Abbott was the driver of these spotted horses that pulled the hearse at all Milan funerals. To Abbott's left is the movable Banner Photo laboratory. A man named Roberts was a photographer in Milan, Delaware, and Osgood. Roberts could up and move his shop with ease. (Possibly a Banner Photo.)

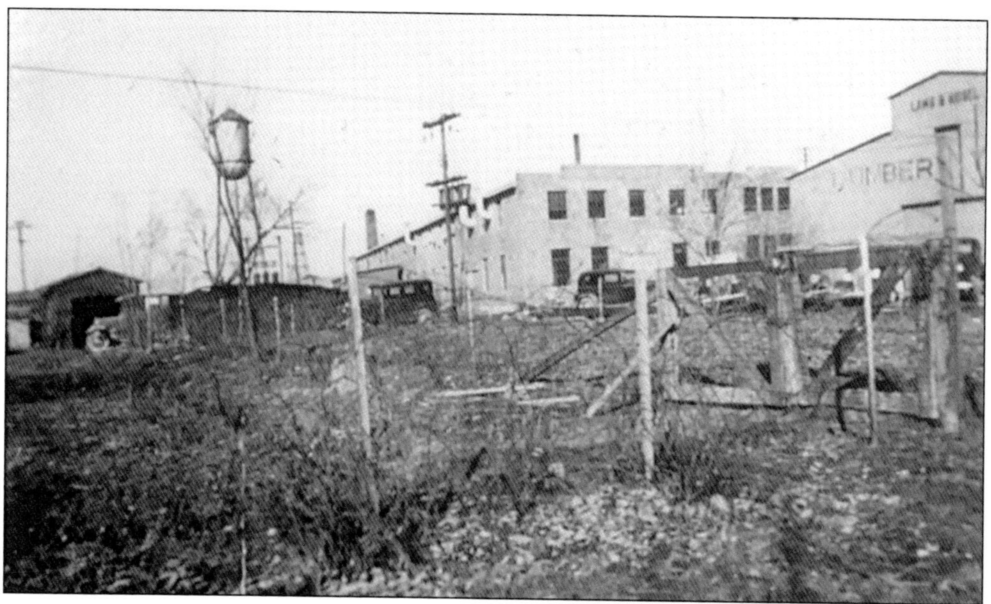

Milan Furniture Factory. This 1937 Milan Furniture Factory photograph shows the rear of Milan's largest industrial building. The company's water tower and Law & Kissell's Lumber Yard are also visible in this picture. In 1902, T.H. Thompson & Edward Abbott purchased Arkenberg & Stite's Sawmill. Abbott retired, and Thompson formed the Veneer Mill and Furniture Plant. For many years this was Milan's largest employer. (Photograph by unknown photographer.)

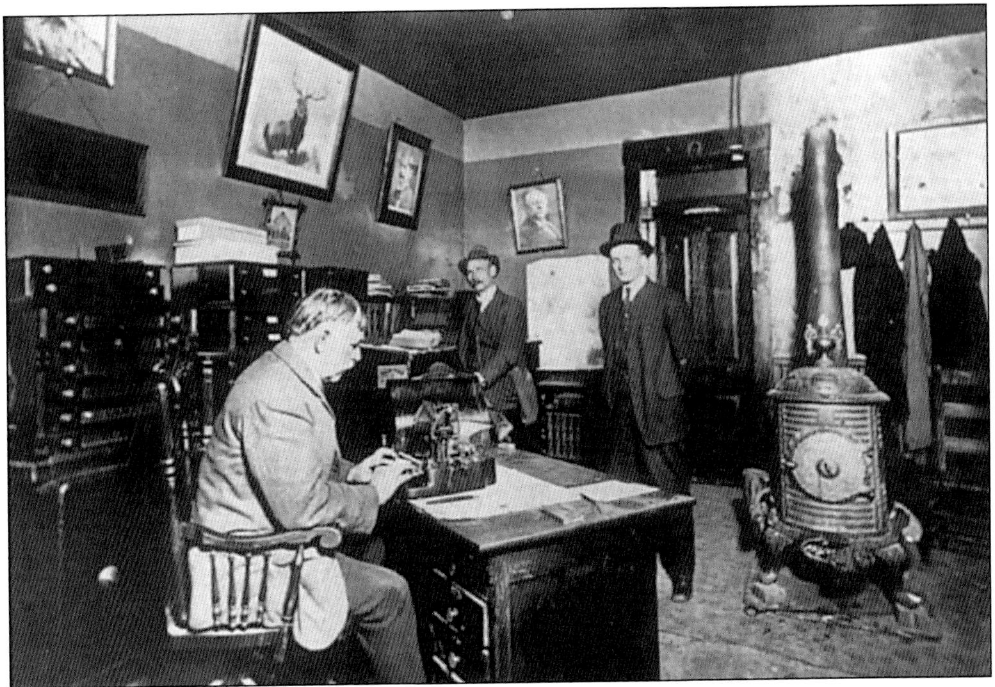

Insurance and Law Office. A lawyer's interesting office in Milan has the ever-present pot-bellied stove with conspicuous pipe, and modern typewriter in plain view. The wall picture shows an elk or moose, most probably representing the Hartford Insurance Company. This was no doubt a wintertime photo. (Photograph by unknown photographer.)

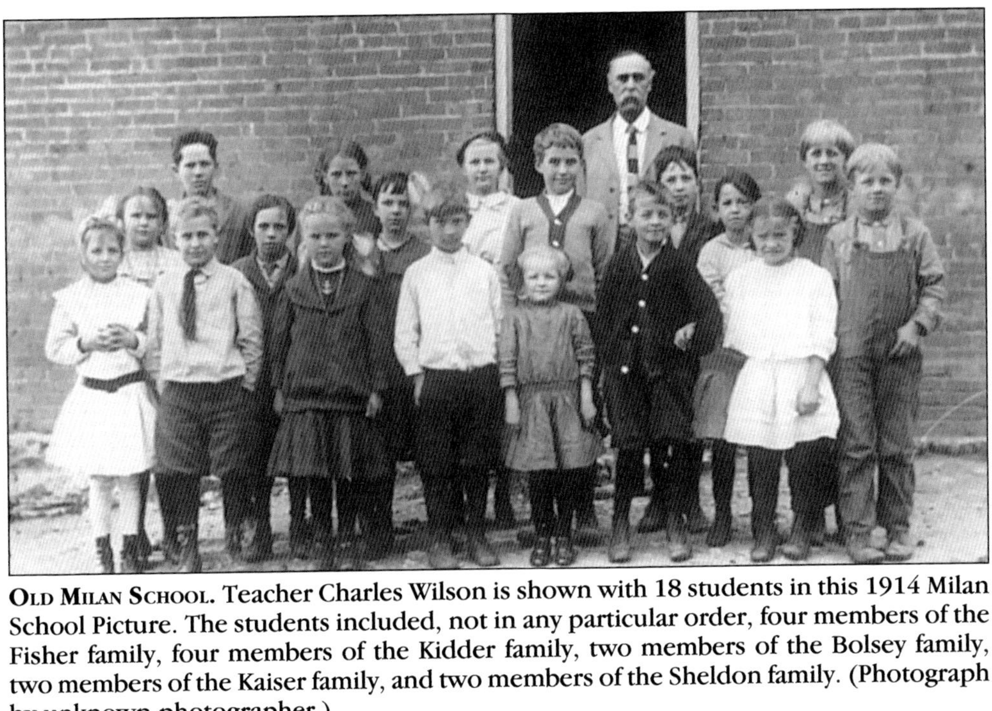

Old Milan School. Teacher Charles Wilson is shown with 18 students in this 1914 Milan School Picture. The students included, not in any particular order, four members of the Fisher family, four members of the Kidder family, two members of the Bolsey family, two members of the Kaiser family, and two members of the Sheldon family. (Photograph by unknown photographer.)

Ten

Adams Township

In May 1825, Franklin Township was divided, and the northern half was named Adams in honor of President John Quincy Adams. In 1815, Richard and Dorcas Wortman settled in what is now Adams Township. Spades, Sunman, and Pennsylvaniaburg (Penntown) were the three villages located in the township. The Cincinnati–St. Louis Railroad traversed the township. Today, Super-Highway 74 crosses the northern portion of the township.

PENNSYLVANIABURG. Pennsylvaniaburg (now called Penntown) was platted in 1837 by James McCreery, William Cheeney, and George Ferguson. The town was at its zenith in the 1850s. A *Versailles Dispatch* newspaper article at the time related "It contains three stores, and some seven places of dealing out intemperance." A post office was established before 1850. Today, it is a corner on Highways 46 and 101.

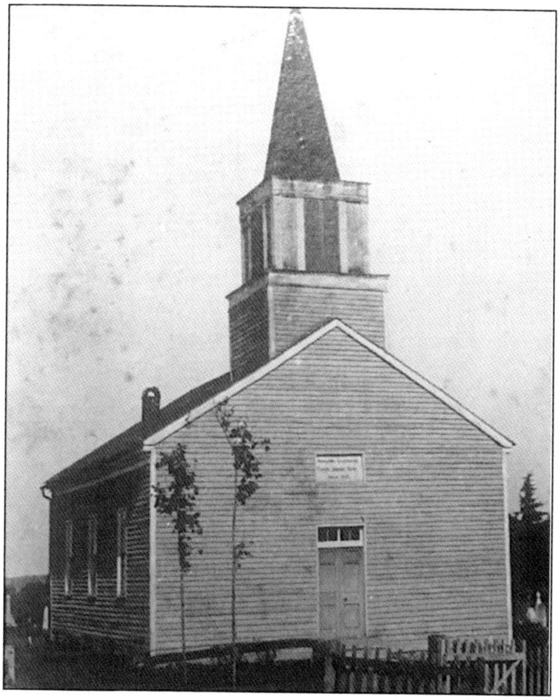

St. John's Church. In 1841, this frame church replaced an older log structure. Both these churches were located behind the brick building presently on that site, in what is now a cemetery. The pictured church was named the Evangelical Protestant German St. John's Church in January of 1841. The church was a little south of the intersection of Roads 46 and 101. (Photograph by unknown photographer.)

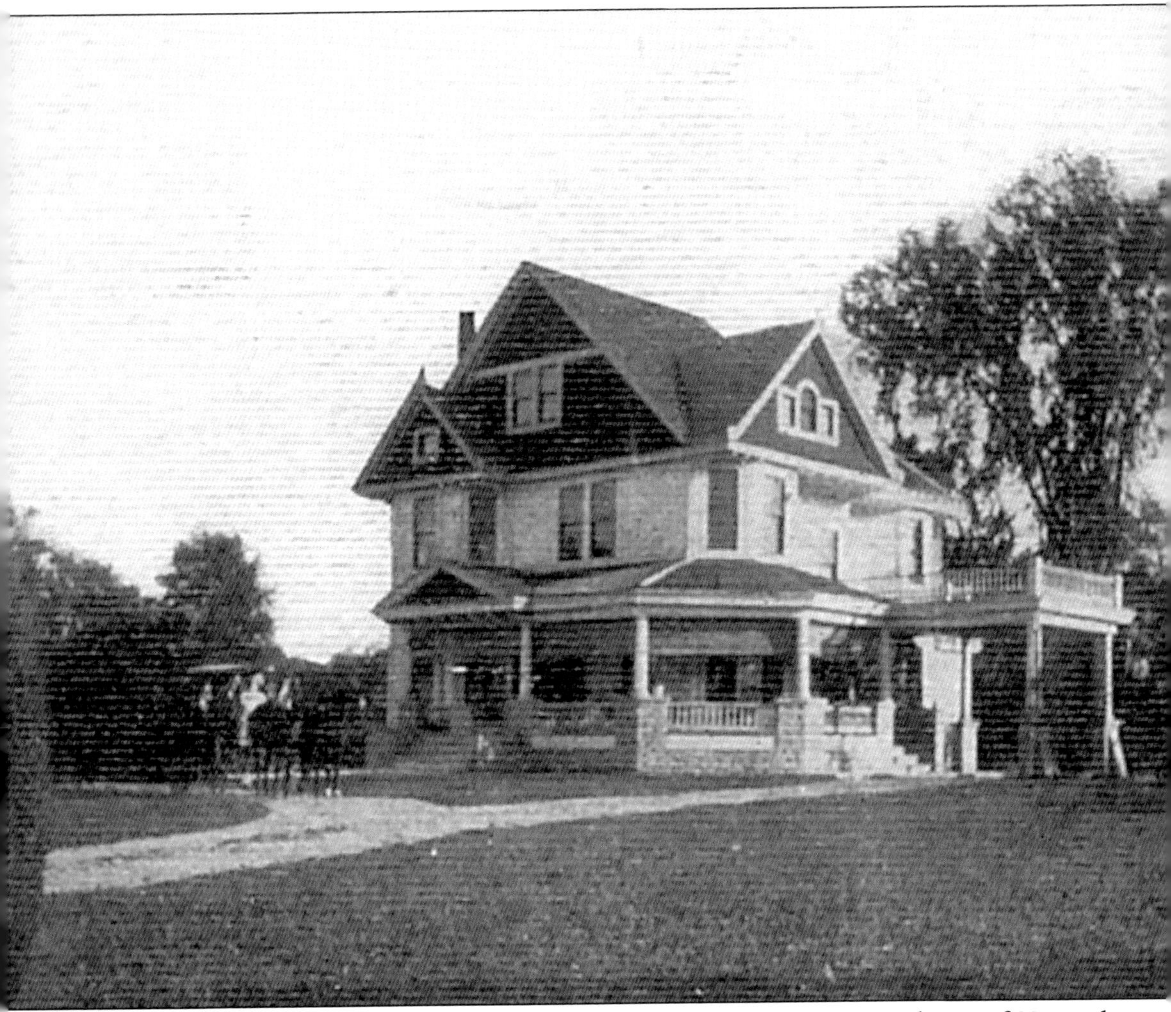

Flow-Mah, Spades, Indiana. Flow-Mah was the name of the fancy residence of Mr. and Mrs. Walter H. Fitch of Spades, Indiana. Walter's occupation is not known, but it is possible that this was a funeral home. Surely this was the show-place of Spades. (Tom Jones Card Co., Cincinnati, Ohio.)

SPADES

Spades was laid out in 1855, by George Miller. An early settler was Jacob Spades, thus the name of the town. After the coming of the railroad, the village grew and once had a saloon, post office, clothing store, general store, mills, and the "Enterprise Bracket Co." Today, a few homes and a railroad crossing are all that remain of the once flourishing town.

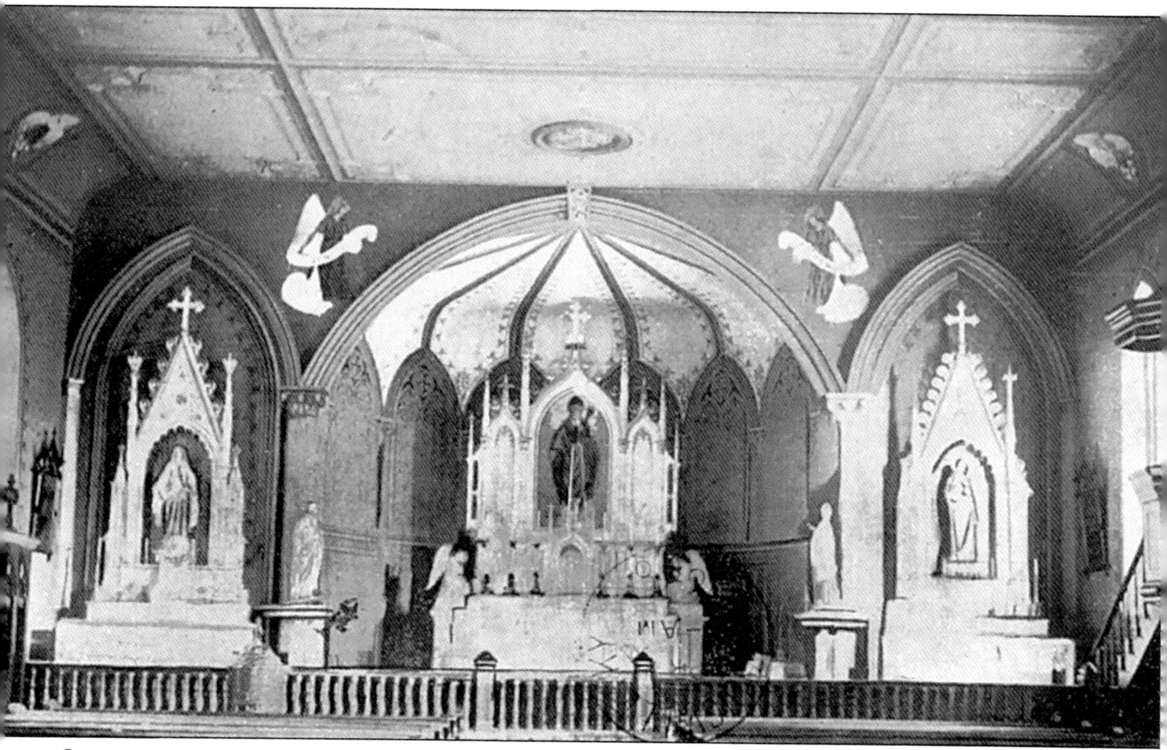

Sanctuary of St. Anthony's Church. This German settlement formed in 1840, and soon the neighborhood was called Springfield. Later, in 1856, this village was named Morris. Bishop de St. Palais consented to build a 60 foot by 40 foot stone church, and the first mass was said on June 13, 1857. The original fixtures in the sanctuary remain today as viewed in this picture. The priest and altar boys are shown in the center of the sanctuary. (Kraemer Art Co., by J.H. Bohland, Batesville, Indiana.)

MORRIS

Morris was first called Springfield, but it was soon discovered that there was already a larger town and post office by that name, so the new village was named Morris. In 1858, D.J. Wright platted the town, and named it Morris in honor of citizen George Morris. The Cincinnati, Chicago, and St. Louis Railway (C.C.C. & St. L), known as The Big 4 R.R., built a depot in the young town. Morris thrived with the railroad's help, and even today is a busy little community.

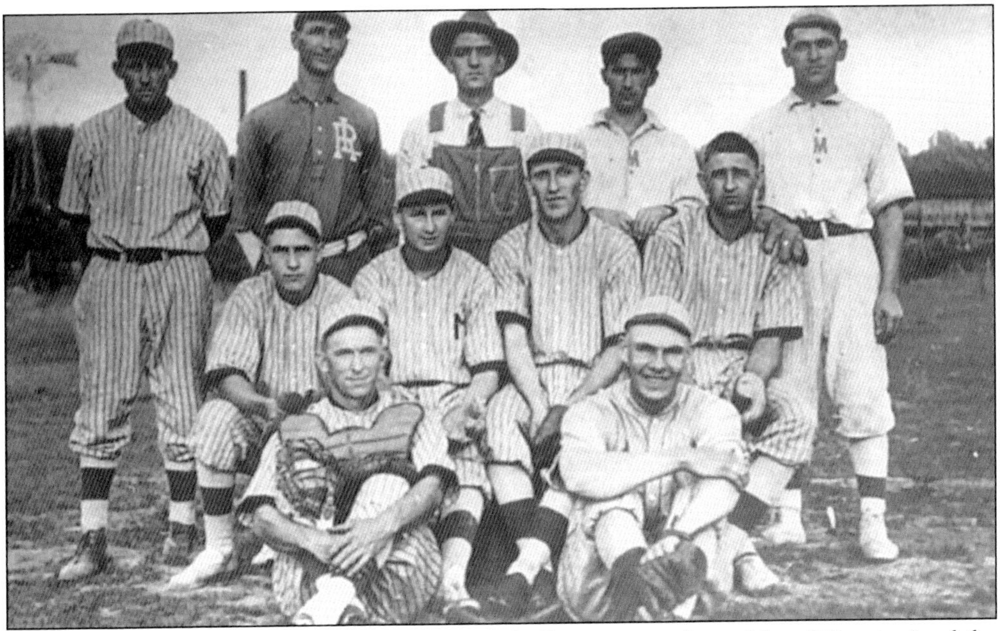

Morris Baseball Team. This 1920 men's baseball team was the pride of Morris. Luckily, the names of these players are remembered. Pictured in the front row, from left to right, are: Al Weisenbach and Harry Bohman. In the second row are, from left to right: Charles Schroeder, Joe Hahn, Nick Prickle, and Ben Schroeder. Finally, in the back row from left to right, are: Oak Wolter, Otto G. "Blackie" Roell, Charles Winkler, Mfg. Edward Hahn, and Gue Wiesenbach. (Photograph by Otto Roell.)

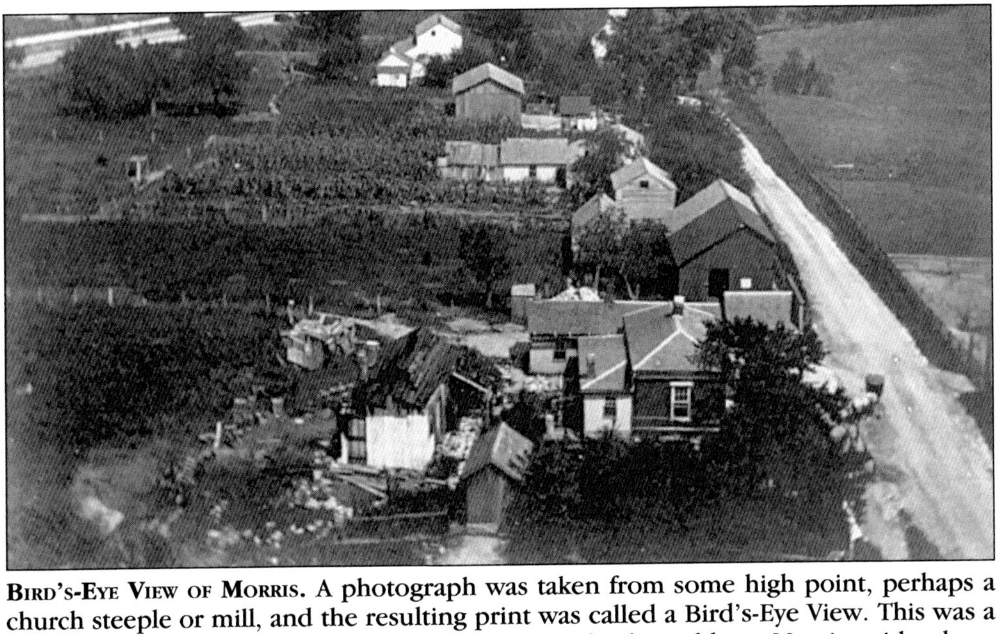

Bird's-Eye View of Morris. A photograph was taken from some high point, perhaps a church steeple or mill, and the resulting print was called a Bird's-Eye View. This was a common practice in early 1900. On this card, the bird would see Morris, with a busy depot, and McDonald's Lumber Yard. A saloon, school, and the Keg & Bucket Factory are also in this photo. (Photograph by Otto Roell.)

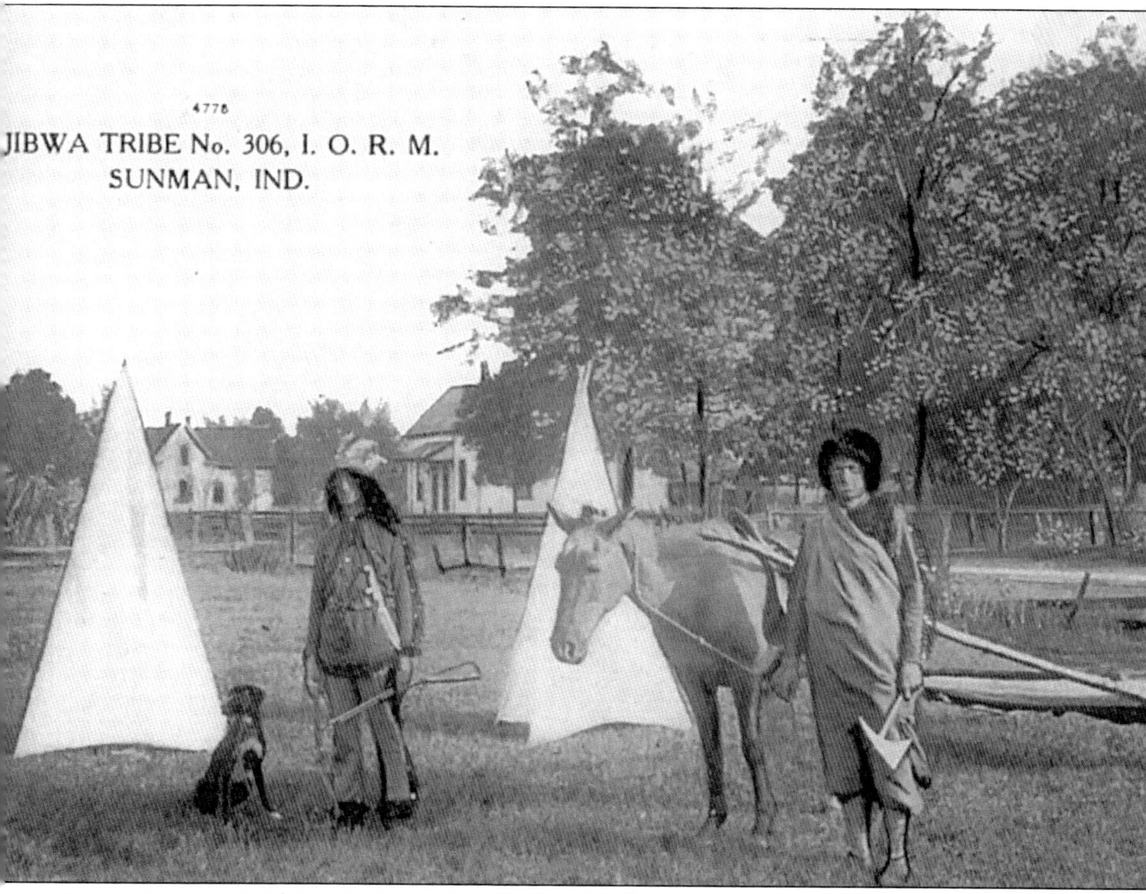

OJIBWA TRIBE NO. 306. The Independent Order of Red Men was a very popular organization for a time. These lodges existed in most towns and cities. Each lodge had an Native American name, and Sunman's was called the "Ojibwa Tribe." Two members with their dog, horse, and tepee are shown on this card. The lodge had its own insurance program for members. (Card #4775 by T.C. Co., Chicago, Illinois.)

SUNMAN

In 1819, John Sunman, father of Tom Sunman, settled in Adam's Township. He was later joined by a few more families and a new town was formed. This town was named Sunman in honor of the Sunman Family. In the 1850s, the Lawrenceburg–Indianapolis Railroad laid its tracks through Sunman, and this gave the young town an enormous boost. For years, Sunman shipped great numbers of turkeys and poultry, causing the town to celebrate a "Turkey Day" each year. In 1905, a fire devastated the thriving town, but the thrifty citizens have rebuilt and created a very livable community to this day.

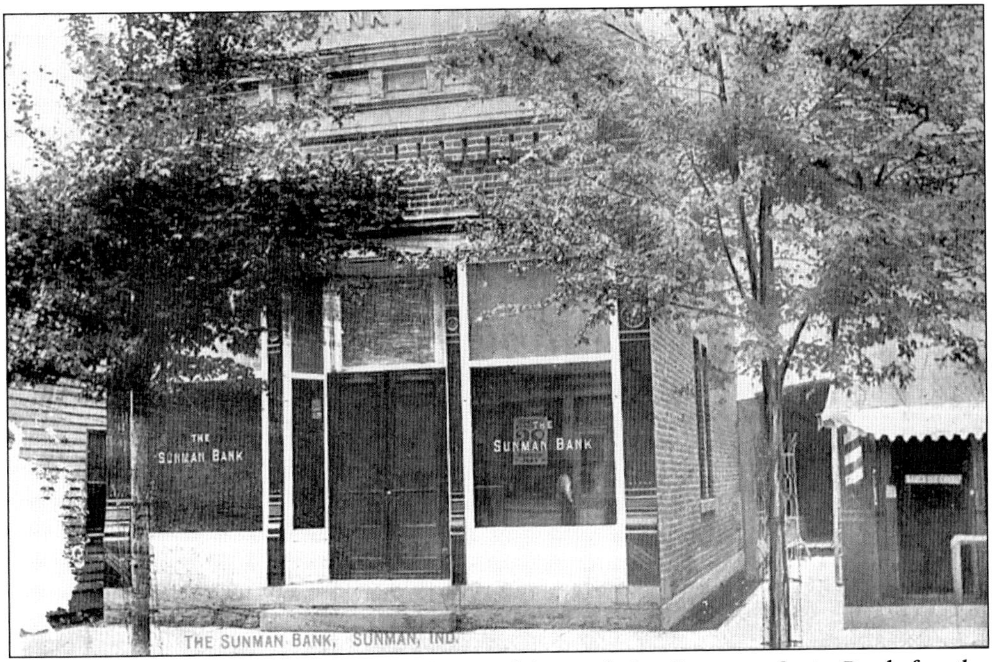

State Bank. The brick building on this card housed the Sunman State Bank for the many years the bank operated. The bank, like so many banks large and small, closed as a result of the Great Depression in the late 1920s. This card was sent by Bigney's Drug Store as an advertising card. (Card by unknown printer.)

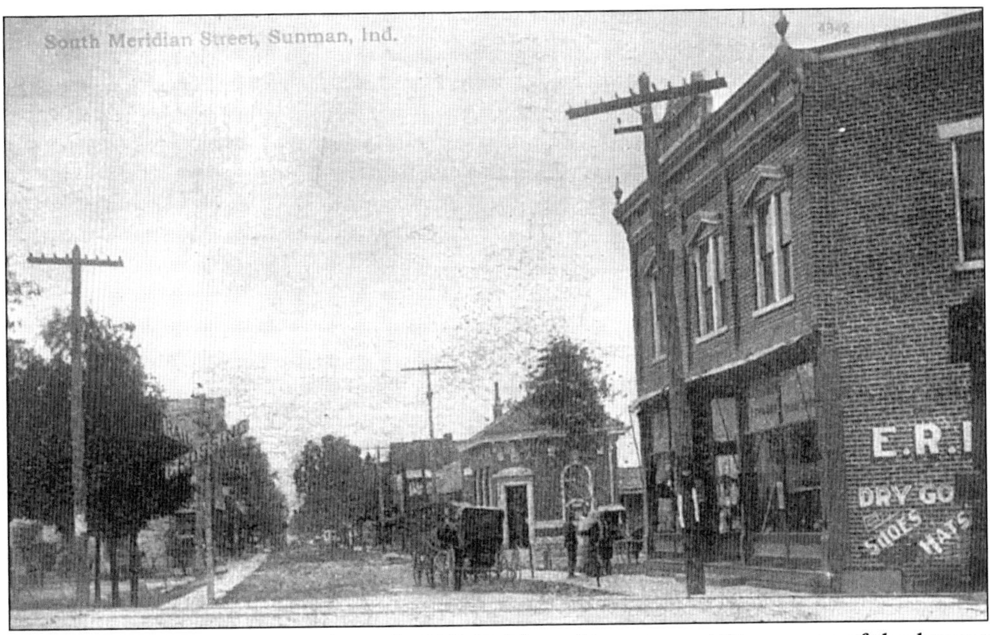

South Meridian Street. At right is the E.R. Behlmer Department Store, one of the largest brick business buildings in Sunman. The small bank building in back of the buggies was located south of the railroad crossing. Sidewalks and telephone lines indicate that the time period is the early 1900s. (Colored Card by Art Mfg. Co., Amelia, Ohio.)

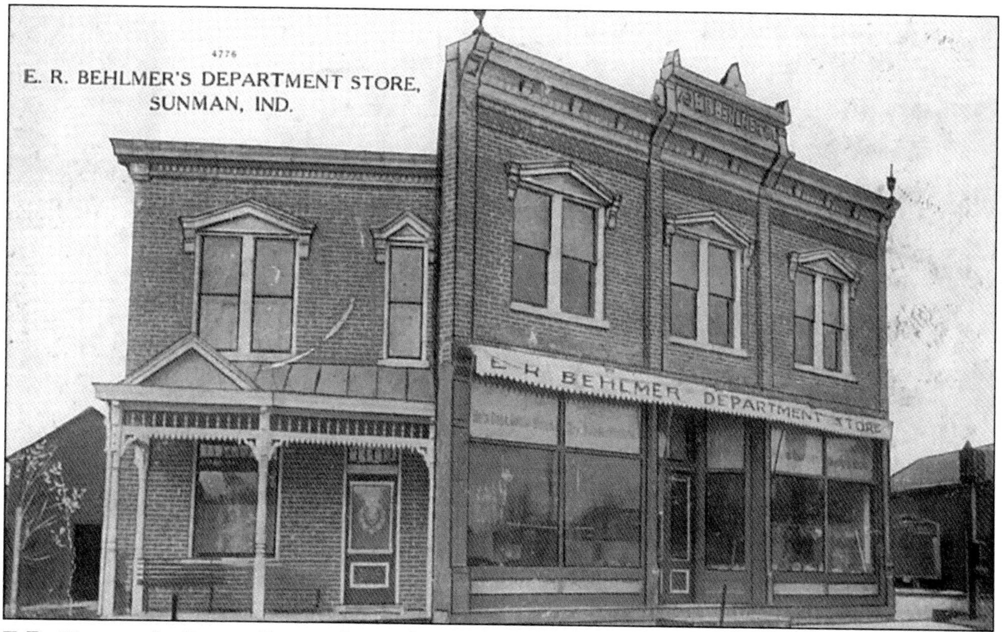

E.R. Behlmer's Store. Located on the west side of Meridian Street was the home and business of E.R. Behlmer. The Behlmer Family was very influential in Sunman as this card reveals. (Card #4776 by T.C. Co., Chicago, Illinois.)

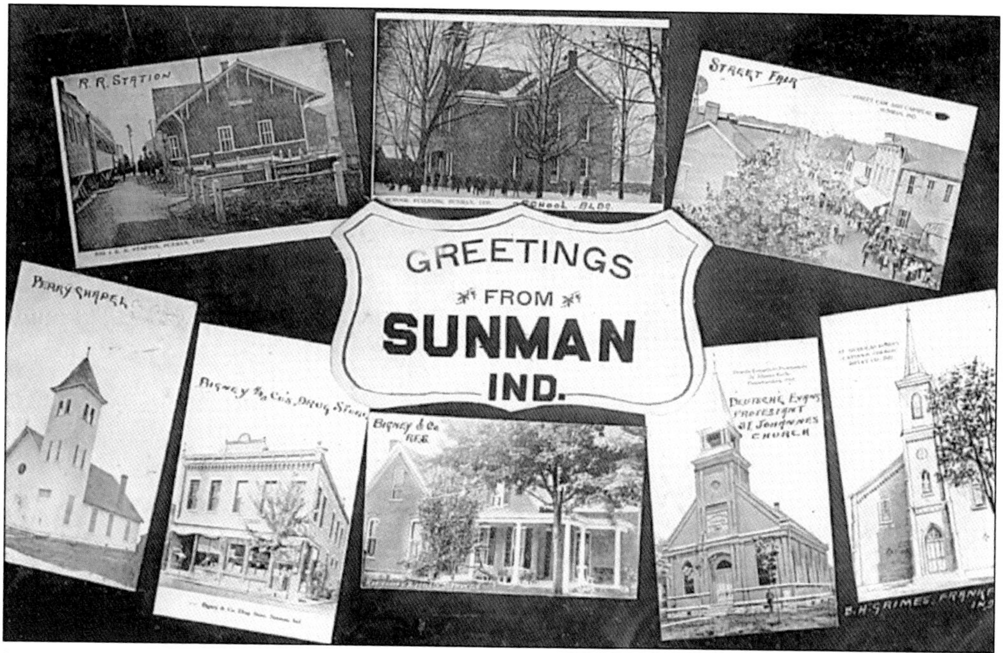

Multi View of Sunman. This 1911 greeting card proudly shows seven interesting points in the town of Sunman. In the top view one can see the Railroad Station, the Old School, and a street fair. In the bottom view are Perry Chapel, Bigney's Drug Store, St. John's Deutsch Church, and the St. Nicholas Catholic Church. (E.H. Grimes Co, Frankfort, Indiana.)

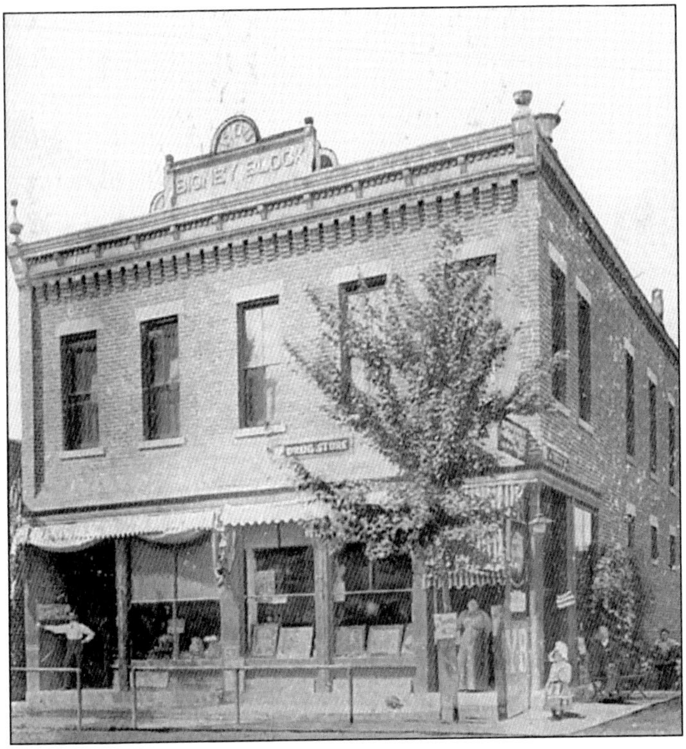

Bigney & Company. High above this prestigious brick home is the slogan Bigney Block. The Bigney Family resided upstairs, while the drug store was on the first floor. This popular store was Sunman's only pharmacy, and served a large surrounding area. Mrs. Bigney is standing in the doorway while an unidentified child and two adults are at one side. (Card #4771 by unknown printer.)

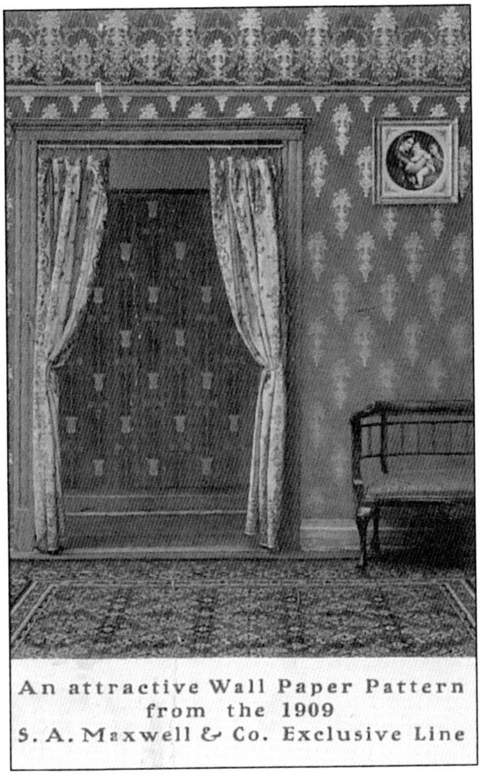

Advertising Card. Bigney's Drug Store mailed this 1909 card to a prospective customer. Wallpaper patterns used by the Maxwell & Co. paper company are displayed on the card. Many small-town drug stores sold wallpaper and paints to supplement their income during these times. The cards plugged Bigney's Store. (Card by unknown printer.)

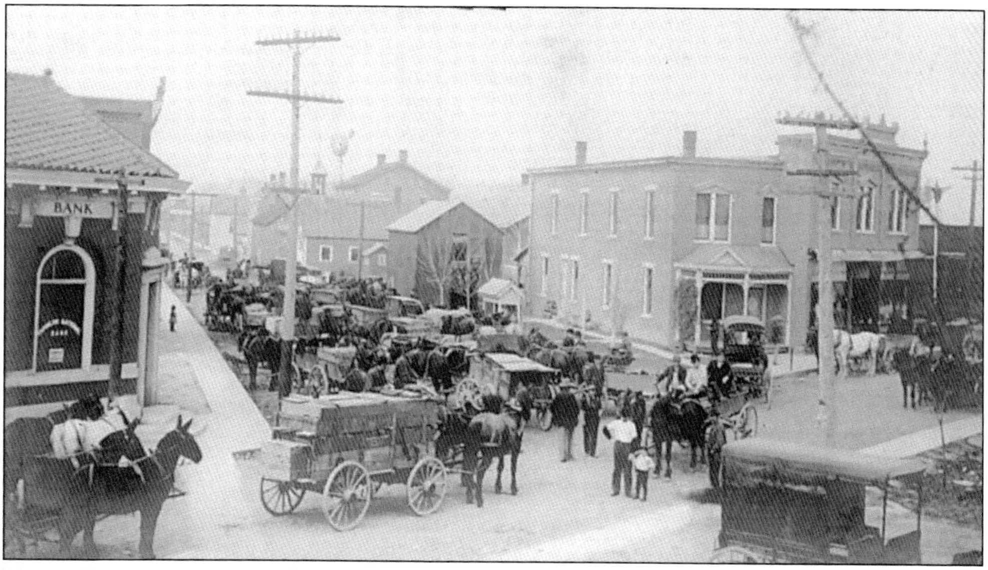

Turkey Day. In 1908, "Turkey Day" was special at Behlmer's Store in Sunman. Hundreds of turkeys were killed and dressed before Thanksgiving Day, and shipped by rail to both Cincinnati and Indianapolis markets. The streets teemed with horses, buggies, and wagons waiting to sell their birds. It was a festive day in Sunman. (Card by unknown printer.)

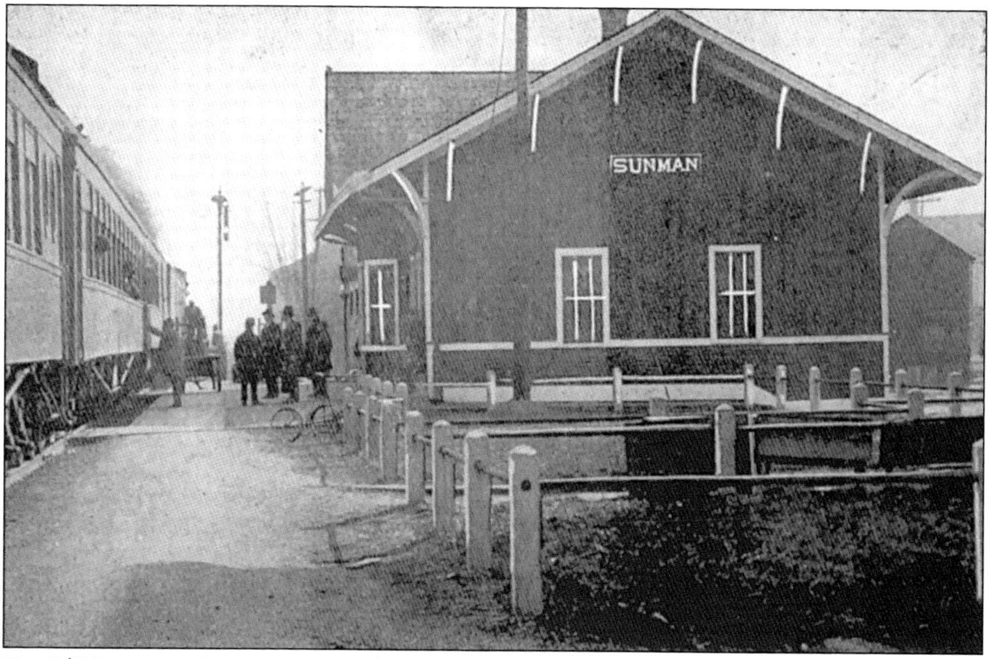

Big "4" Railroad Station. In 1854, Sunman's citizens first saw a train on the new tracks in Sunman. The depot was a focal point in Sunman, and freight, passengers, and mail were transported by this fast, efficient service. The card was made in 1912, and depicts a busy scene at the depot. (Unnumbered card by unknown photographer.)

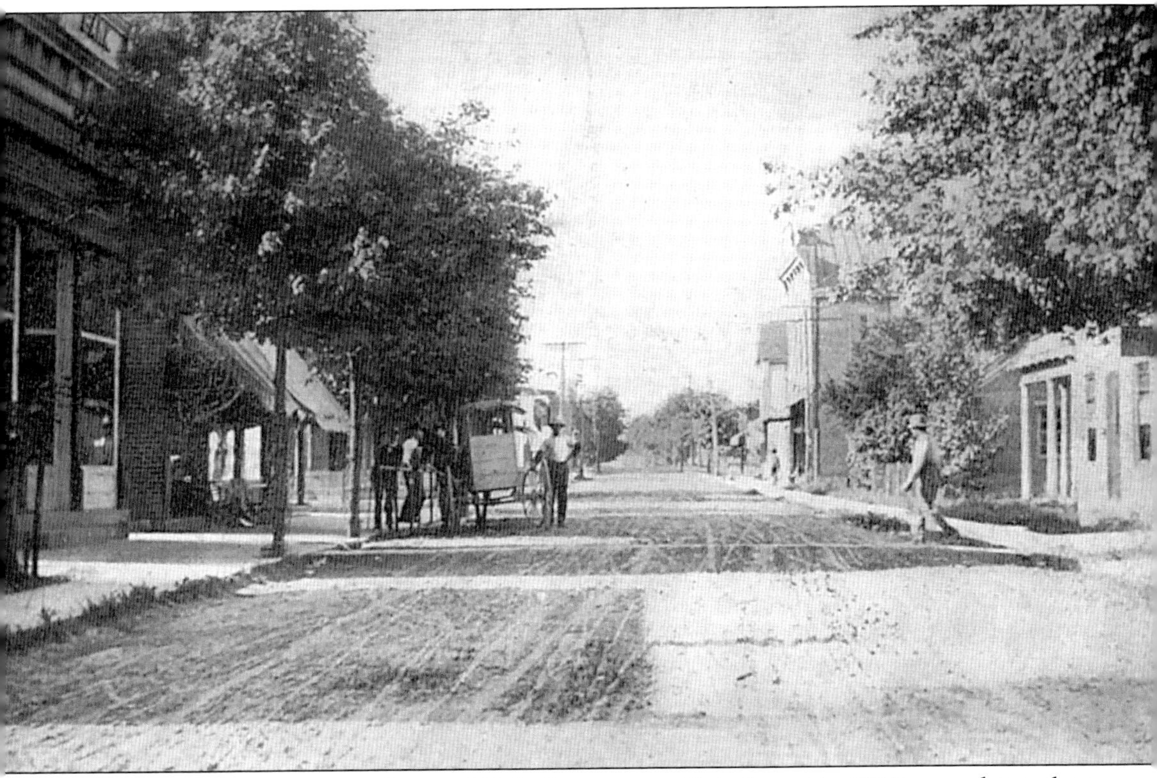

Looking North on Main Street. Life in Sunman on Main Street in 1910 moved at a slow pace. The small horse and carriage hitched to the rack may be a mail wagon. At right, a man saunters across the street toward the local bank. (Colored Card by E.C. Kropp Co., Milwaukee, Wisconsin.)

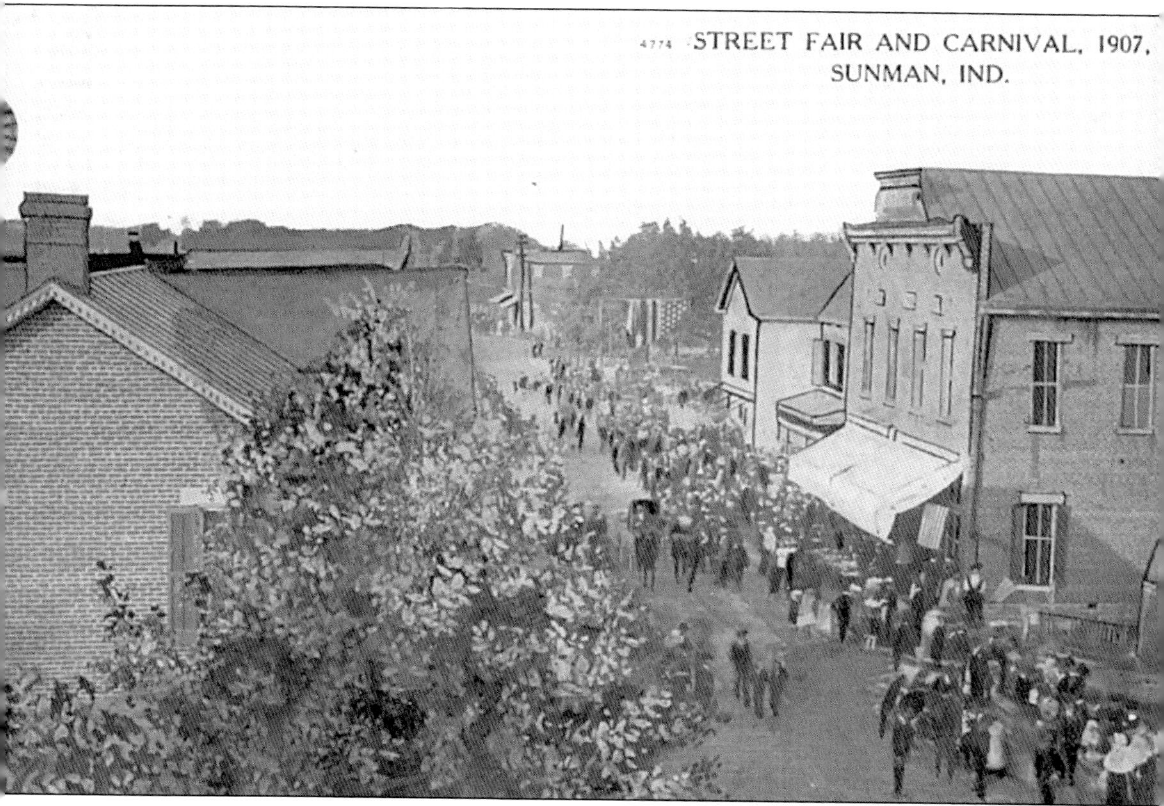

Street Fair. On this Sunman Street Fair advertising card dated October 19, 1907, eight characters are pictured. The reader is told to bring the "Whole Dam Family." Even the dog is a part of the logo. O.C. Beer, Sunman's jeweler, used these complimentary cards as a means of promoting both the fair and his store. (Private mailing card, May 19,1898. Authorized by Congress.)

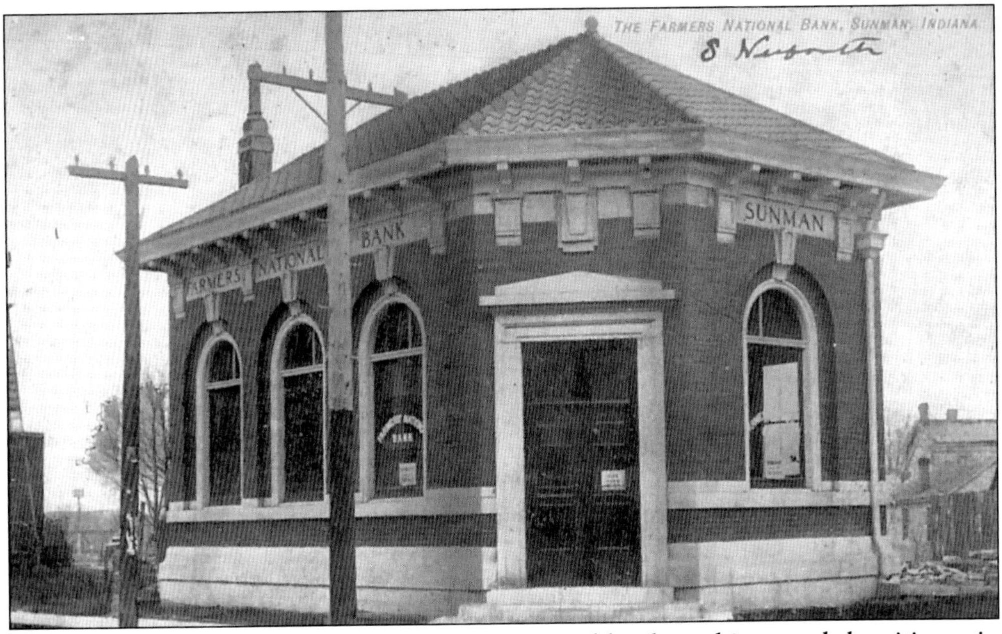

Farmer's National Bank. This was Sunman's second bank, and it served the citizens in and around Sunman from 1907 until 1933. The Depression also claimed this financial institution. After both banks in Sunman failed, the Peoples Bank & Trust was organized and remained in business. (Colored Card #3163 by Allied Printing, Chicago, Illinois.)

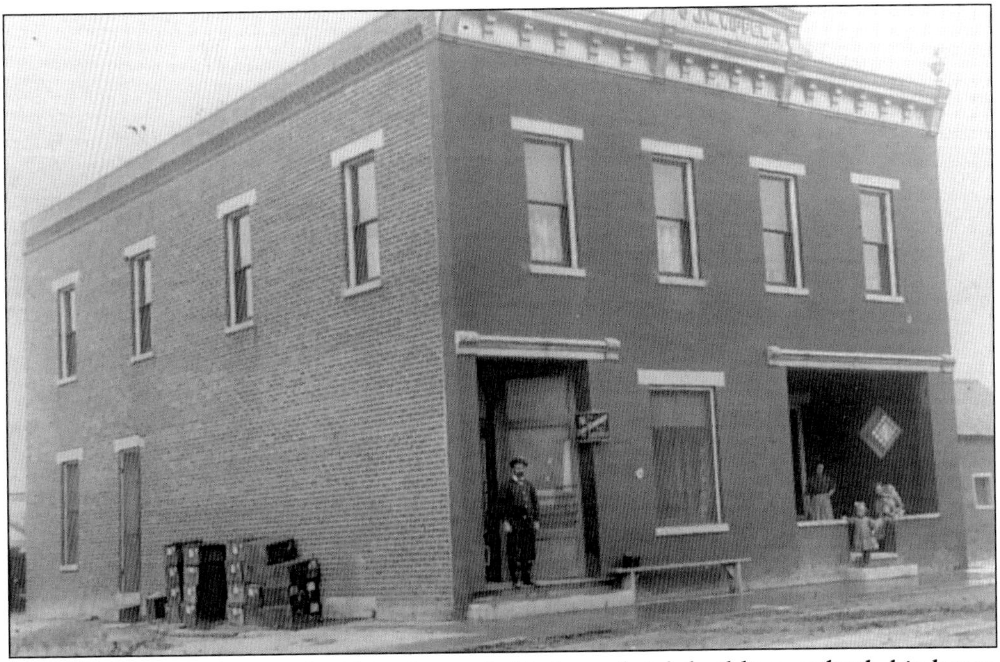

J. Whipple's Saloon. Joseph Whipple used this large brick building as both his home and his saloon business. On the porch can be seen Whipple's family, while Joe himself stands in the doorway of the saloon. Under the front windows, unused at this time, is a "Loafer's Bench." (Glossy card by unknown photographer.)

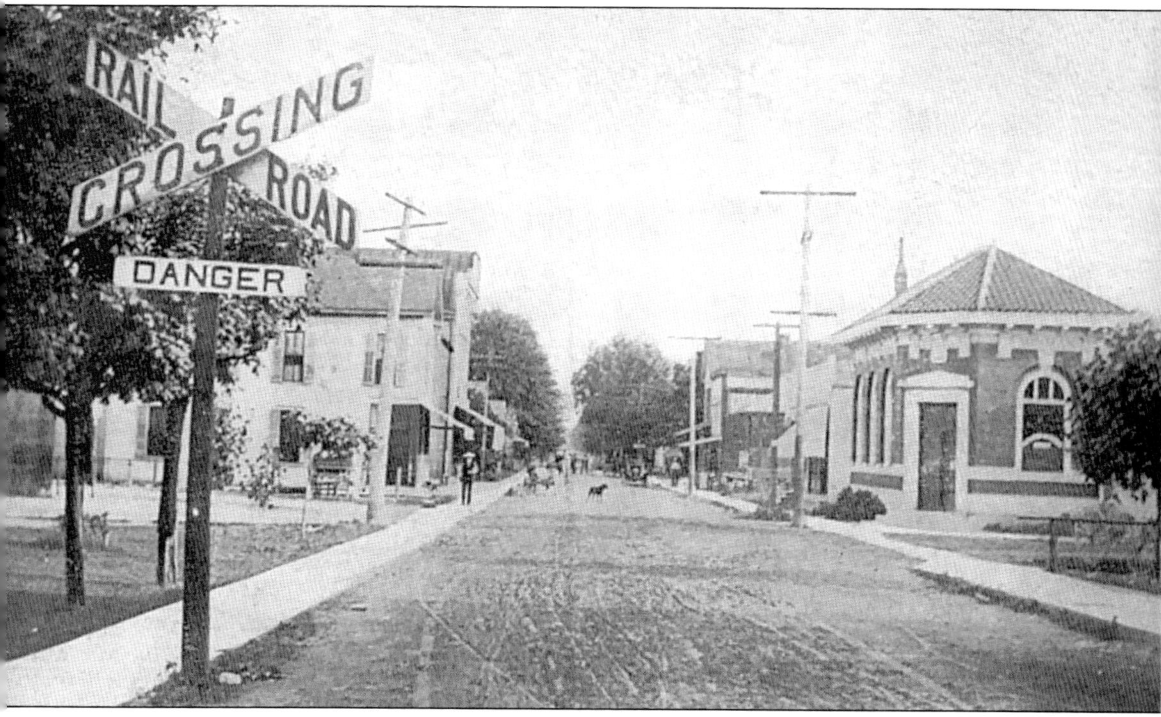

Street Scene. In the middle of the street a dog can be seen safely crossing, but they can't do that today. On the right, looking south, is the Sunman Bank, and in plain view a large sign warns one of the danger at this railroad crossing. (Card by E.C. Knopp Co., Chicago, Illinois.)

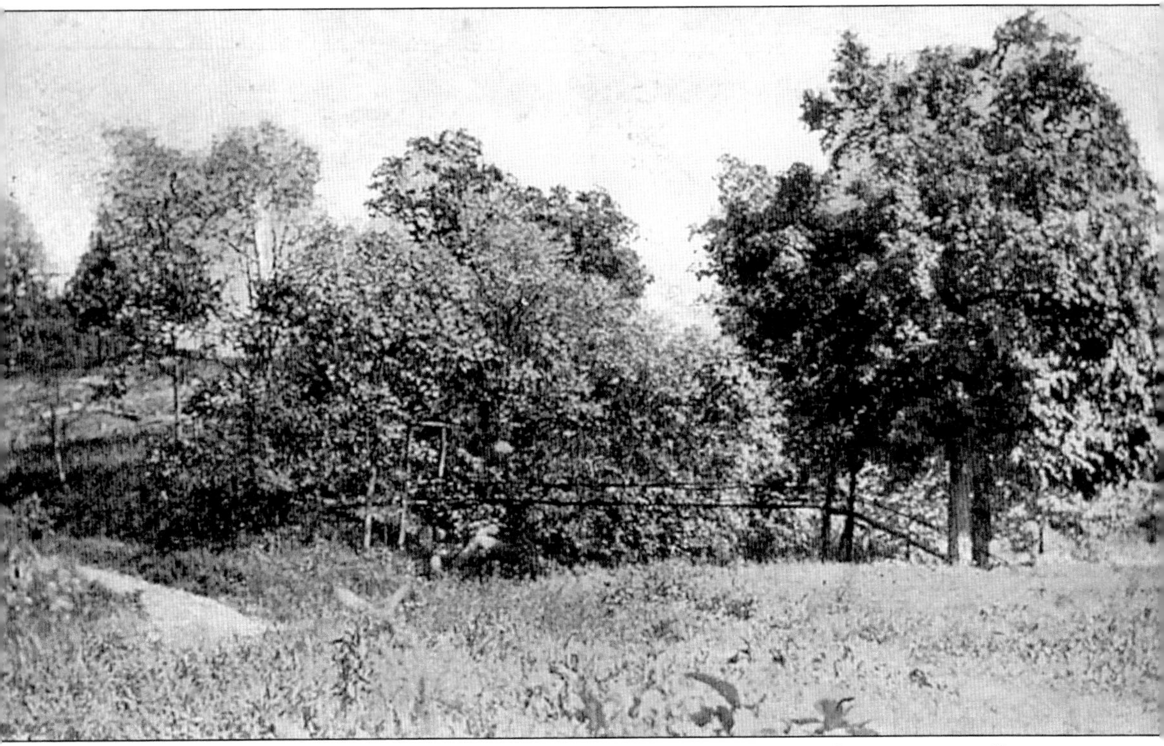

Foot Bridge. Foot bridges were once a fairly common means of crossing small streams and creeks; now they are a scarce article. This wire bridge provided a crossing over Pipe Creek near Sunman. (Colored card by E.C. Knopp Co., Chicago, Illinois.)

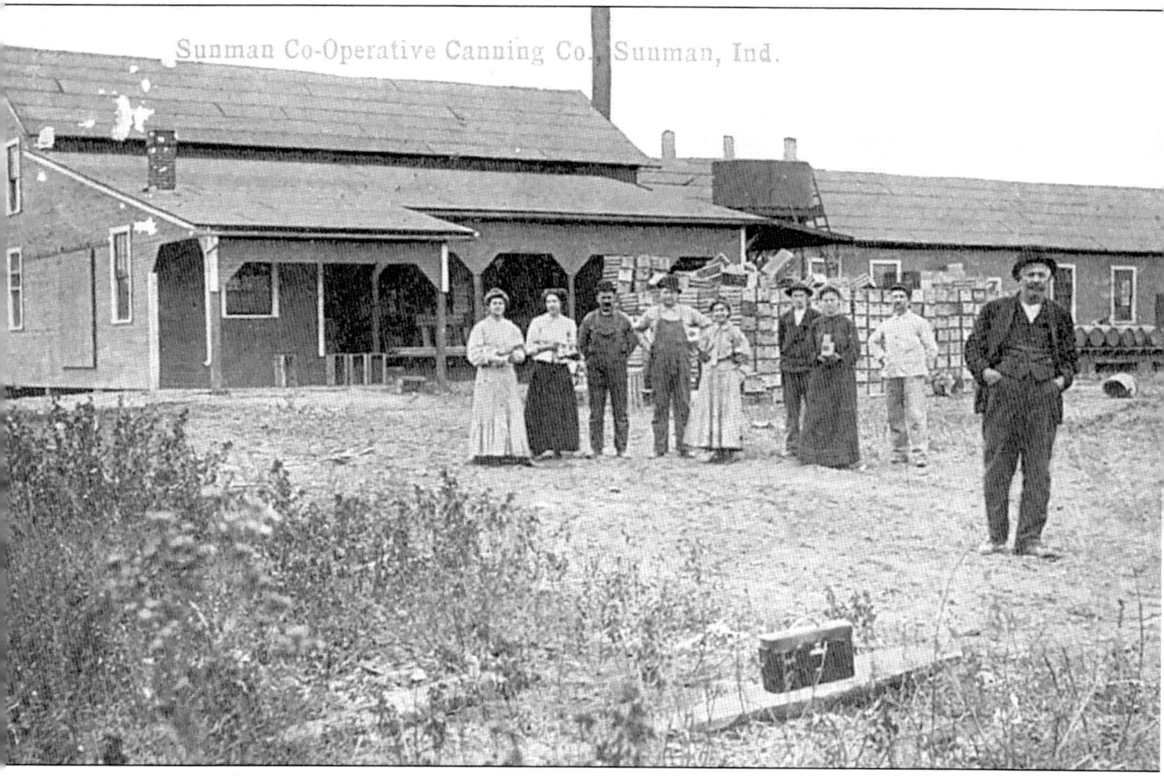

Sunman Coop. The Sunman Canning Company was organized in 1905 as a stock company. It was named The Sunman Co-operative Canning Company, and the business thrived for some time. In later years it bottled mostly catsup. Today it is owned by Pri-Pak Bottling Company. (Sepia Card, by American Card Makers, Chicago, Illinois.)

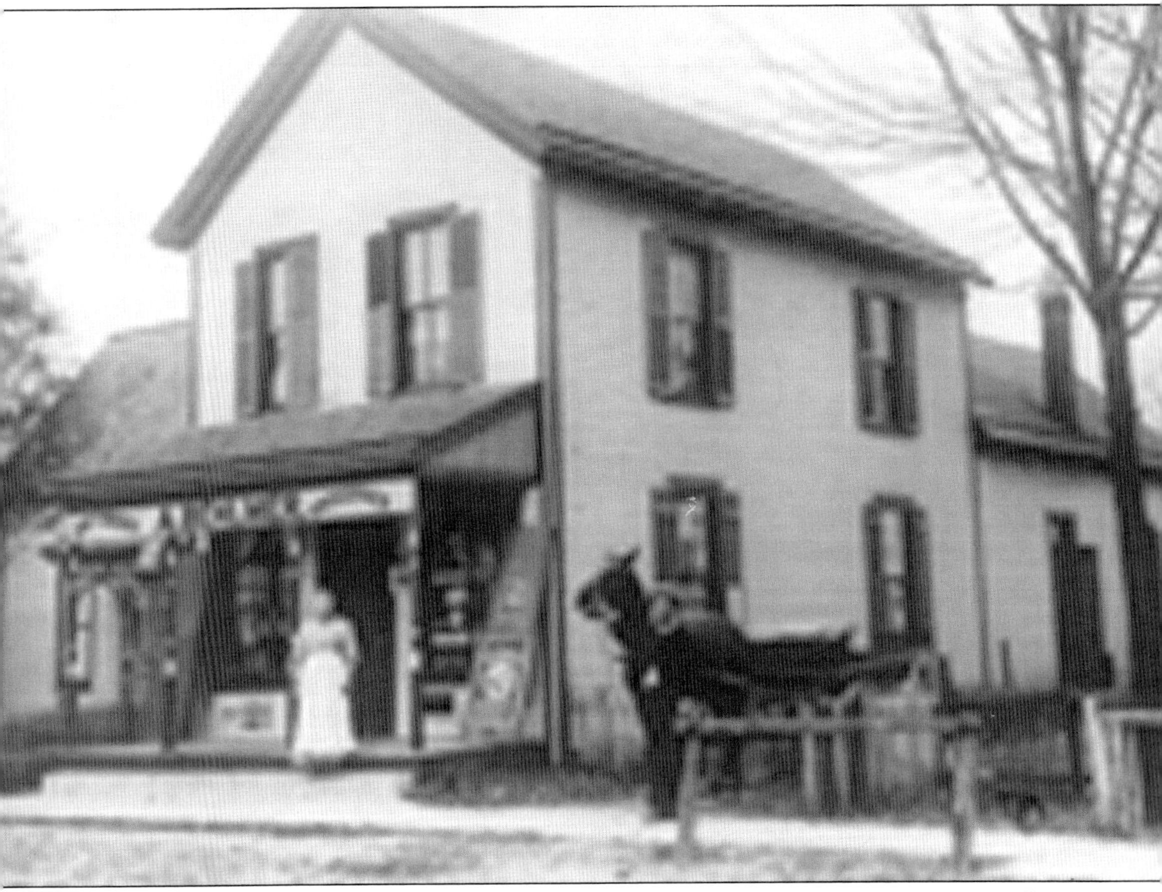

A. Behlmer's Grocery. A. Behlmer's Grocery had its beginning in 1895, when Albert, a carpenter, built this frame house on Meridian Street. Al made his home on the side of the store, and his wife Louise operated the dry goods and grocery store in the main part of the building. The business closed in 1927. In the picture, Louise is standing in front, while Al holds their horse. (Photograph by unknown photographer.)